# REAL ESTATE DEVELOPMENT SYNDICATION

# REAL ESTATE DEVELOPMENT SYNDICATION

## Joseph T. Howell

PRAEGER

PRAEGER SPECIAL STUDIES • PRAEGER SCIENTIFIC

**Library of Congress Cataloging in Publication Data**

Howell, Joseph T.
  Real estate development syndication.

  Includes index.
  1. Real estate investment—Syndication.   2. Real
estate development—Finance.   I. Title.
HD1382.55.H69   1983      332.63'274      83-17764
ISBN 0-03-063939-5 (alk. paper)
ISBN 0-03-063941-7 (pbk. : alk. paper)

Published in 1983 by Praeger Publishers
CBS Educational and Professional Publishing
a Division of CBS Inc.
521 Fifth Avenue, New York, NY 10175 USA

© 1983 by Joseph T. Howell

3456789   052   987654321

Printed in the United States of America
on acid-free paper

To Embry

# Acknowledgements

The research on which this book is based was initially done under a collaborative contract between the U.S. Department of Housing and Urban Development (HUD) and the National Corporation for Housing Partnerships (NCHP). At the time, I was the Director of Development at NCHP and was given the responsibility of writing a book which would deal mainly with low-income housing syndication. As luck would have it, the research on the book was done during the fall of 1980 and spring of 1981, just prior to the Economic Recovery Tax Act of 1981, which transformed the syndication industry. In addition, the Section 8 program, the major housing program utilizing syndications, was also abandoned as a national low-income housing production program. The result was that the book had to be almost completely rewritten—not once but twice. Consequently, this version which you are now about to read not only reflects the tax laws of 1981 and 1982 but also deals much more with the basic principles of real estate syndication and development than did the earlier drafts.

Many people deserve credit for helping to bring the book about. First and foremost is Alice Shabecoff at the Office on Neighborhoods at HUD who had the original idea of doing a book on syndication for neighborhood development corporations and who has been a continuous source of help and support for this effort. Though the Office on Neighborhoods at HUD no longer exists, Alice will always be an advocate for development by neighborhood and community-based groups; and her commitment and enthusiasm are an inspiration to me and many in the housing field. The responsibility for coordinating the work of NCHP fell into the lap of Carol Mills, who did her usual magnificent job of keeping things moving and on track. Many other people at NCHP gave me a great deal of support as well—Bill Comings and Bob Tracy, who gave me the initial task and provided encouragement throughout the writing process; Neil Churchill, who reviewed the initial draft; and tax attorneys Linda Davenport and Tom Tweel, who provided useful suggestions

vii

on the technical side of tax law and accounting. While I am deeply grateful to the folks at NCHP for their support and contributions, any mistakes or errors in the book are mine, not theirs, and I am entirely responsible for whatever shortcomings are contained in this book.

Most of the writing of the initial draft of the book was done while I was at The George Washington University (GWU) as Banneker Professor of Washington Studies during the spring semester of 1981. I will always be indebted to Professor Rod French at GWU, whose leadership inspired the Banneker Professorship and who is responsible for much of GWU's involvement in neighborhood affairs in the Washington area.

I am grateful to several people who read and responded to various drafts—Bill Black, Chuck Edson, Mike Stegman, Ann Bauman, Kris Weilbacker, and Marie McGuire Thompson—and especially grateful to Howard Sumka, whose comments and recommendations were extremely valuable in helping me revise the final manuscript. Also, I appreciate the assistance from attorney Bill Harris, who provided an illustrative Certificate of Limited Partnership, which is included in Appendix E, and the help from Marilyn Gaizban, who typed portions of the text. The final draft was edited and typed by Kathy Dour, who did an exceptionally good job under difficult circumstances; and finally, thanks to my associate, Faye Godwin, also an editor in her own right, who provided a great deal of support and helped edit and get the final manuscript in decent order.

# Contents

# Appendixes

# List of Tables

# Introduction

The primary purpose of this book is to explain syndication and describe its role in the development of real estate projects. Syndication is, quite simply, the process of bringing in people (besides the original developer) as owners of a real estate project. In order to become an owner, an individual will purchase shares of ownership, usually by making capital contributions to a limited partnership in which he or she becomes a limited partner. Selling limited partnership interests in a real estate project is what syndication is all about.

Having been involved in this field for a number of years, I have often been made aware of the lack of understanding about the real estate development process in general and about syndication in particular. Syndication seems to take on an aura of mystery and is sometimes viewed as modern-day alchemy, whereby "losses" are magically turned into gold by strange men in black hats calling themselves syndicators. In this book I hope to shed some light on the real estate development mystery so that the reader can better understand the process.

First, a word of warning. We are now in a time of fundamental change in the real estate development industry. The persistence of inflation has forced major changes in the way all real estate development projects are financed. In addition, major changes have recently occurred regarding federal assistance to housing and the federal tax code.

Because we are in a time of transition, I have tried to stress the basic principles of syndication and real estate development rather than dealing exclusively with specific regulations. While items such as government housing programs, depreciation schedules, and below-market financing will continue to change, the fundamentals of real estate development syndication will not change. A project will always cost a certain amount to develop. Funds will have to be provided to build the project—both by the owner and by lenders. User charges (rents or sales prices) will have to be sufficiently high so that those providing the sources of funds get their money back and make an acceptable profit for their effort, time, and the risk they have incurred. In order for someone to want to be a limited partner in a real estate project, there obviously has to be something in the project which the potential owner considers economically valuable—the opportunity to receive a regular cash return, to sell the project for a profit in the future, or, in the case of most low-income housing developments, to receive a tax shelter. These items will always be present in the development industry.

This book is primarily about the financial aspects of real estate development syndication and as such focuses on the way money is made by the various participants. The first chapter presents an overview of syndication and the syndication process, followed by a chapter dealing with the legal aspects of syndication. Because the various laws and regulations affecting syndication are in constant change, only the basic principles are introduced in Chapter Two; and perhaps the best advice in the entire book is emphasized here: if you plan to syndicate a project, before you get too far down the road, get a good attorney involved early in the process.

Chapters Three and Four deal with, respectively, the investor and developer sides of real estate development and syndication. Chapter Three deals with what investors look for in a real estate syndication deal and explains two important concepts in the syndication industry—the concept of the "losses to investment ratios" and the concept of "internal rate of return." Chapter Four deals with the developer side of syndication and goes into considerable detail in explaining how developers determine the basic economic feasibility of a project without spending very much money. Chapter Five follows up where Chapter Four leaves off by describing all the steps in the development process, once initial feasibility has been determined.

Chapters Six, Seven, and Eight present examples of real syndication deals. Chapter Six presents an "old Section 8 deal" syndicated prior to 1981 under the laws and regulations of the old tax law. While the laws are now different, the syndication process is basically the same; and the case study provides a good example of how a "two-step" syndication deal works. In addition, the same deal is analyzed using the 1981 tax law with the impact shown on both the investors and the developer. Chapter Seven deals with an older rehabilitated commercial property, which was offered for syndication in late 1981, the economics of which were based on the 1981 Economic Recovery Tax Act. Chapter Eight is a case study of a residential rental property which was classified as an historical structure and thus eligible for the 1981 tax provisions for historical properties. The analysis undertaken for this property was for the feasibility stage only, not the actual syndication, since when the information on the project was gathered, the actual syndication had not yet taken place. An interesting thing about this project, however, is that the basic economic feasibility was predicated on a planned conversion to condominiums some five to seven years into the future, after the tax benefits had been realized. These three examples, taken together, give you a good idea of the types of development and syndication opportunities which are available and the varied types of deals that apply to specific projects. Rarely are two business deals the same, although in all instances the basic underlying principles are the same.

As you read this book you will discover that much of the material, especially in the later chapters, is somewhat complicated and quantitatively oriented. In order to understand the material, it will help if you follow the numbers yourself using a calculator to check the figures and see how the numbers fit together.

This book is really not a "how to" book. Accordingly, no effort has been made to include all the technical rules and regulations that must be mastered if one is going to syndicate a real estate development project. Rather, the book's purpose is to enhance one's understanding of the development and syndication process.

The needs of our cities are in many respects more serious and more pressing today than ever. Despite the significant gains made in the 1960s and 1970s in housing and community development, many neighborhoods are still in decline. Bad housing still exists. Many downtown areas are decaying. In order to rehabilitate housing or revitalize a business district or build new housing which is affordable (or any new construction, for that matter), first and foremost the numbers have to work. The specific project under consideration has to be feasible. Being feasible means that the project must produce enough revenue to satisfy the various participants who have put their own resources into the project—that is, the lenders and the owners of the project. If a project does not make sense from a financial perspective, it will probably never be implemented. Or worse, if it is implemented, it will fail in later years. For this reason it is very important that people involved in housing and community development understand what determines the feasibility of real estate development projects and specifically how real estate syndication often plays a major role in this process. The purpose of this book is to give you a better understanding of real estate development and syndication and enable you to evaluate specific projects from the perspective of developer, lender, investor, or public official.

# *O n e*
## How Real Estate Development Syndication Works: An Overview

The real estate syndication process begins with the development of an income-producing real estate development project. The income-producing real estate project is usually put together by one development firm or individual. The developer spends time and money and takes risks to bring the real estate project to the point where it is real. The developer acquires a site or obtains site control, develops a building concept, hires an architect to prepare plans, and obtains necessary local approvals and loan commitments. At the point that the project becomes real—usually defined as the time that the lender advances funds to finance the project—the developer often elects to raise additional capital by selling shares of ownership interests in the project. When shares of ownership interests are sold, the event is commonly referred to as syndication.

## THE BASIC SYNDICATION PROCESS

The way that syndication usually works is this: the developer —who up to this point may be the sole owner of the project— will form a limited partnership. Every limited partnership must have at least one general partner who has unlimited liability for the debts of the partnership (a more detailed description of this appears in the next chapter), and one limited partner, whose liability is the extent of his or her initial investment. The original developer usually becomes the general partner in the newly created limited partnership. The general partner then sells (or someone else sells on the developer's behalf) partnership interests to other individuals, who become limited partners in the partnership. Limited partners will pay cash to own partnership shares, entitling them to share in the financial benefits produced by the project. The shares are expressed as percentages of ownership in the project. The cash that they pay to become limited partners is referred to as capital contributions.

The cash raised through syndication, combined with the cash available through loan proceeds, is often more than is required to develop the real estate project. When this is the case, there is extra cash available for developers to pay themselves back for all of the risk capital they have put into the project (site options, architectural fees, loan commitment fees, etc.) plus to pay themselves a fee to compensate for their hard work, effort, and risk. Money flows into a limited partnership through capital contributions from limited partners and through loan proceeds. Money is taken out to pay for the cost of developing the project, including a development fee to the original developer—or, in most syndications, several fees, including not only a development fee but usually a development syndication fee, marketing fee, lease-up guarantee fee, overhead fee, etc. At the conclusion of syndication, the original developer emerges as the general partner of a limited partnership. At this point, the equity or owner's cash in the deal will no longer be the developer's but rather that of the new limited partners; and, if things go well, the developer will also end up with some of their cash in his pocket. Since most of the ownership interests have been sold to others, the cash taken out in the form of development fees is the primary profit made from the undertaking. This in a capsule is what syndication is all about—selling ownership shares in income-producing projects in order to produce up-front cash for the original developer.

Usually the capital contributions from limited partners are paid-in on an installment basis, typically over a three to five year period. The structure of syndications also varies, depending on whether the limited partners make capital contributions directly into the partnership or whether the ownership interests are purchased by a third party (that is, a syndicator) and then resold to limited partners. Notwithstanding these variations, the basic process of obtaining capital from limited partners and using the capital to develop the project and receive fees or profits at the beginning of the construction period is the essence of syndication. The basic formula is shown below.

**SOURCES OF FUNDS**
**Loan proceeds**
**Capital contributions from limited partners**

**USES OF FUNDS**
**All project development costs:**
   **site acquisition costs**
   **construction costs**
   **financing costs**
   **all other project soft costs**
**All syndication costs:**
   **legal fees**
   **syndication fees**
   **sales commissions**
**Developer fees:**
   **developer fee**
   **construction guarantee fee**
   **operating-deficit guarantee fee**
   **development management fee**
   **reporting fee, etc.**

Another way of stating the equation from the point of view of the developer or general partner is this:

**TOTAL SOURCES OF FUNDS**
**Loan proceeds**
**Capital contributions**
   *Less* **all project development costs**
   *Less* **all syndication costs**
   *Equals* **amount of money available to the general partner for profit, overhead, and related fees.**

## THE ROLE OF THE SYNDICATOR

Because syndication is a complicated process, there is frequently the need for a third party or middleman, who is responsible for bringing the developer and the limited partners together. This middleman is the syndicator. A syndication typically works in one of two ways. The most frequent way is for the syndicator to arrange for individuals to become limited partners in the limited partnership. The syndication firm in this instance is not an owner of the project but rather uses its best efforts to sell the partnership interests to others on behalf of the general partner. The syndicator receives a fee that is usually determined as a percentage of the gross proceeds raised from the sale of the partnership interests. This fee may range from 20 percent to 25 percent of the capital contributions, depending on the services and the guarantees provided by the firm. Syndication legal fees and sales commission fees are also often involved and usually are included in the total syndication fee. The firm will be responsible for preparing the necessary offering materials and, through its legal counsel, appropriate legal documents. Since the ownership interests are classified as real estate securities, in instances where the interests are sold to individuals who do not have direct access to all the original documents, the "retailing" of the interests to potential limited partners can be undertaken only by a registered broker-dealer securities firm.

The second way that syndication works is for the syndication firm to purchase the ownership interests from the developer, thus itself becoming an owner of the project. It then resells the partnership interests to third parties. Because the syndicator acquires the project, the business deal with the original developer involves more than a best efforts arrangement. Under the equity purchase method, the syndicator becomes the new general partner or cogeneral partner, and the original developer is usually out of the picture altogether.

## SYNDICATION APPROACHES

In the sale of the limited partnership interests to limited partners, one of two approaches is usually followed. The first is an informal technique which can be called the *good-old-boy network* approach. The second is formal and can be called the *big-business* approach. In the first, the local developer—who has managed to get a project to the point of starting construction—is someone who has several high-income friends who understand the value of tax deductions. These people trust one another and the developer, who has developed similar projects, knows what he is doing and is, by all accounts, a good-old-boy.

In this transaction, the syndication is relatively uncomplicated and inexpensive. The risks, however, are no less than the risks incurred in syndicating via the big-business route; and the developer is legally obligated by the Securities Exchange Commissions (SEC) regulations to present to associates all the risks, as well as the merits, of the investment. The developer should rely on a competent attorney to draft the partnership agreement and provide advice on the tax opportunities and risks. In addition, an accountant should be hired to prepare depreciation schedules showing projected tax losses. The developer's associates may rely on the developer's attorney and accountant; but, more than likely, they will rely on their own attorneys and accountants. Nevertheless, once the tax losses are determined and the financial needs of each person defined, a price is determined and the group negotiates an agreement. All partners then execute a limited partnership agreement which obligates them to make capital contributions to a limited partnership. The developer will remain the general partner and the developer's associates will become limited partners; or, in some instances, they may also be general partners.

Of course, many such transactions are not necessarily limited to friends or associates. Sometimes people in the same community who know each other only by reputation are involved. Naturally, if the parties are less acquainted with each other, there is need for more formal negotiations and documentation. However, there is usually no need for a formal offering memorandum, and the only pieces of paper that are created are the partnership agreement and the projection of financial benefits and tax losses by a qualified accountant. Often it is the accountants or attorneys or bankers who bring some of their other clients into the deal.

While this approach is quite appropriate in many instances, in most cases there are not enough good-old-boys interested in and able to participate in the deal. In such cases, the developer is faced with broadening the market to bring in strangers. This is when matters begin to get complicated.

First, the developer is usually not a tax expert. The complexities of the tax code are only slightly less baffling and confusing to most developers than they are to the average investor. They understand how to acquire a site, put together a development team, and get the project financed or, in the case of low-income housing, ultimately approved by HUD. The last thing that they have time for is to become experts in tax law and all of the accounting that goes with it. In short, if they want to include other investors besides good-old-boys, they have to rely on someone else to do it for them. They must go the big-business route.

Enter the syndicator, an individual or firm specializing in the securities aspects, not the development aspects, of real estate development projects.

The developer and the syndicator first must negotiate a business deal. The most important aspect to the developer is how much money will be made for selling the limited partnership interests and when it will come in.

The price offered by the syndicator is based on several factors. First, it depends on the specific type of project being offered (low-income housing, conventional rental housing, or historical or commercial property). Each type of property produces a different mix of financial benefits.

In the case of low-income housing, because the primary financial benefit has been the tax benefit, the key determinant of a project's worth has been the tax shelter it produces. Investors are presented information on the ratio of dollars invested to tax shelter generated by the project. Low-income housing, however, has been unique in the extent to which tax benefits have been emphasized. Most other projects offer potential for both cash flow and appreciation. When these other financial benefits are present in a potential project, typically the investor is presented with anticipated rates of return on the initial investment. The investor will be shown how much cash is likely to be received each year, what the after-tax benefits will be, and what potential gain will be received upon resale in the future.

The syndicator will first analyze the development project and the basic material provided by the developer and determine what the project is worth to potential investors. The developer will be advised as to how much equity capital can potentially be raised and then will offer an agreement to sell the securities.

The negotiations between the syndicator and the developer inevitably boil down to a question of money. How much money the developer receives as a fee in exchange for passing the benefits (which otherwise are only the developer's) to others depends on three factors. The first, and probably most important, factor is how much capital can be raised for the portion of the project the developer is willing to sell. This amount is a function of the total financial benefits produced by the project and the market for those benefits. The second factor is the demand on available capital. After applying the total source funds to the total cost of developing the project, is there anything left for the developer? If the combination of equity capital and debt capital is greater than the total cost of developing the project, what is left is available to the developer for fees. The third factor is the amount of risk the developer is willing to take.

In most instances, the developer will remain as general partner. Although the developer may sell as much as 99 percent of the project, as general partner the developer will have unlimited liability for obligations of the project.

In all probability the developer, now the general partner, will be required to guarantee to the limited partners coverage of all construction cost overruns and initial operating deficits. In some cases the developer may be required to cover operating deficits for an additional period. To the extent that the general partner agrees to these guarantees, the exposure (future risk) of the limited partners is reduced and the developer, thereby, can expect more capital contributions to come into the limited partnership. As a practical matter, the project probably could not be syndicated without a construction overrun and initial operating deficit guarantee.

## AN EXAMPLE OF SYNDICATION

Let us look at an illustration of how this would work. A developer has put together a project, the total costs of which are almost $2,600,000, excluding the potential developer's fee. For this illustration, let us assume that the project is a residential rental property. The total costs of the project include all the costs of development, syndication, initial lease-up, and so on.

After examining the project on its own merits, the syndicator determines that the benefits produced by the project are sufficient to attract total equity contributions of approximately $650,000. The equity contribution is related only to the financial benefits produced by the project. These could be tax benefits exclusively, probably expressed in terms of a ratio of dollars invested to tax shelter received, or they could be a combination of benefits, probably identified separately as cash flow, tax shelter, and appreciation. For the project to be feasible, the equity capital from the limited partners plus the financing must cover all project costs and provide a reasonable fee to the developer. The developer wants to retain a five percent ownership share as general partner. Thus, the value of the limited partnership interests is 95 percent multiplied by $650,000, or $617,500.

**PROJECT COSTS**

| | |
|---|---:|
| Land | $ 100,000 |
| Construction costs (including architect and fees) | 1,800,000 |
| Contractor's profit | 80,000 |
| Interest | 160,000 |
| Financing fees, taxes, insurance | 200,000 |
| Permanent loan discount | 50,000 |
| Working capital/lease-up expenses | 40,000 |
| Cost of syndication and syndicator fee | 150,000 |
| Total costs, excluding developer's fees | $2,580,000 |

The sources of funds to meet these total project costs are the mortgage loan and the equity capital provided by the limited partners. The mortgage in this case is approximately $2.2 million. Based on the financial benefits produced by the project, the total equity raised from limited partners is $617,500. The total sources of funds are:

| | |
|---|---:|
| Equity capital (from limited partners) | $ 617,500 |
| Mortgage loan | 2,200,000 |
| Total | $2,817,500 |

Since $2,817,500 has been raised to meet the project costs and only $2,580,000 is required to cover costs, exclusive of the developer's fees, $237,500 is available for the developer's fees, net of all other costs. This would be the income to the developer in the venture.

The developer's fees may vary considerably from deal to deal, depending on the economics of the specific venture. Since the economics of projects vary greatly, almost every developer will talk to more than one syndication firm to get a clearer understanding of the size of the fee available to him. In the case of low-income housing, typically these fees are expressed as a percentage of the mortgage amount.

The example shows capital contributions being made by the limited partners directly into the partnership. As stated earlier, usually the contributions of the limited partners are paid-in over a three to five year period. Also, since the general partner is obligated to cover construction cost overruns and initial operating deficits, many agreements will require the general partner to escrow (put aside in a separate account) a portion of the development fee or secure a letter of credit to assure the limited partners that funds are available to cover these potential problems should they arise.

**TOTAL SOURCES OF FUNDS**

| | |
|---|---:|
| **Equity capital (from limited partners)** | $   617,500 |
| **Mortgage loan** | 2,200,000 |
| | |
| **Total** | **$2,817,500** |

**TOTAL APPLICATIONS OF FUNDS**

| | |
|---|---:|
| **Land** | $   100,000 |
| **Construction costs** | 1,800,000 |
| **Contractor profit** | 80,000 |
| **Interest** | 160,000 |
| **Financing fees, taxes, insurance** | 200,000 |
| **Permanent loan discount** | 50,000 |
| **Working capital/lease-up** | 40,000 |
| **Syndication costs and fees** | 150,000 |
| **Developer fees** | 237,500 |
| | |
| **Total** | **$2,817,500** |

## ISSUES IN SYNDICATION BUSINESS DEALS

When a developer or sponsor negotiates with a syndication firm, it is important to know at the outset what kind of business deal is being proposed and what kinds of risks are involved. Some of the important factors to reach agreement on are these:

1. *Best efforts versus guaranteed price.* Most syndicators will quote a price (or developer fee) based on "best efforts" to sell the limited partnership interests. Should the syndicator fail to perform either in raising the estimated equity capital price or in selling the securities the risk is the developer's. The syndicator may quote one price, only to return at a later time to renegotiate the deal.

In the case of a purchase and resale, a syndication firm will quote a guaranteed price, thus taking the risk itself if it is unable to sell the securities at the estimated price. A developer should know whether the syndicator is talking about best efforts or a firm underwriting.

2. *Role of the developer.* Developers' needs vary tremendously. Some developers want to continue to own the project and remain indefinitely as general partner. Others prefer to get out as general partner once the project is completed, so that they can turn their attention to developing another project. Some prefer to manage the project, others do not.

When the investors make contributions directly into the partnership, the developer will remain as general partner. When a syndication firm purchases the equity, the developer usually will be replaced, although some lenders or insurers require that he remain a partner through the construction period. What route a developer chooses depends on factors such as his own financial picture and his long-term business objectives.

3. *Financial assistance provided by the syndicator.* Many developers find that, for a variety of reasons, they do not have the financial strength to put up the cash or to post letters of credit required by the lender or insurer at the closing of the construction loan. In some instances, they are rejected at the last minute for not having adequate assets. In these cases, the syndicator may be able to assist the developer by providing additional working capital and, if the syndicator is a cogeneral partner, by providing additional financial strength to satisfy the lender's or insurers' mortgage credit requirements.

4. *Exposure of the developer.* Once construction begins, everything is still not over. There is considerable risk, not only during the construction period, but also once the project is in operation. Some developers are prepared and willing to take the risk for covering construction

cost overruns and operating deficits and to offer the guarantees required to syndicate the project. Others prefer to reduce this exposure as much as possible. Most syndication agreements require that the developer be responsible for these risks; some agreements will provide for a sharing of these risks between developer and syndicator.

How all these matters are handled will be covered in the partnership agreement and, in the case of the syndicator's purchasing the equity, the purchase agreement, whereby the syndicator agrees to purchase the limited partnership interests.

All of these items have an effect on how much money the developer makes. Generally, the more the syndicator contributes financially to the developer and the more risks assumed, the less there is available for the developer. This is not always the case, however, and the developer should carefully weigh all the aspects of the proposal before making a final decision.

Once the deal has been negotiated between the developer and the syndicator, the syndicator prepares to offer the securities to potential investors. Usually, the deal is completed prior to the construction loan closing. In any event, once loan closing has taken place and the project is under construction, the syndicator works to sell the limited partnership interests. The key vehicle for accomplishing this is the offering memorandum, as discussed in Chapter two.

## WHY THE PROCESS WORKS

Given the enormous complexities involved and the risks that have been identified, one could ask how such a cumbersome process could possibly work. The fact is that in recent years there has been a large volume of real estate syndications, especially federally assisted housing syndications, and such securities are now generally accepted within investment markets. There are four principal reasons for the general success of these syndications.

First, there are increasing numbers of high-income individuals who feel the tax bite every April. These people, many of whom are doctors, lawyers, and other professionals, have managed to keep their incomes ahead of inflation, only to find themselves in the 50 percent bracket (or higher prior to 1982, since their income from other investments was taxed at the 70 percent rate). For these people, a tax shelter translates directly into dollars saved.

Second, previous tax reform acts eliminated many avenues for tax-shelter investments. Besides energy-exploration investments, income-producing real estate in general and rental housing in particular have offered the primary opportunities for reducing tax exposure.

Third, because the industry is heavily regulated, the likelihood of a catastrophe is generally considered remote. In the case of federally assisted housing syndications such as those involving the Section 8 program (covered in Chapter six), the projects usually have had HUD insurance or were financed by state housing finance agencies. This means that most have been subjected to thorough underwriting procedures by public agencies. The investor has the assurance that it is not just the developer who says the project is feasible. Since these public agencies have a great deal to lose if the partnership defaults on the loan, one could assume that they have given it careful analysis. Most importantly, these projects have had long-term rental commitments in terms of Section 8 Housing Assistance Payments Contracts, thus reducing much of the real estate market risks associated with such projects.

Finally, many of the firms involved have proven ability. Over the past 10 years a fairly large number of firms have developed specializations and earned reputations for reliability. There is nothing more important to an investor than having the assurance that the syndicator and the general partner are competent and financially secure. In instances where these proven abilities are lacking, the market for the limited partnership interests is questionable.

# *T w o*
## The Legal Side of Syndication

There are two basic requirements of any syndication. First, it must make economic sense: The numbers must work. In other words, there must be reasonable assurance that within acceptable risk parameters the project will produce sufficient financial benefits to attract investors. The second basic requirement is that the syndication must be legal. The entity which is established to own the project—that is, the limited partnership—must be legal. The tax deductions and investment tax credits promised to the limited partners must be legal. And, perhaps most important of all, the syndication process itself must be legal. This chapter is concerned primarily with this second requirement; meeting legal requirements and complying with required syndication procedures.

Because real estate syndication covers so many areas, it involves tax law, partnership law, securities law, and basic real estate law. In addition, the tax and securities aspect of syndication involves not only tax law but also IRS regulations, administrative rulings, and court decisions. Because each of these elements is subject to change, the most important recommendation that can be made is this: before you consider syndicating a project in which you are involved, get a good, experienced attorney and a good, experienced accountant (or similar expert in the field). Because the field is changing so rapidly, it is quite possible that many of last year's rules are no longer applicable. While the basic principles of real estate syndication are likely to remain the same, the details and the mechanics surely will not. And it is the details and mechanics that ultimately determine the legality and often the profitability of the undertaking.

## PROJECT OWNERSHIP ISSUES

***The ownership entity must be legal.*** The most common form of ownership is the limited partnership, as discussed in Chapter One. A partnership is an organizational relationship or arrangement whereby two or more people join together to conduct business without forming a corporation. The profits and losses are shared according to contributions of capital and expertise or as otherwise stipulated in a partnership agreement. A limited partnership must have at least one general partner who conducts business for the partnership, plus one or more limited partners.

A partnership certificate is filed with appropriate state officials. Partnerships are not subject to any federal or state income tax. Rather, *pro rata* shares of the tax items are allocated to the partners. This pass-through provision is the key to the entire process. Because having a valid limited partnership in place is a legal requirement, any syndication should provide an opinion by a qualified attorney stating that the limited partnership is legal. An illustrative Certificate of Limited Partnership is included in Appendix E.

## TAX DEDUCTIONS AND TAX CREDIT CLAIMS

***The tax deductions or credits generated by the project must be valid and legal.*** One of the most important factors in determining the tax deductions is the concept of *tax basis.* Tax law provides that investors in a project are allowed to take deductions as long as the deductions do not exceed their *basis* in a project. Generally, basis refers to the actual amount of money an investor has invested or the extent of the investor's liability. Usually the two are the same. For limited partners, who have their liability limited to their actual investment, this would mean that if a person invested $100,000, the actual claim in losses would be $100,000, regardless of any greater paper losses. The only way to benefit from the excess losses would be to change from a limited partner to a general partner. For this reason, some syndications involve general partnerships, whereby all investors are potentially liable for all debts and therefore all partners can participate in additional, otherwise excess, tax losses.

Limited partnership syndications do not work this way, however, because of another key provision called the *non-recourse loan*. Since a non-recourse loan gives the lender no recourse to the borrower (in the case of a mortgage default), the lender cannot take action against the borrower personally. To seek the legally due funds the lender must go only to the property. If there are insufficient funds available upon sale of the property, then the lender loses.

Since no one is personally liable for repaying a non-recourse mortgage loan, the mortgage obligation liability of each partner, both general and limited, is considered to be the percentage of ownership interests in the property. When a non-recourse mortgage is in effect, the tax basis of each limited partner is based on the percentage owned in a limited partnership. If 10 percent is owned in the project, then typically the limited partner is entitled to claim 10 percent of the losses which are generated by depreciation and interest (although these allocations may vary, as spelled out in the partnership agreement). Because the liability has been expanded, tax losses can be claimed in excess of the actual dollars invested in the project. The key provision making this possible is Section 1.752.1(e) of the Federal Income Tax Regulations. It provides for an increase in basis only "where none of the partners have any personal liability with respect to a partnership liability." Without this provision, there would be little syndication of low-income housing properties or other properties that failed to produce substantial cash flow or appreciation.

In other words, unless a non-recourse loan is in place, the tax benefits associated with a project are not available to limited partners. In such an instance, real estate syndication via the limited partner route would not occur.

The total tax basis of a property is the value that can be recovered (formerly depreciated) for tax purposes under the Accelerated Capital Recovery System (ACRS). Tax basis does not include the value of the land on which the building is located, nor does it include syndication costs. Generally speaking, it is determined by the purchase price of an existing property plus all project costs associated with rehabilitation, excluding land costs and syndication costs. In the case of a new construction project, it generally includes all project costs—both hard costs and soft costs—incurred in developing and building the project, excluding land and syndication costs. Since this may not always be the case, however, it is important to consult with an expert in the field to determine which costs constitute the tax basis of a property. To determine the amount allowable under the ACRS method, the formula is as follows:

> **TOTAL COST OF THE PROPERTY**
> **(either purchase price or development cost)**
>    *Less* **land cost**
>    *Less* **any disallowed project costs**
>    *Equals* **tax basis**
>    *Divided by* **15 (the capital recovery period permitted by the IRS)**
>    *Equals* **capital recovery amount for each of 15 years, using a straight-line method**

A limited partner, therefore, in determining tax deductions would claim the *pro rata* share of the capital recovery plus the *pro rata* share of interest due on non-recourse project financing and the *pro rata* share of any fees included in the mortgage.

The tax law also permits the use of declining balance accelerated depreciation of 175 percent declining balance (or 200 percent declining balance in the case of low-income housing). To calculate the amount allowable under the declining balance accelerated depreciation method, this formula is used:

> **FIRST YEAR**
> **Initial tax basis**
>    *Divided by* **15**
>    *Multiplied by* **the appropriate accelerated depreciation percentage (175 percent Declining Balance (DB) for all properties except low-income housing; 200 percent DB for low-income housing)**
>    *Equals* **ACRS in year 1**
>
> **SECOND YEAR**
> **Initial basis**
>    *Less* **amount of ACRS taken in year 1**
>    *Divided by* **15**

*Multiplied by* 175 percent DB
*Equals* ACRS year 2

**THIRD YEAR**
**Initial basis**
    *Less* amount of ACRS taken in years 1 and 2
    *Divided by* 15
    *Multiplied by* 175 percent DB
    *Equals* ACRS year 3

This basic approach is continued through the 15-year capital recovery period, after which time there is no longer any ACRS permitted. At some point the amount allowed under the ACRS accelerated cost recovery system is less than the annual amount allowed using the straight-line method (the adjusted basis divided by the number of years in the remaining life). When this point occurs, the IRS requires the owner to switch to the straight-line method. In calculating these numbers, it is advisable to seek professional assistance, and in no event does the IRS allow an owner to claim more in total capital recovery than the amount of the total tax basis. Appendix Tables A and B show the annual ACRS percentage using the accelerated capital recovery method. These figures, provided by the IRS, should be used in determining the annual amounts allowed for ACRS.

For low-income substantial rehabilitation projects, Section 167(k) of the Code allows straight-line, five-year recovery of rehabilitation costs up to $20,000 per unit. This provision, which has profound effects on the amount of tax losses during the early years, was expanded in the 1981 act to provide for a five-year write-off up to $40,000, if a certified program is in effect for transferring ultimate ownership to tenants.

While the IRS allows accelerated capital recovery, there is the provision that when the property is disposed of, either through sale or foreclosure, the difference in depreciation between the accelerated method and the straight-line method is subject to recapture at the tax rates which would apply to the individual's ordinary income. In the case of commercial properties, if acceleration is utilized, all depreciation, not just the excess, is subject to recapture.

For recapture purposes, a foreclosure is treated like a sale. Probably the most serious adverse event that could befall a limited partner would be a foreclosure, especially in the project's early years, because the IRS would consider all the excess losses as ordinary income. Although most partnership agreements obligate the general partner to guarantee to cover operating losses until a specified point, typically the end of the initial lease-up period, investors should be prepared to put additional money in the project at any time, should it get into operating difficulties.

Also, many projects now qualify for an investment tax credit. Since an investment tax credit comes directly off the tax liability rather than the taxable income, to an owner or investor it is worth the full amount of the credit rather than the amount times the investor's marginal tax rate, as is the case with deductions.

Prior to 1981, an investment tax credit was available for a portion of the costs incurred in rehabilitating older commercial properties and purchasing personal property and equipment for commercial and industrial buildings. The 1981 tax act increased the credit for rehabilitation costs incurred in older commercial buildings and historical structures.

The most important tax acts which currently affect real estate syndications are the Economic Recovery Tax Act of 1981 (ERTA) and the Tax Equity and Fiscal Responsibility Act of 1982 (TEFRA). These are summarized in Appendix F.

## THE LEGAL SYNDICATION PROCESS

*The syndication process must comply with strict federal and state full-disclosure requirements.* The limited partnership interests sold to investors are legally classified as securities. Therefore, the Securities and Exchange Commission's (SEC) rules affecting securities must be adhered to in the offer and sale of the interests to investors as do individual state blue-sky laws. While generally the securities laws require that securities be registered with the SEC, several exemptions from those requirements are available. Because there is a great deal of expense and time involved in registering limited partnership interests with the SEC, many syndicators use the available exemptions.

Whether the interests are syndicated under an exemption or through the registration process, the principle of *full disclosure* remains constant. That is, the SEC wants investors to receive full disclosure concerning the securities that they are asked to purchase. Thus, before the securities can be offered or sold to potential investors, counsel for the promoter has to determine that all of the material facts have been made available to an investor, either through a written offering memorandum or by providing the investor underlying files and permitting the investor to ask questions of the promoter.

In addition, the securities laws govern those persons who actually sell the securities. All brokers who sell securities must be registered in any state in which they make sales. Moreover, the securities themselves must be cleared before each offering can be made in a particular state.

Having reached an agreement with the developer, the syndicator must put the ownership interests in the proper form to sell to investors. The syndicator may choose to have a prospectus written and registered with the SEC, or may choose to write a *private placement offering memorandum* and sell the interests under an exemption from the registration requirements. In extremely limited circumstances where all the underlying documents are made available directly to a sophisticated investor, a private placement offering memorandum may not be necessary.

Most syndicators use the offering exemptions that require a private placement memorandum. Most offering memoranda contain similar kinds of information. The goal is to provide investors with all important information about the project and the people who will be involved with the project, including the syndicator. All compensation to any parties in the offering must be disclosed, as well as information describing how the investors' money will be spent. The major risks—tax, market, and development—and operational aspects of the project must be disclosed to potential investors.

The offering memorandum satisfies two requirements. The first is the legal requirement to present all the pertinent information about a project to the investors. The second is the practical requirement to get the information out to the potential market. Because of the securities laws and regulations, however, an offering memorandum is a formal document which is required to present the bad along with the good about the project. For this reason, the memorandum is required to state at the outset what risks are associated with the investment.

Though the risks vary from project to project, various risks are associated with most real estate securities. The first kind of risk is the *real estate risk* inherent in the development and operation of any income-producing real estate project. Another is the *tax risk* that the IRS might disallow certain deductions that could be declared in future years. There is also the *illiquidity risk* of not being able to transfer or sell the interests (what might be called the risk of not being able to get out of the deal). Another is *partnership risk*, the possibility that the general partner will not perform adequately or meet legal obligations, including fiduciary responsibilities to the limited partners. A *political risk* also sometimes exists, arising from uncertainties about governmental actions. The final risk is the *financial/economic risk* associated with highly leveraged loan-to-value ratios, fluctuating interest rates, and the down side of economic cycles. Most offering memoranda will deal explicitly with each of these areas, in addition to presenting complete information about the project, the developer, and the syndicator, and will present detailed financial projections. The contents of a typical offering memorandum are shown in Appendix C.

## OTHER TAX CONSIDERATIONS

There are other important considerations which, though technical, significantly affect the investor's tax situation, including the tax risk, and which therefore are required by the SEC to be reported to potential investors. One is the warning that Section 183 of the Tax Code provides that as a general rule no deductions (except for interest and real estate taxes) are allowable to an individual for activities not engaged in for profit. In theory, to get the benefit of a tax shelter, the shelter cannot be the only motivation for an investment. So far, investment in federally assisted low-income housing has not been affected by this ruling. Other types of tax shelter investment, however, may be more suspect. Since the Code specifies that for an activity to be engaged in for profit the gross income for two of the five years (ending with the current taxable year) must exceed the deductions, there is the possibility that investment in some tax shelters could be challenged by the IRS.

While limited partnerships provide tax shelters, the Code still imposes a minimum tax on tax preferences which exceed either

$10,000 or 50 percent of taxes paid by the individual. Investors must treat the excess depreciation as a tax preference item which is subject to the minimum tax of 15 percent.

The legal provisions affecting tax deductions are complicated. They are based on a number of factors—tax laws, IRS regulations and rulings, and court cases—each of which is subject to change. In addition, many of the key provisions are open to varying interpretations. Competent professional help is required in putting together any syndication, and this assistance should be sought early in the syndication process.

Syndication must also be marketed and sold to the right kinds of people. Because of the risks associated with most real estate syndications, if the private placement route is followed, as is most often the case, the SEC requires that investors maintain substantial net worth requirements and be "sophisticated investors." The assumption here is that, even though the syndicator is required to present a full disclosure of all the pertinent information, there is no assurance that a particular investment is sound; and only those who can afford to take a loss should be allowed to play the game. This restriction does not apply to offerings registered with the SEC, where there is a thorough review of the offering. An important modification of who can and cannot participate as a limited partner in private placement was published in 1982 as Regulation D, which substantially loosened the procedures for private placement offerings and established the concept of an *Accredited Investor*. An Accredited Investor is essentially someone who has substantial net worth and who presumably is very sophisticated. When accredited investors purchase the real estate securities, the required procedures are considerably more lax. Since these regulations are subject to periodic change, legal counsel should be consulted prior to any decision regarding how a project might be syndicated.

In summary, the legal aspects of syndication are extremely important and have a significant impact on both the economics of a real estate syndication and the ability to undertake the syndication in the first place. Because laws, regulations, rulings, and court decisions are always changing, it is advisable to seek qualified tax and legal assistance at the beginning of any contemplated syndication deal.

# *T h r e e*
## What Investors Look For in a Real Estate Syndication

Limited partners in a real estate limited partnership are silent investors. While they will be given the opportunity to cast a vote on major decisions such as selling the property or replacing a general partner, limited partners are precluded by law from having any say in the day-to-day management decisions of a limited partnership. Few limited partners care about such matters. What they are concerned about is getting a reasonable return on the money that they have invested. Most limited partners probably never see the properties in which they have ownership interests or have any interest in seeing them. It is akin in many ways to owning stock in a corporation. As long as the company does all right, investors are happy. The major difference, however, is that it is relatively easy to sell or transfer shares of stock. It is very difficult to get out of a limited partnership. In addition, if the project does get into trouble and is threatened with foreclosure, not only will the limited partner probably lose all of his initial equity investment, all excess depreciation (the difference between the straight-line and the accelerated declining balance method) is subject to tax at ordinary income rates. The result could be disastrous. For this reason, most investors are concerned about two major items. The first is the financial benefit that the project itself promises to produce. The second is the strength, track record, and reliability of the general partner who will be in charge of managing the development and operations of the project. Both are very important.

## FINANCIAL CONSIDERATIONS

This book uses the term *financial benefit* rather than cash, profit, or money. While ultimately financial benefit translates into cash at some future point, there is an important distinction between financial benefit and cash return. Basically, there are three types of financial benefits which affect real estate investment decisions. The first is cash return, or cash flow. Someone invests money to own a project, and he gets back cash flow each year generated by the profit of the operation. Terms like *return on equity* (ROE) or *return on investment* (ROI) express the ratio of dollars received (on an annual basis) to cash invested. Return on equity is the ratio of cash flow after debt service to the difference between the appraised value of the property and the total debt financing. Return on investment is the ratio of after-debt service cash flow to the amount of actual cash invested in the deal.

A second kind of financial benefit is appreciation; that is, the realized increase in value of a project over its original price when the project is sold. Some projects may not generate very much in the way of cash return, but because of their potential for long-term appreciation in value they will be attractive investment opportunities and demand a much higher investment than would be the case were the financial benefits expressed solely in terms of annual cash return on investment.

The third kind of financial benefit is the legal deferral of what would otherwise be income tax dollars to the federal or state government. Quite simply, investors view these tax dollars saved as dollars earned, and there are very few investment decisions made without taking into consideration the income tax consequences.

While all three types of financial benefits are important, real estate syndications often emphasize the federal income tax benefit. What makes the tax benefit in income-producing real estate investments is the concept of depreciation or, as it is now labeled in the Economic Recovery Tax Act of 1981, *capital recovery*.

Since depreciation is an accounting concept and does not affect the actual cash flow of a project, an income-producing building typically will show an accounting loss even when it may generate income to its owner. The owner may apply these accounting "losses" to shelter income he or she receives from other sources.

The basic formula is as follows:

**TOTAL GROSS INCOME**
  *Less* **operating costs**
  *Less* **interest on the mortgage loans**
  *Less* **capital recovery (or depreciation)**
  *Equals* **profit or loss for tax purposes**

Thus, a limited partner who owns a portion of a real estate project is entitled to include in his tax return his *pro rata* share of the losses generated by the project each year. These tax benefits available to limited partners are very important in most real estate syndications and in some instances determine virtually the total financial benefit of certain types of properties.

Syndication enables a developer to raise capital by selling these benefits to higher-income investors who are in a position to, and who perceive a need to, use these benefits. Moreover, in the case of projects that generate substantial accounting losses, the tax benefits are often so significant that they far exceed many developers' abilities to use these losses themselves. For this reason, it makes economic sense (in many cases it is imperative) for the developer to sell portions of the project so that the tax savings are fully utilized. Basically, this is what syndication of federally assisted low-income housing always has been about and what the syndication of historical and older commercial, rehabilitated properties now will achieve: sharing the tax benefits produced by a project with individuals who can use those benefits.

Potential investors in a limited partnership are people who have many opportunities to use their money—investing in stocks, bonds, commercial paper, Treasury bills, commodities, foreign exchange, and the like—each of which offers some promise of financial benefit. Real estate investment must compete for their dollars. The financial benefits of real estate investment will be compared with returns from alternative types of investments. After-tax yield will be a principal point of comparison between various investment alternatives.

Most investment opportunities offer some combination of all three types of financial benefits. How a specific investor weighs the types of benefits is influenced primarily by the individual's own tax situation, the amount of money available to invest, and two other very important factors: the risk of the investment and the timing of the financial benefit. Generally, the longer an investor has to wait to realize financial benefits, the less willing the investor is to invest at the outset in order to receive those benefits. Similarly, the greater the perceived risk, the less one is willing to invest to receive project benefits. Another way of stating this relationship is that the greater the risk, the higher the required return.

The financial benefits, their timing, and the risks associated with them determine whether or not an investor will purchase ownership interest in a real estate project. Accordingly, unless the investment opportunity combines these factors in such a way that the result is competitive with other investment opportunities—taking into consideration the timing and risk of the benefits—syndication is not feasible. For comparing the various opportunities which are available, two useful concepts are often used by syndicators and investment firms. These are the investment loss ratio and the internal rate of return concepts.

## Investment/Loss Ratios

Most low-income housing syndications are priced to investors on the basis of a straightforward and relatively simple concept which presents the tax losses generated by the project each year and shows the relationship of the dollars invested each year to the total tax losses generated each year by the project. The reasons for this relatively simple formula are that few low-income housing projects can demonstrate assurance of generating much in the way of cash flow distributions to partners (and cash flow distributions to partners are often limited by law) or can be expected to appreciate in value. The one thing that is certain, however, is the availability of tax benefits. Because these tax benefits are relatively secure and can be determined easily, they are the primary basis for pricing the limited partnership interests.

Suppose, for example, that an individual or family had a net taxable income of $100,000 a year. The marginal federal income tax rate of the individual is 50 percent, so that 50 cents on every additional dollar earned goes to the federal government, with additional dollars going to the state and local governments. Since the losses generated by a real estate project can be passed through to the individual's tax return, ownership interest in a real estate limited partnership defers his tax liability. In simplistic terms, the relationship works as follows:

|  | No Tax Shelter | Tax Shelter |
|---|---|---|
| Taxable income | $100,000 | $100,000 |
| Pass-through losses from limited partnership | 0 | $ 20,000 |
| Net income, subject to tax | $100,000 | $ 80,000 |
| Marginal tax rate | 50% | 50% |
| Tax (from 1982 tax tables) | $ 37,449 | $ 27,505 |
| Net savings | 0 | $ 9,994 |

The value of the $20,000 tax write-off in this case, therefore, amounts to almost 10,000. If the individual invested, for example, $7,500, the return on investment would be 33 percent, even if the project did not generate any cash flow and the initial equity was not recovered when the project was sold.

This is the basic concept behind practically all low-income housing syndications. Chapter Six presents an example of how the information for a low-income housing syndication typically is presented to investors. The standard industry norm is to show pretax ratios of dollars invested to total losses generated. Usually the information is also presented showing the after-tax consequences to taxpayers in the 40, 45, and 50 percent marginal income tax brackets. The losses are shown for both a five-year pay-in period, over which time the investment is made in installments, and a 15 to 20-year anticipated holding period.

Since there have been a very large number of tax-shelter syndications on the market, brokerage houses often carry several offerings, thus giving investors the opportunity to pick and choose. The result has been that market demand has a strong effect on how the securities are priced, and the pricing tends to be fairly similar for similar types of properties. Affecting the ratios are such items as location, market risks such as the lack of Section 8 for some units, the length and types of government assistance, the potential for appreciation or condominium conversion, and the strength and track record of the general partner.

Ratios are also affected by changes in the tax law, which affect marginal tax rates and the length and duration of the tax losses generated. When the tax law was changed in 1981, for example, the ratios of losses to investment were increased, since maximum tax rate was reduced from 70 cents on the dollar to 50 cents on the dollar. The ratios used in tax shelter limited partnership pricing are shown below:

### RATIO OF TAX LOSSES TO DOLLARS INVESTED
### (NEW CONSTRUCTION PROJECT)

| Year of Investment | Typical Ratio (pre-1981) | Typical Ratio (post-1981) |
|---|---|---|
| 1 | 1.5 to 1 | 2.0 to 1 |
| 2 | 2.1 to 1 | 2.4 to 1 |
| 3 | 2.1 to 1 | 2.3 to 1 |
| 4 | 1.9 to 1 | 2.0 to 1 |
| 5 | 1.7 to 1 | 2.0 to 1 |
| 6 | 1.6 to 1 | 1.8 to 1 |
| Avg. 1–6 period | 1.8 to 1 | 2.08 to 1 |
| Avg. 1–20 period | 3.1 to 1 | 3.2 to 1 |

The other major factor is when the losses are experienced and how long they last. Low-income housing substantial rehabilitation projects, for example, generate a large number of losses over the first five years because $20,000 of rehabilitation costs per unit can be written off over a five-year period (and up to $40,000 in some cases). After the five-year period is up, however, the losses drop very quickly; and—often as early as year 8 or 10—the projects may start showing taxable income. The result is that the pricing for substantial rehabilitation projects shows a ratio of losses to investment much higher than a new construction project over the five-year pay-in period. For the overall 20-year holding period, however, the ratios are usually similar. The pricing of substantial rehabilitation projects has not substantially changed from the pre-1981 pricing, which was as follows:

### RATIO OF TAX LOSSES TO DOLLARS INVESTED (SUBSTANTIAL REHABILITATION PROJECT)

| Year of Investment | Typical Ratio |
|---|---|
| 1 | 2.4 to 1 |
| 2 | 2.5 to 1 |
| 3 | 2.6 to 1 |
| 4 | 2.7 to 1 |
| 5 | 2.4 to 1 |
| 6 | 2.4 to 1 |
| Avg. 1–6 period | 2.5 to 1 |
| Avg. 1–20 period | 3.0 to 1 |

Ratios will likely change over time as tax laws change and as conditions of supply and demand change. If many such securities are on the market at one time, for example, there is greater likelihood of having to show larger losses in order to attract investors. Since the pricing of these real estate securities is influenced by market factors, the people best suited to price the securities are those actively involved in the syndication field.

## Internal Rate of Return

Internal rate of return is a fancy word for translating all the financial benefits produced by a project over time—cash flow, tax benefits, and potential appreciation—into one lump-sum investment amount which takes into account the interest that an investor could be making on his money on other investments. The key to understanding this concept is the fact that real estate projects produce potential benefits over time. A dollar produced by the project five years from now is not worth a dollar today for the simple reason that if you had a dollar today you could invest that dollar (at whatever the market interest rate is) and have more than a dollar five years into the future; at 12 percent compounded annual interest, for instance, a dollar today would be worth $1.76 at the end of year 5, as shown below:

| Year | Calculation | Amount Compounded at 12% |
|------|-------------|--------------------------|
| 1 | $1.00 × 1.12% | 1.12 |
| 2 | $1.12 × 1.12% | 1.25 |
| 3 | $1.25 × 1.12% | 1.40 |
| 4 | $1.40 × 1.12% | 1.57 |
| 5 | $1.57 × 1.12% | 1.76 |

The reverse of compounding interest is *discounting.* It divides the financial benefit received in a given year by the appropriate discount rate, which is a function of the interest rate that the money could be earning today. In other words, $1.76 earned in year 5 discounted at 12 percent is worth $1.00 today. Examples of discount tables are shown in Appendix D and are included in most financial textbooks.

| | |
|---|---|
| Year 5 discount factor (from table) | .567 |
| *Multiplied by* amount in year 5 | 1.76 |
| *Equals* present value | $1.00 |

Discount rates can now be easily calculated by many pocket calculators or computers. The discounted value of an income stream over time, which includes cash flow, after-tax benefits, and net profit at the time of sale, is commonly referred to as *net present value*. To calculate net present value, the interest rate is known. The question that is solved for is what is the present value of the income stream over time.

In order to figure the present value of an income stream which is produced over a period of time extending into the future, each amount of income received is discounted to the present by multiplying the figure by the appropriate discount amount. Generally it is assumed that the cash flows are received on an annual basis at the end of each year. The discount rate is the desired rate of return to the investor or the rate of interest that the investor believes he could earn on an investment of similar risk. The discount figures for a 12 percent and 15 percent return, for example, are shown below. (See Appendix D for a complete table.)

### DISCOUNT FACTORS

| Year | 12% | 15% |
|------|------|------|
| 1 | .893 | .870 |
| 2 | .797 | .756 |
| 3 | .712 | .658 |
| 4 | .636 | .572 |
| 5 | .567 | .497 |

In other words, assuming a 12 percent discount rate, a dollar received in year 5 is only worth about 57 cents today under a 12 percent rate, and only 50 cents under a 15 percent rate. Why? Because, if you had the dollar today and invested it at 12 percent, at the end of year 5 it would have generated interest compounded annually amounting to $1.76, as shown above.

Net present value, therefore, is the sum of all the annual cash flows, with each cash flow discounted to the present. Let us assume, for example, that a project was presented to an investor which promised to produce the following cash flows over a five-year period:

| Year | Amount |
|------|--------|
| 1 | $100 |
| 2 | 150 |
| 3 | 125 |
| 4 | 200 |
| 5 | 210 |
| **Total** | **$785** |

In figuring the net present value of this income stream, at a 12 percent interest rate, the wise investor would discount these cash flows as follows:

| Year | 12% Discount Factor | × | Cash Flow | = | Present Value |
|------|---------------------|---|-----------|---|---------------|
| 1 | .895 | | $100 | | $ 89 |
| 2 | .797 | | 150 | | 120 |
| 3 | .712 | | 125 | | 89 |
| 4 | .636 | | 200 | | 127 |
| 5 | .567 | | 210 | | 119 |
| | Totals | | $785 | | $544 |

In other words, while the actual total cash produced $785, the discounted amount, taking into consideration the interest that the money could be earning if the money were in hand today, is only $544. Using a 15 percent discount rate, it would be even lower:

| Year | 15% Discount Factor | × | Cash Flow | = | Present Value |
|------|---------------------|---|-----------|---|---------------|
| 1 | .870 | | $100 | | $ 87 |
| 2 | .756 | | 150 | | 113 |
| 3 | .658 | | 125 | | 82 |
| 4 | .572 | | 200 | | 114 |
| 5 | .497 | | 210 | | 104 |
| | Totals | | $785 | | $500 |

The concept of internal rate of return is exactly the same as net present value, except in this case both the initial investment and the income stream are known; but the discount rate is not known. The question that is solved for in internal rate of return calculations is what is the discount rate that is required to discount the income stream to a present value number which is equal to the initial investment amount. In figuring the internal rate of return for real estate transactions, the net after-tax cash flow to the investor is used (including tax shelter benefits); and it is assumed that the project is sold at the end of the period, with the net after-tax proceeds shown as the final number in the project's income stream.

The useful thing about net present value or internal rate of return is that they are numbers that can be used for comparing alternative investments. Another way of stating this is that it tells the investor that the future benefits produced by the real estate investment are roughly the same as having X dollars today on which the investor could earn a given interest rate. If the given interest rate (or internal rate of return) is more attractive than the interest rate that he could earn on the money today (and the risks are acceptable), the investor probably will make the investment. If not, the person more than likely will decline to invest.

To calculate net present value of $100 received in year 1, $150 received in year 2, $125 received in year 3, $200 received in year 4, and $210 received in year 5, at a discount rate of 12 percent, you look up the discount amounts in the table in Appendix D, multiply each income figure in the given year by the discount factor, and then add the results together, as calculated earlier.

Calculating the internal rate of return, you begin with an initial investment of, say, $544, with a projected income stream of $100 in year 1, $150 in year 2, and so on; but you do not know what the discount rate is. Unfortunately, calculating the internal rate of return is based on a trial and error method of first guessing what you think the discount rate ought to be and then calculating the net present value and comparing the results with the initial investment. When the net present value amount equals the initial investment amount, you have figured out the internal rate of return. Fortunately, computers and even many hand calculators instantly now can calculate the internal rate of return (IRR) easily and quickly.

The problem with internal rates of return and net present value is that the results are profoundly affected by the assumptions that go into the model. A minor change in the projected increase in rents, operating costs, or sales price at the end of the projected holding period often has a major impact on the net present value or internal rate of return. For this reason, the IRR is not appropriate for most low-income housing syndications and is often suspect in other syndications as well—and no IRR is any better than the assumptions on which it is based.

What is important, however, in any real estate securities offering is for all the financial benefits to be presented for a long period of time (usually 15 to 20 years) or the projected length of the holding period. Equally important is for the assumptions on which the benefits are based to be clearly spelled out. This information, which is the essence of any offering memorandum, must be accurate and complete; and it is largely on the basis of these financial projections that an investor will choose to participate as a limited partner in a syndication deal.

## INVESTOR RISKS

As stated in the previous chapter, offering memoranda are required to state what risks are associated with a particular investment. In many cases, the risks are very real and should not be taken lightly. There are three major risks. The first is the market and economic risk inherent in the real estate aspects of the project. The second is the tax risk, alluded to earlier, that the IRS may disallow certain deductions that could be declared in future years. The third is the risk of not being able to transfer or sell the interests, or what might be called "the risk of not being able to get out of the deal."

### The Real Estate Risk

It is sometimes assumed that once a project goes into construction most of the problems have been solved and relatively few risks remain. This assumption is only partially accurate and depends in large part on the nature of the project. The fact is that the project still must be built on budget and on time; and, once completed, the project must lease-up on schedule and operate at close to full occupancy at rents that are high enough to meet debt service requirements and the cost of operating and maintaining the building, and to produce a cash flow for the owner.

The real estate risk is present even though a limited partner has only limited liability. While in theory the partner has only limited liability, because of the IRS recapture provision, if a project does fail and is foreclosed on by the lender, the IRS treats this the same as it would a sale and requires all excess depreciation to be treated as ordinary income for tax purposes. In the case of accelerated depreciation on a commercial building, all depreciation is subject to recapture. Nothing could be worse for an investor in a tax shelter limited partnership.

For this reason, it is extremely important that the project be on a sound economic footing from the outset and have as a general partner an individual or firm with a proven track record and, equally important, with the capacity to provide the financial resources to prevent a foreclosure in difficult situations. While the general partner may technically be on the line to provide additional cash, the limited partners may have more to lose financially in the event of a foreclosure. The general partner could come back to the limited partners and present them with a rather difficult decision: they put in the extra cash required to complete the project or cover operating deficits or the general partner walks off, leaving them with the IRS breathing down their necks for several hundred thousand dollars in taxes due. It is not a happy situation.

And projects do get into trouble, even the best of them with the best sponsors. A typical problem sometimes encountered is discovering subsurface soil conditions which require much more construction work than was budgeted for. Also, since the cost of rehabilitation projects is very difficult to estimate, rehabilitation projects are often subject to cost overruns. There is no guarantee that the lender will increase the mortgage to cover these cost increases. If the general partner will not provide the additional funds the limited partners may have no practical alternative other than to provide additional funds themselves.

One way that such difficult problems are often handled is for the general partner to loan money to the partnership and to be repaid with interest over a period of time out of rental proceeds. Also, general partners are often required to provide guarantees to the limited partners to cover construction overruns and operating deficits for a limited time period. Absent a formal guarantee, the investor should be aware that, if problems occur, a limited partner may get an unwelcome call from the developer discussing a few unanticipated problems involving "this project which they are all involved in together."

The other false assumption is that once the project is completed there is very little risk, especially if the project consists of government rental support such as Section 8 Housing Assistance Payments Contracts, whereby "the government is footing the bill." There is no question that the Section 8 Housing Assistance Payments Contract provides a great deal of security to the owners. Without such a contract, new or substantial rehabilitation projects serving low-income people would be on extremely shaky ground in inflationary times—as rents inevitably increase while incomes of many low-income households do not—and probably could not be syndicated. The built-in "automatic adjustment factor" in the Section 8 program gives owners assurance that the basic mechanism is in place for meeting increases in fuel, utilities, and staff salaries. There is no absolute assurance, however, that the automatic adjustment will in fact be adequate to cover legitimate operating-cost increases in every situation. While there is the provision that owners can petition HUD for specified rent increases to cover unanticipated energy costs or real estate tax increases, there is no assurance that such an increase will be granted or, if granted, that it will be in time to avoid a catastrophe.

There is also the problem of poor property management. The management of low-income housing, in particular, is extremely difficult even under the best of circumstances. Many management firms are simply not capable of dealing with the day-to-day problems encountered in this type of housing. Often when the partners become aware that a problem exists, it is already too late to remedy the situation without a major infusion of funds. Equally important from an investor's perspective is that the limited partners can have no say in the management of a project, including the selection of a management firm. HUD or a state financing agency can replace a poor manager, but a limited partner cannot since to do so would jeopardize his limited partnership status. A general partner's associates may find themselves in utter shock when they learn that the worthless brother-in-law has been hired to manage the property. There is nothing, however, that they can do about it.

For projects which do not involve Section 8 assistance—and, in future years, this will increasingly be the case—an additional dimension is added: the market factor. An investor must ask these questions: "Is there in fact a market for the project?" "Will households pay the required rent?" "Will firms execute the required leases for office buildings?" At the very least, market-rate projects will take longer to lease initially and will likely experience an initial operating deficit. It should be completely clear how the initial deficit is covered. Is the deficit capitalized and considered part of the total development cost, or will it come out of the general partner's fee? The real estate factors, such as the metropolitan area, the location of the project, and the rents of competitive apartment or office buildings, enter the picture when one is dealing with a market-rate building. In such projects, unless the investor understands the real estate market himself, he should insist that general partners or syndicators provide him with a market study by a reputable real estate consulting firm. This market study should also be an important part of any offering memorandum.

## The Tax Risks

These risks, which were identified in the previous section dealing with legal provisions affecting syndication, are by no means insignificant. A valid partnership must be in place. There must be a non-recourse loan to enable the partner to increase his basis with regard to the mortgage obligations. Also, there is the risk that an IRS audit might disallow some of the deductions and that an IRS audit of the partnership might trigger an IRS audit of the individual's personal tax return. Some of the less clear deductions include the deductions usually claimed for guarantees against construction cost overruns and operating deficits, and the deduction of certain construction period expenses. There is the risk that Congress might pass future legislation which could modify the tax consequences of earlier investments and, finally, the potentially disastrous risk that the IRS could rule that insufficient "profit motivation" is involved to warrant the deduction for depreciation or cost recovery.

## The "Getting Out" Risk

The ownership interests in assisted housing are frequently sold without being registered with the Securities and Exchange Commission. One of the requirements of a private offering of securities is that the security not be sold to anyone who intends to resell the interest publicly. That is, investors are required to represent that they intend to hold the securities for a long period. Generally speaking, individual partnership interests can be resold only under very limited circumstances (as spelled out in the partnership agreement), and not without the consent of the general partner, and then only if an opinion of reputable counsel is obtained that the transfer does not require registration with the SEC. In many instances, consent is also required by the lender or insurer for individual limited partners to get out of a deal. In other words, once you are a limited partner, you may not be able to resell your partnership interests.

The primary way out is for the entire project to be sold. The partnership agreement spells out the consent that is necessary in order for this to happen. Approval of partners owning more than half the project is usually required. In addition, in most instances, approval to sell the project or repay the loan is also required by HUD and state financing agencies (or other tax-exempt bond issuers); often, in bond-financed projects there is an absolute prohibition against selling a project through a specified time period. Such provisions, however, must be presented to the investor prior to his participation.

When, for tax reasons, it is important that the project be sold some 15 or 20 years into the future, it may be that at that time there will be few economic benefits associated with the project. In such instances, syndicators are required to point out that there may not be a market for resale of the partnership interests and to state that it is probable that the investor will receive less than his original investment. While this pertains more to government-assisted projects than to market-rate projects, investors should be forewarned that opportunities for appreciation may not be present in the case of many syndications—especially tax-shelter syndications—and that they should not necessarily count on getting back their initial cash.

## LONG-TERM TAX LIABILITY RISKS

One frequent misconception about real estate syndications, especially those syndications emphasizing the income tax benefits, is the notion that participation in a real estate limited partnership is a way of avoiding income taxes. This is not the case. Rather, it is a way of deferring taxes. The day of reckoning ultimately comes when the project is sold. At this point, capital gains taxes will be paid based on the difference between the selling price and the initial purchase price (or total development cost), less all depreciation taken. In addition, all excess depreciation taken (the difference between the depreciation using the accelerated method and that using the straight-line method) is subject to taxes at the ordinary income rate in the case of residential properties. All accelerated depreciation is subject to the ordinary income tax rate in the case of commerical properties. Since the capital gains rate is currently 20 percent, the tax rate is lower than the ordinary income rate which would have been applied to the investor's ordinary income, had it not been sheltered. Also, since the taxes are deferred many years into the future, if inflation occurs during the period, the tax liability will be paid back with deflated dollars. In this sense, tax-shelter syndications do provide long-term tax savings. At the same time, investors should beware that in many instances—especially in the case of low-income housing syndications—there is likely to be a substantial tax due without any proceeds available to pay the tax. You might respond, "What is there to worry about? If the project doesn't appreciate in value, I won't have any capital gains." Wrong. The taxes due are based not on the difference between the project's selling price and its *initial tax basis,* but rather on its *adjusted tax basis* (initial basis less depreciation). If the value of the project remains the same, you would still owe a capital gains tax equal to 20 percent of all depreciation taken. If any excess depreciation had been taken, the tax rate would be 50 percent of the excess amount (or the entire amount in the case of commercial properties).

Let us examine a project which was initially developed for $1 million and sold for $1 million 10 years later. (For this example, no land value is assumed.) Using the straight-line 15-year ACRS, in year 10 the adjusted basis of the property would be $333,333 ($1,000,000 – $666,667). Even though the property had not increased at all in value, the owner would owe the federal government $133,333 (.2 × $666,667). If the project were financed with a long-term loan, it is quite possible that insufficient funds would be available to pay off the initial lender and meet the tax obligations.

While the tax liability issue is identified in most offering memoranda, it rarely is played up. Investors at the very least should carefully weigh the long-term consequences of taxes due on sale.

## KEY INVESTOR CONSIDERATIONS

Given the complexity of a real estate syndication and the risks involved, what should an investor look for? Three things are important. The first thing to look for, of course, is the financial return that is likely to be received. However the financial return is expressed, either as a ratio of losses to investment, an internal rate of return, or simply an identification of the likely financial benefits, the benefits should be competitive with those of other investment opportunities with similar risks. Second, the investor should carefully review the assumptions behind the financial projections and should be reasonably comfortable with those assumptions. If the investor does not have sufficient information to form an opinion about the assumptions or the real estate risks of the undertaking, additional professional assistance should be sought before investing in the deal. Finally, the investor should feel comfortable with the ability of the general partner to perform and live up to promises and obligations. Without a capable general partner, many a great deal has gone sour. Since there is virtually nothing a limited partner can do regarding day-to-day management decisions in a development project, if the limited partners are unhappy with management decisions, the only recourse is to replace the general partner, an action which is extremely difficult. If there is any doubt about the general partner's ability, you should not invest. This concept holds true both with regard to the partner's ability to develop the project *and to manage* the project on a long-term basis.

## THE ECONOMIC RECOVERY TAX ACT OF 1981 AND OPPORTUNITIES FOR INVESTMENT

There are numerous varieties of real estate syndications. Prior to the Economic Recovery Tax Act of 1981, the main area of tax shelter real estate syndication was federally assisted low-income housing. However, the 1981 Tax Act significantly altered the tax aspects of real estate investment. That fact, coupled with the significant reduction of the HUD Section 8 and FMHA programs for new construction and substantial rehabilitation, affects the opportunities available for syndication. While the opportunities for syndicating low-income housing have been significantly reduced, new syndication opportunities have been created for rehabilitating older commercial and historical properties.

### Low-Income Housing

Between 1974 and 1983, there were many low-income housing syndications. What made such syndications possible were these factors:

- a strong market for tax-shelter investments due to high nominal incomes and high marginal tax rates;
- the security offered investors by government-guaranteed rents for low-income projects for up to 20 years through the Section 8 program;
- government-assisted financing for Section 8 projects at below-market rates of 10 percent interest or less through the Government National Mortgage Association (GNMA) program and through tax-exempt permanent financing by state or local housing agencies; and
- a tax policy that generally favored investment in housing and especially favored investment in low-income housing.

Few of these factors exist today. The Section 8 program is dead, and the nature of permanent financing has radically changed. Yet because of the Economic Recovery Tax Act of 1981, new opportunities have arisen, primarily in the area of syndicating older low-income housing projects. The basic process works like this:

A syndicator will approach the owner of an older government-assisted housing project—most often a HUD-insured Section 236 or older HUD 221(D) (3) project. The existing owner may be either a for-profit, a limited dividend, or a nonprofit sponsor. The syndicator will offer to acquire the project under terms and conditions similar to the following:

1. *Assumption of existing project financing.* HUD as the loan insuror must agree to a transfer of physical assets (TPA). The syndicator will assume responsibility for obtaining HUD's approval in this area.
2. *Cash to cover tax liability.* The syndicator will pay cash to the owner to cover the owner's tax liability at the time of the transfer. The existing owner comes out of the deal with no cash, but with no money owed the federal government.
3. *A negotiated purchase price based on an appraised value using a modified "current replacement cost" method of appraisal, subject to approval by HUD.* In other words, the syndicator offers to buy the property for an amount related to what it would cost to build the identical project today. Since this amount is considerably higher than the original development cost of the project, and since it is probably higher than the economic value of the project (based solely on the income it is producing), the offer normally sounds pretty good to an owner who wants to get out of what is probably not a very good deal anymore anyway, since the tax shelter benefits have been exhausted and his project is probably not generating much, if any, cash flow. Of course, if the owner is a limited partnership, as is most often the case, the limited partners must agree

to the sale. For most older government-assisted properties, this will not be a problem.

4.  ***A non-recourse purchase money second trust at a negotiated interest rate.*** While interest is charged, no interest or principal is due until the project is sold. This is typically called a deferred interest mortgage. Here, of course, is the key to the transaction. The seller must wait a long time before realizing any cash benefits; and, if sufficient funds are not available at the time of resale, the current owner will never see any real cash benefits. At the same time, the current owner gets out from owning what may no longer be a very good investment. What does the owner have to lose?

How can the syndicator afford to make such an offer? The answer has to do with the Economic Recovery Tax Act of 1981, which eliminated the distinction between first-user and second-user properties in figuring depreciation, and substantially shortened the capital recovery period of all real estate (see Appendix F). Using the basic losses-to-investment formula presented earlier, the syndicator will turn around and syndicate the property. Since the tax basis is defined as what is paid for the property, the purchase price will determine what can be written off each year. In addition, there is a new deferred loan held by the seller. This loan carries an interest charge, which is a deductible item for tax purposes. The overall result is that the property is now attractive again as a tax shelter and can be syndicated using the losses-to-investment pricing mechanism.

Investors should look on these properties with considerable caution, however. For one thing, the properties are older properties which may require capital expenditures in the future in order to maintain the property. If the rehabilitation expenditures cannot be financed (and, if the property does not produce sufficient income, it will be difficult to obtain financing), the limited partners may be called on to make additional capital contributions. In addition, most older properties do not contain long-term government rent guarantees in the form of Section 8 payments, thus subjecting the property to real market forces. Also, the purchase price paid for the property could turn out to be a very real tax risk if the IRS determines that the value cannot be upheld or that the appraisal is not valid. While it is clear that there will be a large number of these recycled low-income housing syndications, the risks associated with them are considerably greater, both to the syndicator and the investor.

## Older Commercial Properties in Need of Rehabilitation

While the Tax Code previously favored investment in low-income housing, it now also favors older commercial properties by allowing for an investment tax credit for rehabilitating these properties. Also, since the Code provides for a shorter "recovery period" of 15 years for all real estate and for the use of accelerated depreciation with all real estate, significant tax benefits are available in rehabilitating older commercial properties. In addition, since such properties tend to generate greater cash flow than do residential projects and to increase in value to a greater degree than do apartment houses, older commercial properties in need of substantial rehabilitation now offer very significant total financial benefits and are increasingly attractive as investment opportunities.

## Historical Structures in Need of Rehabilitation

Also affected by the Economic Recovery Tax Act of 1981 are all properties on the historical register and properties in an historical district which are determined to be significant to the historical district in which they are located. A larger investment tax credit is available for the rehabilitation of historical structures, and the rules for capital recovery are more lenient. Accordingly, the financial benefits are potentially the highest of all for historic properties and offer especially appealing opportunities for developers of these properties.

The only constant pertaining to tax laws and rulings is the statement that all these items will surely change. New tax laws will be passed as Congress perceives the need to plug remaining loopholes or encourages special types of investments. As these laws change new types of investment opportunities will be created while former opportunities will disappear. What will not change, however, are the basic principles underlying the economics of real estate investment analysis, as identified in the chapter. It all, quite simply, boils down to a question of money: how much you will receive (or save by deferring taxes), when you will receive it, and how much risk is involved in the undertaking. If you understand this basic principle, you understand what investment in real estate deals has always been about and always will be about.

# *F o u r*

## Getting Started on a Syndication Deal: Making Sure the Numbers Work

Now that you have a general understanding of syndication and how it works, if you want to develop and syndicate a real estate project, where do you begin? You begin with a feasible real estate development concept. All projects must start with an idea, but how do you know that the idea will work? The problem in the real estate development business is that while a project may ultimately produce substantial financial rewards, it also involves substantial risk. To get to the point where a project can produce financial benefits, someone must spend a lot of money. Prior to the start of construction, the money typically is provided by the developer. At the start of construction, a lender enters the picture, as do the limited partners. Prior to this, the developer is in a high-risk situation. Thus, it is extremely important that you know at the outset whether a potential project is likely to make economic sense. It is equally important for you to determine this without spending a great deal of money. Therefore, the first step in any development project is the preliminary economic feasibility stage, when you determine whether a basic development concept is feasible and makes financial sense.

For two reasons this initial stage is the most important in the development process. First, it will establish the basic assumptions for estimating financial benefits. Although there will be many refinements to the basic economic model and to much of the data as the project progresses, the initial assumptions will shape the concept and will largely determine the outcome. If the basic assumptions

43

and economic relationships of the project significantly overstate returns or understate costs at the outset, the project is likely to fail at some future point in the development process. Second, the initial assessment of basic feasibility can be done relatively quickly and cheaply. The further you progress along the development path, the more money you spend and the more you commit both financially and emotionally to the project. If a project does not make sense, you are far better off finding it out earlier rather than later. This is what a preliminary economic feasibility analysis is about.

The preliminary steps required to answer the feasibility question are as follows:

1. A building program is conceptualized and a market survey is conducted to determine whether a market exists for the intended use. The basic program requirements (such as unit mix and sizes for rental apartment units, number of parking spaces, amenities, etc.) and the anticipated income from the project depend on these factors. The market survey may be informal and focused on short-term considerations, or it may be very thorough—but it is *always* the starting point.
2. Future operating costs are calculated.
3. The economic value of the project is determined.
4. Potential sources of funds are identified, including loans and equity capital.
5. The cost to develop the project is calculated.
6. A preliminary go/no-go decision is made on the basis of whether the sources of funds are equal to or greater than the cost to develop the project. Let us look at each of these steps in detail.

## MARKET STUDY AND PRELIMINARY PROGRAM PARAMETERS

To test feasibility, there must be something specific to build, referred to as a *building program*. The building program should be formulated by the developer, not the architect. The role of the architect is to fit the building program to a specific site. The design phase of the project does not get underway until the initial building concept is determined to be feasible.

How can you determine that a project is feasible without any drawings or specific architectural design concept? This can be accomplished by dealing with basic units of the development industry: housing units and square feet. Once the numbers are determined with regard to values and costs per housing unit or per square foot, it is relatively easy to expand them to accommodate whatever size building is being contemplated.

The first step, therefore, is to formulate a hypothetical building program which results in the typical unit of the project you want to build. The starting point is to gather detailed information regarding similar projects in your market area. An inventory of these projects should be prepared, showing for each project the following information:

- name and location
- date completed
- number of units (or size)
- unit sizes and mix (for residential projects)
- unit rents or rents per square foot
- utility combination
- amenities
- initial absorption (of units or square footage of recently completed similar projects in the area)
- current vacancies (or waiting list)
- estimates (if available) of construction and land costs, and operating expenses
- type and terms of available financing

By visiting projects and talking to the owners or management agents, you get a feel for similar projects. In addition, if a more thorough market study is to be undertaken, you will need to compile background data on basic economic and demographic conditions in the area such as population and household trends and projections, employment trends and projections, and annual production trends of whatever use is being considered (housing, office space, retail space, etc.) If you are uncertain about the market support for the project or want to develop a project which is untried in a given market area, you would be wise to engage the services of a professional marketing firm to undertake a detailed market study for you.

After gathering and analyzing this preliminary market information, you then refine your initial concept and address the issue of whom you want your project to attract and serve. This question must be answered if the project is market-oriented or if it is government-assisted because it significantly affects such things as size of project, types of units, size of units, unit mix, project location, project amenities, and project value. It is true both for residential and commercial properties.

After making an initial determination of market orientation, your next step is to develop a basic concept for your own project. This should include the following types of items (depending on whether the project is commercial or residential):

- type of building (commercial or residential; garden, townhouse, mid-rise or high-rise
- unit mix
- net unit sizes
- parking requirements
- amenities
- utility combination
- common areas and net rentable area
- rents per unit (residential) or per square foot (commercial)

It is easier to formulate a hypothetical project for new construction than for rehabilitation, which always involves a specific existing building. However, it is possible to undertake a similar conceptual analysis for rehabilitation, if you make assumptions about the typical structural features and layouts of target rehabilitation buildings. The purpose of this preliminary analysis is to test the basic feasibility of the concept, not to fit a specific design to a site or a specific rehabilitation concept to an existing building. The latter exercise comes later, at which time the preliminary numbers will be refined. The preliminary numbers are especially useful, however, because they give the developer a good idea of what the parameters are. In other words, they serve as a target for the more detailed design work to follow and are a useful guide as the development process continues.

At this stage the income that can be generated from the project is the most critical variable. The potential income should be projected forward to when the space will be initially rented. For Section 8 projects, the potential income is based on the allowable fair market rents (as determined by HUD). For all other projects, the income is determined by the market rents currently existing for competitive projects and projected forward to the time when the project should be completed.

## DETERMINING FUTURE OPERATING COSTS PAID BY THE OWNER

By estimating the rents of the project (projected at the midpoint of the first year's operation), you can determine the potential gross income of the project. However, the critical figure is not gross income, but *net* income—the amount of money available to you after all the bills for real estate taxes, insurance, maintenance, and operations have been paid, and after taking into consideration losses for normal vacancies and collections. The equation is as follows:

**POTENTIAL GROSS INCOME**
   *Less* **five percent vacancy and collection loss (percentage may vary)**
   *Equals* **effective gross income**
   *Less* **operating costs, maintenance costs, real estate taxes, and insurance**
   *Equals* **net income available to pay lender and owner**

The next key question therefore is what it will cost to operate the building when the project is at the midpoint of its first year of operation.

There are two ways to estimate operating costs. The first is to determine the current *per-unit* (either per residential unit or per gross square foot) operating costs for similar projects already in operation and to project those costs into the future. Most developers start with current per-unit operating cost figures, which they obtain from a management agent if the figures are not otherwise readily available. The problem is that there often is a very wide range in operating costs. Local real estate tax rates and assessments vary enormously, as do utility rates, employee payroll taxes, and other costs. Individual projects also differ as to the type of utility combination, on-site staffing, energy-saving concepts, and so on. The typical per-unit figures are helpful as a starting point, but only as a starting point.

The second way, clearly the more reliable of the two, is to prepare a detailed first year's budget, line item by line item. Typical types of operating costs are:

- management fee
- advertising
- legal, accounting, and audit fees
- elevator maintenance
- fuel
- electricity
- licenses and permits
- telephone
- water and sewer
- gas
- garbage and trash removal
- payroll
- security
- decorating
- repairs and maintenance
- insurance
- grounds expense
- reserve for replacements (future capital expenditures)
- real estate taxes
- personal property taxes
- employee payroll taxes
- payroll benefits
- char or cleaning service (for commercial space)

## ESTABLISHING ECONOMIC VALUE

Deriving economic value from *net rental income* is accomplished by dividing the projected net rental income from a project (the potential *gross income less operating expenses*) by the *capitalization rate*. The capitalization rate is the key to determining the value of income-producing real properties. The rate can be determined from tables, by formula with a calculator, or in consultation with a lender.

The concept of the capitalization rate is similar to the concept of the discount rate described in the preceding chapter. The difference is that in the calculation of present value presented earlier, we assumed that the financial benefits differed each year and that the income stream ended upon sale at a discrete time in the future. In this analysis, in determining economic value, no future sale is presumed and the net income produced by the project is presumed to extend indefinitely into the future and to be constant for each year. The economic value of the income stream is the net income figure (total realized income less all operating costs paid by the owner), divided by the capitalization rate. For all practical purposes, economic value means basically the same thing as *net present value,* that is, the value of a future income stream, which in this instance is presumed to extend indefinitely into the future without variation.

While this concept is very simplistic, it avoids the problems of having to develop assumptions regarding inflation, future sales prices, etc. Moreover, the concept is used primarily by permanent lenders in determining how much money they are willing to lend. Since their loan is based on how much is likely to be available to pay them back, using the capitalization concept is a quick and generally reliable way to accomplish this.

For example, let us assume that a project concept was presented to a permanent lender which showed $100 available free and clear in year 1 after all bills had been paid. If all this money were available to repay the lender (assuming the owner did not require a profit or return on equity), and assuming that the lender wanted to receive 10 percent each year interest only, then the lender would be prepared to make a loan of $1,000, as calculated below:

| | |
|---|---:|
| **ANNUAL INCOME TO BE RECEIVED BY THE PERMANENT LENDER** | **$ 100** |
| *Divided By* **lender interest rate** | **.10** |
| *Equals* **loan amount** | **$1,000** |

Each year the permanent lender receives $100. Since he made an initial loan of $1,000, his rate of return is $100 divided by $1,000, or 10 percent each year.

Of course, the real world is somewhat more complicated since the owner also wants a portion of the $100 to obtain a financial return on his equity. It is further complicated by the fact that the permanent lender typically wants to get back more than just interest. Typically, loan repayments are based on a distribution of interest and repayments to principal. This amount, commonly referred to as debt service, is a function of the interest rate and the length of the mortgage loan.

The capitalization rate is therefore a composite rate based on the requirements of the permanent lender and the requirements of the owner. It is determined as follows:

| Bank's portion | Percentage loan to value ratio | × | Debt service constant |
|---|---|---|---|
| *Plus* Owner's portion | Percentage equity portion | × | Owner's desired rate of return |
| Equals | total capitalization rate | | |

In the case of the project producing a $100 annual net cash flow, let us assume that the loan term was 25 years, producing a debt service constant (equal debt service payments of principal and interest at 10 percent) of .1158. (This amount must be looked up in mortgage tables or calculated with a programmed calculator.) Let us also assume that the lender was prepared to offer a loan based on 75 percent of economic value. Let us finally assume that the owner desired a 15 percent return on cash equity before taxes. Twenty-five percent of the value of the project would be in the form of owner's equity capital. The capitalization rate would be as follows:

| Bank's share: | 75% (loan-to-value ratio) | × .1158 | = | 8.685% |
|---|---|---|---|---|
| Owner's share: | 25% (owner's equity) | × .15 | = | 3.750% |
| | | Composite total | | 12.435% |

Under this set of economic assumptions, therefore, the capitalization rate is 12.435 percent and the new economic value of the project is:

| Net Income Available | $ 100 |
|---|---|
| *Divided By* capitalization rate | .12345 |
| *Equals* economic value | $ 804 |

The economic value has been changed because the basic terms

and conditions of the deal have been changed. The term of financing directly affect the economic value of income-producing properties.

For example, most Section 8/221(d) (4) HUD-insured properties financed under Government National Mortgage Association (GNMA) tandem programs and developed in the late 1970s had 40-year loans with a 7.5 percent interest rate, providing a capitalization rate of .0839685. The rate is derived as follows:

| | | |
|---|---|---|
| **90% (loan-to-value ratio)** | × **.0839685 (constant including .005 mortgage insurance premium)** | **= 7.55716%** |
| **10% (owner's equity)** | × **8% (owner's return)** | **= 0.80000%** |
| | | **8.39685%** |

Shown below are examples of how the capitalization rate is changed if the sponsor's desired return on equity is increased to 10 percent (as permitted for Section 8 family projects) or decreased to 6 percent (as required for older projects).

**ASSUMPTIONS**
   **HUD financing**
   **6 percent sponsor's return on equity**
   **90 percent loan-to-value ratio**
   **7.5 percent interest rate**
   **.5 percent mortgage insurance premium**
   **40-year term**
   **.0839685 debt service constant (from mortgage tables)**

**TO FIGURE CAPITALIZATION RATE:**

| | |
|---|---|
| **90% (loan ratio) × .0839685 (constant)** | **= .0755716** |
| **+ 10% (sponsor's equity) × .06 (return)** | **= .0060000** |
| **Total capitalization rate** | **.0815716** |

**ASSUMPTIONS**
   **HUD financing**
   **10 percent sponsor's return on equity**
   **90 percent loan-to-value ratio**
   **7.5 percent interest rate**

.5 percent mortgage insurance premium
40-year term
.0839685 debt service constant (from mortgage tables)

**TO FIGURE CAPITALIZATION RATE:**

| | |
|---|---|
| 90% (loan ratio) × .0839685 (constant) | = .0755716 |
| + 10% (sponsor's equity) × .10 (return) | = .0100000 |
| **Total capitalization rate** | .0855716 |

Because economic value is calculated by dividing the net income of the project by the capitalization rate, if the capitalization rate goes up, the economic value of the project goes down. The higher the capitalization rate, the lower the economic value of the project. Since net income remains the same in each instance, the value of the project has been altered simply by changing the sponsor's targeted rate of return. For example, let us consider a rental apartment project renting average units at $595 and costing about $2,280 annually per unit to operate. The economic value under financing as previously existed would be as follows:

**EXAMPLE A**

8 percent rate of return
.0839685 capitalization rate

| | Amount Per Unit |
|---|---|
| Composite unit rent as $595/month | $ 7,140 |
| *Less* vacancy and collection loss at 5% | 357 |
| *Equals* effective gross income | $ 6,783 |
| *Less* annual operating cost at $2,280/unit | 2,280 |
| *Equals* net income | $ 4,503 |
| *Divided By* capitalization rate | .0839685 |
| *Equals* economic value | $53,627 |

The economic value of this project would be $53,627 per unit. The value in this case has been established on the basis of a 40-year, 7.5 percent loan with an anticipated 8 percent annual return on sponsor's equity. The capitalization rate is a function of three factors: the length of the loan, the interest rate, and the owner's desired return on the investment. Note what happens when the capitalization rate changes as shown below:

**EXAMPLE B**

**6 percent rate of return
.0815716 capitalization rate**

| | Amount Per Unit |
|---|---|
| **Net Income** | $ 4,503 |
| *Divided By* **capitalization rate** | .0815716 |
| *Equals* **economic value** | $55,203 |

**EXAMPLE C**

**10 percent rate of return
.0855716 capitalization rate**

| | Amount Per Unit |
|---|---|
| **Net Income** | $ 4,503 |
| *Divided By* **capitalization rate** | .0855716 |
| *Equals* **economic value** | $52,622 |

The economic value of the project is higher with a 6 percent return and lower with a 10 percent return. The total spread is over $2,500 per unit, which would be, $550,000 for a 220-unit project.

These examples illustrate what happens when an adjustment is made only to the owner's return on equity. Changes in the terms of financing usually have a more dramatic effect on economic value. Let us examine two other alternatives: first, financing by a state housing agency which issues a 40-year loan at a 90 percent loan-to-value ratio, with an interest rate of 10 percent; second, conventional financing with an interest rate of 15 percent for 25 years and a loan-to-value ratio of 75 percent:

**EXAMPLE D**

**State Agency Financing**
    **6 percent sponsor's return on equity**

90 percent loan-to-value ratio
10 percent interest rate
.5 percent mortgage insurance premium
40-year term
0.10689951 debt service constant

**To figure capitalization rate:**

90% (loan value) × 0.10689951 (constant) = 0.0962095
10% (sponsor's equity) × 0.06 (return)  = 0.0060000
Total capitalization rate                  0.1022095


**EXAMPLE E**

**Private Conventional Financing**

15 percent sponsor's return on equity
75 percent loan-to-value ratio
15 percent interest rate
no mortgage insurance premium
25-year term
0.1536997 debt service constant

**To figure capitalization rate:**

75% (loan value) × 0.15369967 (constant) = 0.1152747
25% (sponsor's equity) × 0.15 (return)   = 0.0375000
Total capitalization rate                   0.1527747


Note the significant impact on economic value. The economic value of the project with state agency financing is $44,056 per unit, as shown below:

Net Income                              $   4,503
*Divided By* capitalization rate        0.1022095
*Equals* economic value                 $  44,056


The economic value of the conventionally financed project is much lower—only $29,474 per unit:

| Net Income | $ 4,503 |
| *Divided By* capitalization rate | 0.152774 |
| *Equals* economic value | $ 29,474 |

The following table summarizes the economic values under the various assumptions:

| | Economic Value Per Unit (rounded) |
| --- | --- |
| HUD financed at 7.5%, 6% return | $55,200 |
| HUD financed at 7.5%, 8% return | 53,620 |
| HUD financed at 7.5%, 10% return | 52,620 |
| State agency financed at 10%, 6% return | 44,050 |
| Conventionally financed at 15%, 15% return | 29,470 |

The key to determining economic value, therefore, is directly related to the type of permanent financing available. For this reason, it is important at the outset of any development project to have a good idea as to what kinds of financing are available for the proposed project. If the only type of financing produces economic values below what you know it is going to cost to develop the project, then by definition the project is not feasible and there is no need to spend additional time exploring economic feasibility.

## ESTIMATING TOTAL SOURCES OF CASH

Having determined economic value, the next step is to estimate the total sources of cash that can be raised for the project, including loan financing and capital raised from limited partners.

In a project that is to be syndicated, there are two sources of cash. The first is debt capital (loans) from one or more individuals or financial institutions. The second is equity capital (or capital contributions) from limited partners. Together these two sources must equal all the costs associated with the development of the project.

The loan amount is figured first and is established by the lender. The loan amount typically will be based on the economic value of the project and a prescribed loan-to-value ratio. In the illustrative HUD project in Example C, the loan would be 90 percent (loan-to-value ratio) multiplied by $52,620 (economic value under HUD terms with 10 percent owner's return on equity) equals $47,358 per unit. In the case of conventional financing, the loan would be 75 percent (loan-to-value ratio) multiplied by $29,470 (economic value under conventional terms) equals $22,102 per unit.

In addition to the loan, there must be equity capital. The amount of equity capital is a function of the total financial benefits produced by the project. These include cash return on equity, tax benefits (including deductions and, in some instances, investment tax credits), and, finally, the potential for long-term appreciation. In order to figure the equity capital that can be raised from limited partners, it is necessary to estimate the total benefits that are available and to price these benefits according to a losses-to-investment ratio method or internal rate-of-return method, or some similar approach, as described in Chapter Three. The amount of the project loan and the amount of equity capital provide the total sources of funds that are available to support project costs. If the project can be built for this amount (including in this case all costs associated with syndication and required developer fees), the project is feasible. If it cannot be developed for this amount, the project is not feasible. In summary, the process works like this:

1. On the basis of the net income the project produces and the likely available financing, an economic value for the project is established by dividing net income by a capitalization rate.
2. On the basis of the economic value, a loan amount is established.
3. In a separate calculation which takes into consideration all three financial benefits—cash flow, tax benefits, and appreciation—the amount of equity capital that can be raised from limited partners is calculated.
4. The two sources of capital—the project loan or loans and equity capital raised from limited partners—constitute the total source of cash available to cover all project costs, including developer fees and syndication costs.
5. If sufficient capital exists to cover all anticipated project costs, the project is feasible. If insufficient funds exist, the project is not feasible.

## FIGURING TOTAL PROJECT DEVELOPMENT COST

A great deal goes into determining total project development costs. Just as in the case of operating budgets, lenders often have their own formats and methods of determining costs. Some costs are relatively easy to determine and document, such as the cost of the land, the general construction contract, construction loan interest, and fees paid to outside professionals. The difficulties lie in what costs are mortgageable items (what costs the lender will consider legitimate and allow to be covered by the mortgage). In the private sector, generally what is, or is not, a mortgageable item is negotiated between the developer and the lender; and most costs associated with the project are accepted. Since a loan will be based on the economic value of the project, as long as there is sufficient money to support the loan, private lenders are not especially concerned about specific cost items. In HUD or state agency financing, however, the situation is different. There are specific rules stating which items are covered by the mortgage. Regardless of the procedures imposed by the lender, it is important for the developer to keep an accurate total account of all of the actual costs, even if some are disallowed by the lender. In computing the final economic feasibility of the project, it is the actual total cost, not just the costs the lender allows for application of mortgage proceeds, that determines whether the project is workable.

Generally acceptable project development costs include:

1. *General construction contract.* The general construction contract typically consists of a base number, to which a percentage amount is added (6 to 8 percent) for general requirements (or *general conditions*) 2 percent for overhead, and another 4 to 8 percent for profit. The significant number is the total amount paid by the owner to the general contractor. When allowing a developer's fee (called Builder's and Sponsor's Profit and Risk Allowance, or BSPRA), HUD will not allow the developer to claim as a mortgageable item any profit paid to a general contractor, since the BSPRA concept assumes that the builder and the developer are the same entity, and in fact requires a formal identity of interest. (There will be more on BSPRA later in this chapter.)

2. *Other construction fees.* These items include the costs of soil borings, preliminary engineering studies, topographical and boundary surveys, special structural inspections, assessments for off-site improvements, and sewer tap fees.

3. ***Architectural fees.*** Two fees are paid to the architect. The first is the design fee, usually about three-fourths of the total fee, from which the architect must also pay consultants (structural, mechanical, and electrical engineers; landscape architect, and other special consultants). During the design phase, most architects prefer to get paid as their work progresses. Since developers do not have financing at this point, they prefer for architects to wait until the construction or rehabilitation loan closes before being paid. Usually, an agreement is reached whereby the developer pays a portion of the fee as it is earned, with the balance due at construction loan closing. If the project never closes, the developer may negotiate to pay only a portion of the outstanding balance.

The second fee is the supervisory fee for regular supervision of construction and review/approval of the contractor's monthly draw requests. Typically, architects must approve all draw requests before lenders will release funds. Usually, the architect is the developer's principal agent who determines the project has been built according to the plans and specifications. The supervisory fee is generally 25 percent of the total architectural fee.

4. ***Bond premium.*** The purpose of a bond is to assure the lender that if the builder is not able to complete the project, a surety company will provide the necessary funds for completion. The fear is not so much that the builder will have trouble on your project, but that he may have trouble on other projects and find that his business cannot continue. This is a frequent occurrence in the development industry. Although private lenders do not always require a bond (especially if the project is small), HUD and state agencies do. In lieu of a bond, the builder often can post a letter of credit, equivalent to 15 percent of the total construction contract (25 percent if the building is high-rise).

5. ***Carrying and financing costs.*** These include the "soft costs" associated with the project, most notably construction loan interest and loan fees paid by the developer to the lenders and to financing agents.

6. ***Construction loan interest.*** Interest on the construction loan is determined by the construction lender, who in all likelihood is not the same lender as the permanent lender. Most construction lenders will commit a loan only after there is a commitment from the permanent lender to "take out" the construction loan. Two months are added to the length of time of the construction contract to determine the construction loan period. It is assumed that permanent loan closing will occur within two months of project completion, or that at least the project will be generating its own rent and net income, which can be used to cover construction loan interest. The construction loan interest is converted to a monthly interest rate, which is multiplied by the length of the loan period to

determine the total loan period rate. This is multiplied by the average outstanding balance of the construction loan, which typically is half the mortgage amount in the case of a new construction project and higher (55–65 percent) for rehabilitation projects, since acquisition costs generally are greater.

*Example*

Construction loan rate is 16 percent per annum. Construction loan period is 18 months. Mortgage amount is $2,500,000.

| | | | | |
|---|---|---|---|---|
| **0.16**<br>(annual loan interest) | ÷ | **12**<br>(months) | = | **.0133**<br>(monthly interest) |
| **.0133**<br>(monthly interest) | × | **18**<br>(total loan period) | = | **0.2394**<br>(total loan period interest) |
| **0.2394**<br>(total loan period interest) | × | **$1,250,000**<br>(average outstanding balance) | = | **$299,250** |

7. ***Real estate taxes.*** It is often difficult to estimate this since the project is likely to be reassessed during the construction period. The starting point is to estimate the real estate taxes due on the vacant land or the original building (in the case of rehabilitation). This should be figured for the total loan period, based on the market value of the land multiplied by the real estate tax rate. In addition, some jurisdictions will reassess the value of the property periodically and base the new value on how much of the project has been completed at the time of reassessment. Other localities will not reassess until the project has been completed. By calling the local assessor's office, you can find out the practice and base your calculations on this information.

8. ***Property and builder's risk insurance.*** The owner must provide two types of insurance during the construction period. The first is *builder's risk* insurance to reimburse the contractor for materials or items stolen from the site or destroyed before they are part of the building. The second is *general hazard* insurance, which insures the building as it is completed. Should the building burn down during construction, this insurance, which builds in value as work progresses, would provide funds for rebuilding what was destroyed.

Most lenders will provide the owner with detailed insurance requirements. It is best to work with a knowledgeable insurance agent to assure adequate coverage at competitive rates. Most lenders will require evidence of adequate insurance prior to issuing a construction loan.

9. *Financing fees.* There are several financing or financing-related fees that may be charged by lenders or third parties who arrange the financing (mortgages). The fees on HUD projects are typically 4.5 to 5.0 percent of the loan amount (to cover the mortgage insurance premium, inspection, HUD processing, and financing). Fees charged by private lenders usually are negotiable and range from 1.5 to 2.0 percent each for the construction loan and the permanent loan.

The amount of the financing and carrying charges varies with the nature of financing and the locality of the project. While in HUD projects the fees are for the most part established by HUD, in the case of state agencies and private lenders there is more variation and often room for negotiation. Although some financing costs may be disallowed by HUD as part of project costs, they nevertheless must be counted by the developer in figuring his real costs. Most lenders should be able to provide assistance in identifying the financing and carrying costs.

10. *Title and recording costs.* Prior to a construction loan closing, a title company must undertake a title search and examination to determine whether the title to the property is free and clear. At construction loan closing, a title insurance policy must be issued against possible challenges to the title.

During the construction period, the title company will initiate a title *bring-down* prior to the release of funds to the contractor to be sure there are no mechanic's liens against the property. The charges for the initial search, abstract update, bring-down, and insurance policy are based on staff time and the value of the property title that is being insured.

The item most subject to change is the recording fee. There typically is a nominal charge by the local juridiction to record the key closing documents, which include the deed, the mortgage, and—in the case of HUD projects—the Regulatory Agreement. Sometimes there is also a recording tax, which can range from 0.5 to 3.0 percent of the amount of the mortgage. You should determine the local recording tax before making your estimate.

11. *Legal, organizational, and accounting costs.* The first of these is for the real estate attorney (in contrast to the syndication attorney). Legal fees vary enormously and depend on how much work is involved. A lawyer may be involved in legal work to obtain an option agreement and always will be involved in closing the loan. It is wise to reach an understanding with your attorney regarding fees prior to enlisting the attorney's services.

Organizational items are the developer's out-of-pocket expenses during the development and construction period. The amount allowed by HUD is usually very small, averaging from $2,500 to $5,000, and does not take into consideration real staff costs or office overhead. Private lenders often are more flexible.

Finally, HUD requires a cost certification audit by an independent accountant at the end of the job, in order to certify that the HUD-approved costs have been incurred. Should the sponsor not spend all the money allocated in the mortgage, HUD will reduce the mortgage by the amount of savings. Three to four thousand dollars is usually sufficient to pay for the audit for most projects. Audits also will be required by the limited partners (even when HUD insurance is not involved) for tax purposes and to give them assurance that the project is not in trouble and to document their tax basis.

12. *Land or building costs.* This item is the cost of the site or existing building (in the case of rehabilitation). The amount included here is typically the fair market value of the land rather than the actual purchase price. The lender will determine the fair market value on the basis of its own appraisals. As a practical matter, where fair market value exceeds the actual cost to the sponsor, lenders often allow the cost to stand, especially if the overall budget is tight. If the appraisal shows that the cost paid by the developer is greater than its fair market value, the value of the land will be reduced and the developer will suffer a loss.

13. *Other miscellaneous costs.* These include other costs related to the development of the project, such as consultants' fees, site appraisal, lease-up expenses, marketing costs, initial operating deficits, and a contingency allowance. While they are negotiable between a private lender and a developer, HUD has rules as to what is allowed. Typical costs that are part of any development project but that are not allowed by HUD as mortgageable items are:

- fee paid to the builder by side agreement
- off-site construction costs
- cost of working capital letter-of-credit requirements—2 percent of the project mortgage. This fund is meant to assure the lender that the developer has sufficient funds available to meet unanticipated increases in soft-cost items, such as taxes, insurance, and interest.
- escrow deposits required at initial closing for prepaid insurance and real estate taxes
- marketing expenses
- furniture expenses
- developer's overhead during the development and construction period

- change orders
- cost overruns in soft-cost items which cannot be offset by cost savings
- construction loan discounts
- permanent loan discounts
- fees paid to outside professionals other than the architect
- initial operating deficit
- contingency reserve (except in the case of rehabilitation projects)

In addition to these costs are two other major items. The first is the cost of syndicating the project, and the second is the developer's fees. As discussed in Chapter One, these fees are determined by what is available out of sources of funds—after all other costs have been paid—to pay the developer for his time and effort. The fees are a function of the cash available less the costs to develop the project. While the fees may have very little to do with how hard the developer worked, they reflect the developer's skill in putting together a workable deal.

The fee paid to the syndication firm includes the cost of producing the offering memorandum, the legal costs for reviewing the materials and rendering opinions as to their completeness and accuracy, the registered broker-dealer's cost of marketing and selling the securities to the investors, and the profit to the syndication firm. The fee will vary with the type of project involved, the amount of work, and the risks assumed by the syndication firm. Typically, the fee is in the range of 20–25 percent of total equity proceeds raised for complete syndication services, though the fee is greatly affected by the amount of work undertaken by the syndication firm and the responsibilities it takes on.

After all these costs have been subtracted, what is left is available to the developer as profit. Typically, there are different fees—developer fee, construction guarantee fee, lease-up fee, and so on. The primary reason for structuring the fees in this manner is to enable the investor to deduct as much of the fee as possible as an expense rather than to capitalize and amortize the fee as part of total development costs.

Neither the cost of syndication nor the developer's fees are acknowledged by lenders as a mortgageable item in evaluating or underwriting income-producing properties. How the developer raises equity capital is of no concern to the lender, who makes a loan on the basis of the economic value of the project. The lender presumes the developer is knowledgeable and aware of the risks involved. If there is extra money available after the limited partners have signed up, so much the better, but it is not part of the lender's business.

While limited partners' equity is also not part of HUD's business, in some of its insurance program HUD (and state agencies) have provided for a builder-developer's fee (BSPRA) to be a mortgageable line item. In part, this distinction has been required because HUD takes both a cost approach to value (requiring all costs to be justified) and an economic approach to value (allowing any costs so long as income is available to cover the cost). Since private lenders typically are concerned only with the economic approach, the concept of BSPRA is irrelevant to them.

BSPRA is calculated to be 10 percent of all other project development costs except the supplemental management fund, contingency reserve (for rehabilitation only), and land costs. BSPRA inflates the total cost of the project by between 6 and 9 percent, depending on the value of the land. Since the developer does not have to pay anyone, it increases his profit. However, BSPRA cannot be drawn down as cash by the developer. Rather, it can only be used as a credit to reduce what would otherwise be a 10 percent cash equity requirement. The practical result of BSPRA is that, instead of an equity requirement of 10 percent, the actual cash equity requirements of developers are more on the order of from 2 to 4 percent of total project costs, including land.

BSPRA has achieved two objectives. The relatively low rate of return for HUD or state agency projects (6 to 10 percent) has not been sufficient to attract many profit-motivated developers into the program, given the level of effort and the amount of risk involved. Theoretically, the use of BSPRA reduces the cash requirements and increases the effective rate of return to a more acceptable level. In practice, the effect is reduced by additional out-of-pocket expenses required for loan discounts, builders' fees by side agreement, and other nonmortgageable items. The second reason that BSPRA is important is that it has enabled developers to make money through equity syndication. The use of BSPRA enables sponsors to keep their out-of-pocket cost requirements to a level at which they can make a profit from the proceeds from limited partner investors.

Let us consider an example of how these costs are estimated. Since there is no specific site or project in mind, it is useful to put all costs on a per-unit basis (''per square foot'' for commercial properties). The starting assumptions are:

| | |
|---|---|
| **Rent** | **$595 per month (excluding utilities) determined by the market survey** |
| **Net size** | **765 sq. ft. net (also determined by the market survey** |
| **Gross size** | **850 sq. ft. gross (figure includes halls and entrance)** |
| **Likely land cost** | **$2,500/unit (average land cost in area)** |
| **Capitalization rate** | **0.0855716 (assumes HUD or below-market financing)** |
| **Economic value** | **$52,620** |
| **Sources of cash** | **$12,000  capital contributions (determined by the tax losses  generated by the project, utilizing the losses to investment ratio)** |
| | **47,360  financing (90% loan to economic value)** |
| | **$59,360  total per unit supportable costs** |

It is now possible to estimate all the costs. The first category is mortgageable job costs. The second is non-mortgageable job costs, and the third is the syndication fee. The fourth category solves for how much is available to the developer. The distinction between mortgageable and non-mortgageable costs is more appropriate to HUD or state agency projects than to privately financed projects, but it does not make a great deal of difference how the costs are presented as long as all the costs to the developer are accounted for, since what is left over is available to the developer.

The reason for the distinction between mortgageable costs and nonmortgageable costs in HUD-insured or state housing finance agency projects goes back to the dual approach these agencies take in project underwriting. They use both an income approach and a cost approach to determine value. Because there is usually a public subsidy involved (direct rental assistance such as Section 8 or below-market financing), these agencies want to be sure that no more subsidy is used than what is justified by the costs involved. For this reason they have established what in their view are legitimate costs and will allow only those costs to be included in the project mortgage, hence the distinction between mortgageable and non-mortgageable costs. However, because from a developer's viewpoint all costs are real, it is important to account for both mortgageable and non-mortgageable costs. These are shown below in Table 1. The numbers are all expressed in terms of per unit values because there is not yet a specific project.

On the basis of this preliminary analysis, the proposed project appears to be feasible, since about $1,800 per unit is available to the developer, and liberal allowances have been made for all other project costs. For a 150-unit project, the developer would make about $265,000, or more if the various contingency funds were not used. The model, however, is only as good as its assumptions. To the extent that the developer overestimated sources of cash or underestimated costs, the project would change from "worth doing" to "not worth doing."

## PRELIMINARY GO/NO-GO DECISION

You now have all the information required to decide to move forward or to abandon the concept. You have developed a physical building concept or program expressed in terms of a typical unit. Projected initial rent levels have been established on the basis of your market analysis. You have calculated the first year's operating cost by projecting current per-unit operating costs of comparable projects. You have utilized a capitalization rate provided by the lender (in this case, the insuror, HUD) to determine the economic value of the project. Knowing the economic value, you also know the maximum loan amount. Finally, you have completed an analysis of what the total equity funds will be and what the total costs to develop the project are likely to be. You have saved the developer's fee for last, leaving it as an "available amount."

All these figures usually are expressed in a single table called a *pro forma* financial statement. Developers use *pro formas* frequently. They are one of the most useful analytical tools in the de-

# TABLE 1
## MORTGAGEABLE AND NONMORTGAGEABLE COSTS

| Item | Per Unit Estimated Amount (in $) | Explanation |
|---|---|---|
| **MORTGAGEABLE COSTS** | | |
| General Construction contract per gross sq. ft. assume 765 net, 850 gross | $34,000 | Price is based on $40/sq. ft. Price includes general requirements, overhead and bond but *no profit* (paid by side agreement). Assumes start within a year. Also includes amenities as stated in conceptual program. Site work is included. $40 \times 850 = \$34,000$ |
| Other construction fees | 1,600 | Assume 150 unit project with total as follows: |
| | | survey        $ 5,000 |
| | | borings      10,000 |
| | | subtotal      $15,000 |
| | | divided by    $ 150 |
| | | equals         100/unit |
| Sewer tap fees | | sewer tap fees   1,500/unit |
| | | total         $ 1,600/unit |
| Architectural fees | | |
|   Design | 900 | Represents 3.5% of con- |
|   Supervision | 300 | struction contract |
| | 1,200 | |
| Bond premium | — | Included in construction contract cost |
| *Carrying and financing:* | | |
|   Interest at 16% for 18 months | 5,683 | $.16 \div 12 = .0133$ $\times 18 \text{ months} = .24$ $\times \text{loan of } \$47,360$ $\times .50 \text{ (avg. balance)} = \$5,683$ |

| Item | Per Unit Estimated Amount (in $) | Explanation |
|---|---|---|
| Real Estate taxes | 150 | Tax assessor has provided you with this estimate for taxes |
| Insurance | 150 | Insurance estimates provided for 150 unit costing about $8,000,000 and prorated |
| Financing fees and closing costs | | |
| • Mortgage ins. premium | 482 | 1.0% × 48,264 |
| • Exam fee | 145 | 0.3% × 48,264 |
| • Inspection fee | 241 | 0.5% × 48,264 |
| • Construction financing fee | 723 | 1.5% × 48,264 |
| • FHA/GNMA fee | 965 | 2.0% × 48,264 |
| • Title and recording | 832 | Recording tax of 1%. Figure approximately 1.5% of mortgage |
| Subtotal | 3,388 | |
| Total carrying and financing | 9,371 | |
| Legal, organizational, and audit | 167 | Figure $25,000 total for 150 unit project and prorate |
| TOTAL OF ALL OF ABOVE | $46,338 | |
| BSPRA | 0 | Would be based on 10% of "all of the above" items but is not included here because it is not a real cost |
| Land costs | $2500 | |

*(continued)*

TABLE 1 *(Continued)*

| Item | Per Unit Estimated Amount (in $) | Explanation |
|---|---|---|
| **NON MORTGAGEABLE COSTS** | | |
| Builders fee | $ 1,700 | Based on 5% of construction cost |
| Off site costs | 67 | Assume $10,000 for entire project |
| Permanent loan discount | 1,184 | Assume 2.5% of mortgage |
| Working capital letter of credit | 947 | Based on 2.0% of mortgage. Assume money would be used as contingency and for escrows for insurance and taxes |
| Marketing costs | 333 | Assume $50,000 for 150 unit project since project is market rate |
| Contingency allowance for change orders | 1,020 | Assume 3% of construction contract |
| Initial operating deficit and lease up expenses | 500 | Estimate based on experience with similar projects |
| Subtotal other cost | $ 5,751 | |
| **FEE AND PROFIT** | | |
| Syndication fees | $ 3,000 | Figured at 25% of gross syndication proceeds of $12,000 and includes commission to broker, dealer, legal fees, overhead expenses, and profit. Amount could range from 20–25% |
| Developers fees | (not included) | Balance available |
| Subtotal excluding developers fee | 3,000 | |

| Item | Per Unit Estimated Amount (in $) | Explanation |
|------|------|------|
| TOTAL excluding developers fee | 57,589 | |
| **AMOUNT AVAILABLE TO DEVELOPER** | | |
| Total sources of cash | 59,360 | |
| less total cost excluding fee | 57,589 | |
| equals amount available to developer | $ 1,771 | |

**Source:** Illustrative information provided by the author.

velopment industry. The *pro forma* for your project is presented in Table 2.

This tells you that the numbers work using your assumptions on land costs, rents, operating costs, construction costs, and other items. What if no land, appropriately zoned, can be purchased for this amount, or if construction costs are much higher? Typically, in this instance, the developer begins to "massage" the numbers. Additional economic value can be generated in a number of ways:

- increasing the rents, thus increasing income and the loan amount;
- reducing the vacancy ratio, which is probably not wise since the project contains mostly market-rate units (in a project which received rental subsidies for all the units, you could go to 97 percent occupancy and be safe);
- reducing operating costs, which is often wishful thinking since the developer may have to cover operating deficits;
- reducing construction costs by building small units or cheapening the building, but it is not wise to assume that your construction costs will be less than what others experience in the area;
- shortening the construction loan period, thereby reducing construc-

# TABLE 2
## PRO FORMA

| Item | Amount Per Unit |
|------|----------------:|
| **ECONOMIC VALUE AND SOURCES OF CASH** | |
| Potential Gross income at 595 | $ 7,140 |
| Less vacancy and collection loss at 5% | 357 |
| Equals effective gross income | 6,783 |
| Less operating costs and real estate taxes | 2,280 |
| Equals net operating income | 4,503 |
| Divided by cap rate of .0855716 | — |
| Equals economic value | 52,622 |
| Sources of Cash | |
| Loan (90% of economic value) | 47,360 |
| Equity (from syndication) | 12,000 |
| Total Sources of Cash | 59,360 |
| | |
| **DEVELOPMENT COSTS** | |
| Mortgageable | |
| Construction cost at $40 × 850 sf | 34,000 |
| Other fees | 1,600 |
| Architect design and supervision | 1,200 |
| Bond | — |
| Carrying and financing | |
| Interest | 5,683 |
| Real estate taxes | 150 |
| Insurance | 150 |
| Financing fees | |
| MIP (1.0%) | 482 |
| Exam (0.3%) | 145 |
| Inspection (0.5%) | 241 |
| Construction financing fee (1.5%) | 723 |
| Permanent loan fee (GNMA) (2.0%) | 965 |
| Title and recording (1.5%) | 832 |
| Total Carryng and Financing | 9,371 |
| Subtotal | 46,171 |
| Legal and Organizational | 167 |
| BSPRA | (not included)** |
| Other costs | 0 |
| Estimated land cost | 2,500 |
| Subtotal | 48,838 |

| Item | Amount Per Unit |
|------|----------------:|
| Nonmortgageable | |
| Builders fee | 1,700 |
| Off Site | 67 |
| Permanent loan discount | 1,184 |
| Working Capital | 947 |
| Marketing | 333 |
| Change order allowance | 1,020 |
| Initial deficit | 500 |
| Subtotal | 5,751 |
| Total Development Cost (exclusive of fees) | $54,589 |
| | |
| AMOUNT AVAILABLE FOR FEES | |
| Total Sources of Cash | 59,360 |
| Less total development costs | 54,589 |
| Equals total amount available for fees | 4,771 |
| Less estimated cost of syndication and syndication fee | 3,000 |
| Equals residual available to developer | 1,771 |

*Typical Unit* 765 sq. ft. 850 sq. gross
**BSPRA is not a cost item in the pro forma because the developer does not have to pay anyone.

tion loan interest (this may be a possibility; but since there is some cushion in this area, you don't want to do this yet);
- reducing the permanent or construction loan rate;
- increasing the equity contributions from limited partners, by possibly taking a more aggressive tax position. Since such contributions are a function of the market, this effort may be unrealistic.

The easiest thing to do—and also usually the safest from the perspective of overall economic feasibility—is to pass the additional cost on to the consumer in the form of higher rents or prices. It boils down to a market judgment whether the consumer will pay more.

The next step is to redo the analysis using the higher income figures. Developers often will analyze projects many times, changing various assumptions before arriving at an economic model for which the numbers work. In reality, many projects never work and are abandoned.

The *pro forma* compresses all the information and is useful for quick calculations and recalculations. It is also useful because any cost item can be saved for last and "solved for" on a residual basis. For example, the developer can put in a required developer fee and determine how much is available for the syndication fee. Or, the developer can put in the required amounts for syndication and developer fees and determine how much is available for land costs or the construction budget (if land costs are known).

In the process of undertaking this detailed analysis, you are able to achieve an understanding of all the economic relationships of a proposed real estate project. Equally important, thus far you have not spent much money (except for possibly paying for a market analysis). That important step should not occur until you are convinced that the basic project concept is feasible and you are ready to acquire (or option) a specific piece of property or an existing building.

When applying for HUD mortgage insurance the project economics are presented on a special form called FHA Form 2013, a copy of which is shown in Appendix table H.

Let us now turn to Chapter Five to see how the development process fits together.

# *Five*

## Getting the Project to the Closing Table: Steps in the Development Process

You have just completed your initial feasibility study and the overall concept you are considering looks promising. With the help of appropriate professionals, you have determined that the available combination of equity capital and debt financing will generate sufficient sources of cash to cover likely development and syndication costs and return to you sufficient cash as a development fee to make the effort and the risk worthwhile. In addition, you have available to you sufficient funds to cover an option on a site or building and to advance initial fees for architectural and engineering studies. You also have sufficient net worth to qualify for both a construction loan and a permanent loan. You have made enough preliminary inquiries to determine that a market exists for the type of financial benefits which will be available to sell to limited partners, that firms are available to help you in this effort if you need them, and that permanent and construction financing are available.

Your next step is to obtain control of a specific parcel or building (either by purchasing or, preferably, optioning suitable property). Before examining the site control stage in closer detail, let us review all the steps you must go through before the entire process has been completed. In addition to the first step of testing the economic feasibility, there are seven additional steps you must go through to get to the point where you are ready to syndicate the deal:

1.  obtaining site control of a specific parcel or an existing building;

2. fitting a specific project (or rehabilitation concept) to the site and determining the economic feasibility of that specific project;
3. obtaining a preliminary permanent financing commitment and preliminary local approvals (such as, water, sewer, zoning, utilities);
4. preparing construction working drawings and obtaining final construction cost figures;
5. obtaining final permanent financing approvals, final local approvals, and a construction loan;
6. closing the construction loan and starting construction; and
7. raising equity capital (syndication).

While there may be some overlap involved, each of these steps constitutes an important checkpoint for evaluating where you stand. For this reason, a good developer will look at each step as a milestone and ask the "go/no-go" question at the end of each step. If project economics have adversely changed, the project should be aborted or postponed at the end of each step. Let us now examine each of these in detail.

## OBTAINING SITE OR BUILDING CONTROL

Without a specific site or building in mind, it is impossible to go any farther. Lack of a site is the first major obstacle which keeps many developers from moving ahead.

There are three critical questions regarding site control. The first is how to find an acceptable site for the project. The second is how much to pay for property. The third is what kind of option agreement or sales contract should be negotiated.

### Finding the Site or Building

Nothing is more important in determining the success of a project than its location. This is the case for commercial projects and market-rate housing and, to a lesser extent, even government-assisted housing. If the initial market and feasibility study is done correctly, you should have a good idea of the basic physical program parameters: how large the project should be, where it should be located, and what it should include.

Determining ideal parameters is one thing. Finding a site or building that meets all the requirements is another. Rarely will you be able to identify easily the perfect site that is both for sale and affordable. Moreover, if the actual sale price exceeds the limits established in your *pro forma* analysis, you must recalculate project feasibility.

There are several ways developers come up with sites. One of the most common is that they already own one. This is especially the case with first-time developers. Someone owns land or a building and feels that the time is right to do something with it. While a lot of headaches are avoided by already owning land or a building, it is rare that such a buiding or site is without problems.

When the site is already owned, the first step is to tailor the preliminary feasibility study to the specific site to determine if any development is currently feasible (it may not be for a variety of reasons) and, if so, what type of development is most desirable. Many nonprofit groups, especially church groups, have gotten involved in the development of housing projects because they already owned or were donated land that could be used for multifamily housing.

If you don't already own a site or a building, then you have to find one. You can do it yourself or you can use a real estate broker. It is possible to enlist realtors who seek out property for you. In large commercial deals where difficult problems in site assembly are not unusual, this is often done. Realtors will charge a fee for such work, usually contingent upon a sale's being transacted.

A third way is to be designated the developer of publicly owned or controlled land. A number of assisted housing projects have been built on such sites, including urban renewal land, abandoned schools or rights-of-way, and properties acquired through tax foreclosures.

In exchange for large-scale rezoning, some suburban counties require large developers to "proffer" (donate) sites to the local housing authority which, in turn, selects local nonprofit groups to sponsor housing. This process usually involves competition. The local government or community development agency requests development proposals and selects the best development team to be the developer. While the selection process is time-consuming and may involve some expense, often the local government or agency will negotiate a price on the basis of what it takes to make the project work, and the developer usually does not have to acquire the site until construction is ready to begin, when the risk, exposure, and front-end costs are greatly reduced.

As a practical matter, smaller developers or community-based development corporations lacking capital may have no choice but to work with local governments if they do not already own or have access to a feasible site or building.

Neither the difficulty nor the importance of this step in the development process should be underestimated. Developers spend an enormous amount of time seeking out and evaluating properties. The ratio of sites examined to sites selected for various types of projects is very high.

## How Much to Pay

The most important question is how much you can afford to pay for the site or building. This can be determined by using the *pro forma* analysis. If the asking price is at or below what you have determined to be affordable, you can negotiate the acquisition. If the price is in excess of your affordable land value, something has to give. Either:

- the seller will have to come down on the price; or
- you will have to rent the space at higher prices than you originally contemplated to generate higher economic value; or
- you will have to raise additional equity capital; or
- you will have to reduce your developer fees; or
- development costs will have to be reduced in some other cost area such as construction or financing.

You should never make an offer to purchase property unless you are convinced that all the costs can be supported by the total sources of cash to the project.

## Negotiating the Acquisition

Assume that you identify a site or building that seems to come reasonably close to meeting the basic requirements established by your initial feasibility study. Now you are ready to obtain site control. This usually begins by presentation of a written contract to the seller; that is, either an option to purchase or a proposed contract of sale. Generally there will be a realtor involved. Although there will be an asking price for the property, most sellers do not expect to get the full amount. Also, most sellers will agree to terms rather than an all-cash deal. The realtor may give you a general idea of what the seller will likely accept and will invite you to offer a contract. The seller will either accept your proposed contract, reject it outright, or reject it with a counterproposal. In the last instance, you may respond with another proposal or set up a meeting to identify areas of agreement and attempt to negotiate the transaction.

The negotiation process for sites for market-rate commercial or residential properties is significantly different from that for sites involving government-assisted projects. The development timetable for market-rate, conventionally financed properties is usually much shorter than that required for HUD processing. In areas where there is a great deal of activity in the real estate market, sellers will be less willing to wait long periods of time before receiving their cash. This creates a problem for someone trying to develop government-assisted housing, since you are never assured that you have a "real" project until you receive an acceptable firm commitment from HUD. Accordingly, if possible you should delay land settlement to coincide with the construction loan closing, at which time the lender will advance cash to pay for the property. The problem of lengthy processing is handled by an option agreement or a purchase contract with a special provision linking land settlement to construction loan closing. Quite often, however, such lengthy extensions are not available.

Options and purchase agreements vary, but these general guidelines usually apply:

1. Most sellers will give buyers a 45 to 60-day study period to undertake basic engineering studies and obtain a preliminary financing commitment. Usually a good-faith deposit is placed in escrow, all or most of which will be refunded if the buyer elects not to proceed.
2. After the 45 to 60-day period, there usually is a second 45 to 60-day period allowed before settlement. During this period the deposit is at risk; and if the sale does not go through, it is forfeited.
3. At the end of the 90 to 120-day period, most sellers anticipate settlement. If conventional financing is being used, lenders may agree to advance funds at this point, prior to construction. However, this is rare, except in larger commercial deals when the developer and lender are in effect joint venture partners. Also, some sellers may agree

to take back financing for a portion or all of the land price. Such *purchase money* mortgages would have to be subordinated to any loan from a bank, a requirement the seller may not be willing to meet.

## FITTING A SPECIFIC PROJECT TO A SITE OR BUILDING

If you have a site that appears to meet your requirements, you are ready to hire an architect to prepare preliminary schematic plans. You should negotiate a fixed fee for this with an architect experienced in designing the type of project you want to build or rehabilitate. The fee will vary with the size and scope of the project but should not be very high. Some firms will speculate on such work since it does not involve a great deal of design or drafting time (in contrast to preparing actual construction documents). The architect and the architect's consultants should produce the products shown below. They usually can be completed within a three- to six-week period. All drawings at this stage are schematic, not final plans. The products to be produced are:

- a site plan;
- a main elevation;
- a typical floor plan (by building types if several buildings are involved);
- typical unit layouts (in the case of residential properties);
- a sketch rendering of the building (optional but recommended);
- a description of the proposed utility combination; and
- a set of outline specifications.

If the project involves substantial rehabilitation, an ''as is'' description of the existing building should be included (including photographs) with a conceptual before and after comparison.

In addition to the architectural documents, there also should be a soil analysis (or engineering study in the case of substantial rehabilitation) and a survey of the property. If you are dealing with an historical property, you should set up a meeting with the State Historical Preservation Officer (SHPO) to determine what is required to qualify for special tax benefits.

As mentioned earlier, do not assume that the architect should come up with the building program—the size of the building or, for residential properties, the total number of units, unit mix, unit sizes, amenities, utility combinations, and any special features. The developer should provide the architect with the basic program and direct the architect to fit the program to the site or building as best possible. Modifications to the program will be required since a specific site or building is involved, but the basic program should come from the developer. The desired program should be based on market survey information and modeled after the program developed in the preliminary feasibility study. For government-assisted projects, special marketing features may be less important; however, since the development budget may be tighter, the architect should be provided with strict parameters regarding unit sizes, common areas, type of construction, and the like. If you need professional consultation, a real estate or development consultant who understands the financial aspects of the project and the government requirements is usually better than the architect to help you formulate the development program.

Before proceeding, request that the architect initially provide you with several alternative schemes for implementing the basic program. Most good architects will do this routinely, but some will not, especially if the design budget is tight. It is better to spend more money at this stage to assure that you are getting a good concept, rather than to skimp on the design concept. Only by looking at alternative design schemes can you adequately see what can be done with a property.

You must now make two important determinations. The first is whether the architect has developed one or more schemes which are reasonably close to programs you have provided. The second is whether one or more alternatives are economically feasible. Refer to your initial *pro forma*, but in this analysis use numbers based on the actual architectural plans.

At this point you have enough architectural information to get a more accurate estimate of the likely cost of construction. Many developers are also general contractors capable of estimating construction budgets. Other developers will bring in a general contractor at this stage, with the understanding that if the general contractor can work with the architect to assure that the design of the project can be built within the prescribed construction budget, the contractor will have the right of first refusal to be the general contractor for the project. The role of the contractor is to provide estimates of construction costs and recommendations for cost containment and cost control. When a general contractor is not providing cost estimates and cost-control recommendations, an independent cost-estimating firm should be retained during the preliminary design period. If the project cannot be built within the cost budget in the *pro forma*, the basic feasibility of the project is in question. If the construction cost goes up, some other cost must go down or the project must generate more income to produce more economic value.

If at this stage the sources of cash of the proposed project are sufficient to support your anticipated total development costs, you are ready to submit a preliminary permanent loan application to a lender, respond to a government request for a proposal, submit an application for HUD insurance, or submit a preliminary application for state agency financing.

If the numbers do not work at this time, then the project must be modified. You must go back to the *pro forma* and "massage" the numbers to see if adjustments can be made to enhance project feasibility. In some cases, redesign may be necessary. In other cases, you will discover at this point that the project is simply not feasible and will abandon the undertaking. However painful this is, better now than later, after you have spent substantial dollars.

## PRELIMINARY FINANCING AND LOCAL APPROVALS

Most income-producing projects will have two loans. One will be the permanent loan, which goes into effect when the project is completed. The other will be the construction loan, which finances the construction of the project and is drawn down as work progresses.

Permanent loans are often called permanent *take-outs* because they *take out* the construction lender; that is, they replace the construction loan at the conclusion of construction. Except in the case of projects financed through tax-exempt bonds, permanent lenders and construction lenders usually are two different lenders. Historically, construction lenders have tended to be commercial banks, while permanent lenders have been savings and loan institutions, savings banks, life insurance companies, and, in the case of commercial properties, pension funds. While many of these traditional distinctions no longer apply, the concept of two separate loans will continue to apply for most projects.

The most difficult loan to obtain is the permanent loan. Once a permanent loan is in place, it is usually relatively easy to attract construction financing since the loan period is relatively short and the interest rate usually will be pegged at 1 to 2 percent above the prime lending rate.

The permanent loan period is longer-term: 25–30 years for conventional projects and 30–40 years for tax-exempt bond-financed or HUD-insured projects. During the late 1970s, practically all Section 8 projects utilized tax-exempt bonds at a rate of 8 to 10 percent or used the HUD GNMA program, which provided for 7.5 percent interest. Such financing, if available in the 1980s, will take on a different set of terms and conditions.

What has transformed the real estate industry is the change in the way permanent financing works. Two of the most important changes are that many permanent lenders will provide only variable rate loans or loans with periodic call provisions allowing for interest rate adjustments every few years, and that many permanent lenders require substantial participation in the cash flow and equity appreciation of the project.

These requirements add a new dimension to the economic feasibility of any project and pose additional challenges to the development industry. Because of the need for creative financing vehicles to attract permanent lenders, virtually every deal is going to have different financing terms. It is important to approach a permanent lender as soon as you have a real project for the lender to consider. The deal you work out will greatly affect the other items in the *pro forma*.

You begin by preparing a loan package. When only private lenders are involved, there is considerable latitude as to what constitutes an acceptable loan application package. By contrast, government-insured or -financed projects have very specific requirements. In any case, a loan package should include at least the following:

- evidence of site control
- architectural schematic plans;
- a sketch rendering of the project;
- a structural report or site analysis;
- a location map;
- a narrative description of the site and neighborhood;
- a narrative description of the project, including the overall concept, market orientation, type of construction, utility combinations, etc.;

- evidence of market support for the project;
- evidence of permissible zoning;
- evidence of availability of adequate utilities;
- the proposed members of the development team, including the architect, the contractor, and other appropriate consultants, and the experience of each;
- a demonstration of the developer's capability (staff and experience);
- the developer's financial statements (the current one and ones for the last two years) and evidence of ability to fund the seed money requirement;
- a detailed *pro forma* indicating feasibility;
- an explanation of the loan request with specific budget line items identified;
- a management plan or management concept and proposed management agent; and
- a marketing plan.

Upon receiving this material, a private lender normally will react within four to six weeks. If there is sufficient interest, a loan officer will be assigned to the project and you will meet with the officer to go over the project and negotiate various items in the proposal, which then will be taken to a loan committee. With the committee's approval, the lender will issue a financing commitment letter listing the terms of financing and identifying all the special provisions which must be met by the borrower prior to any disbursement of funds. If syndication is contemplated, the permanent financing must be non-recourse, as discussed in Chapter Two.

Once the permanent financing is secured, the developer will approach a construction lender. Since many of the distinctions between types of lenders are now blurred, it is possible that one lender may provide both a permanent and a construction loan, particularly if substantial participation in cash flow and appreciation is involved. Once a workable permanent financing commitment is in hand, the construction loan usually is obtainable. Because the construction loan theoretically involves greater risk, the lender may require this loan to be recourse. If this is the case, the tax losses during the construction period will be affected. Before accepting a recourse construction loan, you should consult with your tax attorney and accountant to assess the impact on the syndication.

In addition to the permanent loan and the construction loan, stand-by loans may be required to cover potential shortfalls in capital. A fee will be required to reserve such loans. If stand-by or gap loans are required, they must be included in the *pro forma* economic analysis; and the revenue generated by the project must be enough to repay all loans, including stand-by loans.

It is generally preferable—and often necessary—to enlist the services of a mortgage banker or financing agent to help you obtain these financing commmitments. The agent is a mortgage company that arranges the financing and assists the developer in preparing loan applications (*packaging*). HUD allows a financing fee of 1.5 percent of the mortgage amount for this service. In contrast to HUD-insured loans, mortgage brokers are not required for state agency loans, which are direct loans.

Unlike the private sector process, which usually has one or two phases, the HUD process has three phases. During the *site appraisal and market analysis* (SAMA) stage, HUD establishes the fair market value of the land (or existing building) and approves the project location. This stage (called *feasibility* in the case of substantial rehabilitation) does not obligate HUD to insure the project but determines whether it is feasible. During the *conditional commitment* stage, HUD commits to insure the project, subject to any special conditions spelled out in the commitment. A maximum loan amount is established in the commitment. The material which must be submitted by the sponsor includes more detailed architectural drawings and more detailed information on marketing and management. During the *firm commitment* stage, HUD issues a final insurance commitment. The firm commitment is based on final plans (working drawings and specifications) provided by the developer and a final construction price provided by the contractor. If the developer accepts the firm commitment, the project can close within a month.

With HUD's permission, it is possible to bypass stages in the loan application process, and this frequently is done. Typically, developers with Section 8 preliminary awards have passed the SAMA stage or, in some instances, have gone directly to the firm commitment stage. Also, it often has been necessary to go back to HUD to request an amended firm commitment in order for the project to be feasible.

At the same time you are pursuing an initial financing commitment, you should determine whether any special approvals are required by the local jurisdiction—rezoning, zoning special exception or variance, sewer or water commitment, easements, subdivision site plan approval, historical certifications, or anything else required for construction to get underway. Prior to moving ahead with working drawings, you should be convinced that the required approvals can be obtained, and you should take the necessary steps immediately to obtain them. Of course, if it is not possible to obtain an acceptable preliminary financing commitment, the project would not move forward; and no additional funds would be spent until such a commitment were secured.

## CONSTRUCTION WORKING DRAWINGS AND FINAL CONSTRUCTION COST FIGURES

Once you have received a commitment for permanent and construction financing, you can direct the architect to begin working drawings. This is a very expensive phase of the project, since a great deal of effort must go into producing these drawings. Any basic changes in concept or design should be made prior to the working drawings phase. Periodic meetings with the architect should occur during this phase to assure that the design work is on track.

The drawings created by the architect and the architect's professional consultants (usually a structural engineer, an electrical engineer, and a mechanical engineer) will be the legal construction documents on which a construction price will be based. The builder will be obligated legally to build the project according to these plans and specifications and for the price agreed to in the construction contract.

The major concern during this period is how much it will cost to build according to the detailed plans and specifications being produced. The question now is whether the project actually can be built for the amount estimated for construction.

The answer will not be known until the end of the design period when the architectural documents are completed and put out for bid. There are two ways to handle the bid process. The first is to bid the project out on the general contractor level. In this instance you have not involved a general contractor in the design of the project but will select bids from several qualified general contractors. Usually, general contractors must be approved before they are allowed to bid on a project. The general contractor with the lowest bid will be selected as builder.

The other way to handle the process is to negotiate with one general contractor, who agrees to work with the architect during the design of the project. The selected general contractor will bid out all or most of the work to subcontractors. Most government-assisted projects are handled in the negotiated fashion because it gives the developer a greater degree of cost control during the critical design and working drawings stage. The understanding with the contractor is that he will have the right of first refusal to build the project as long as his price does not exceed the allowed-for dollar amount in the final financing commitment. Though this does not guarantee that the cost will come in on budget, it does create a teamwork environment where architect, builder, and developer are working together to solve a common problem. It also helps identify cost-saving design solutions during the working drawing phase rather than after, when it is often impossible to make significant changes in the design concept.

Should the contractor be unable to perform, you have the right to bring in another general contractor on a negotiated basis or to use the competitive-bid procedure.

## FINAL FINANCING AND LOCAL APPROVALS

At this point you have a complete set of final plans and specifications, along with the final construction price provided by the general contractor, which you submit to the lender or to HUD. It is here that you have your greatest exposure. You may have incurred several site-option extension fees or may have had to acquire the site. The architect has completed the design work and is due a substantial portion of the design fee. You have paid FHA exam fees or, in the case of private financing, have paid loan reservation fees to lenders. If the project does not move ahead, you are likely to lose several hundred thousand dollars for a moderate-size project costing between three and five million dollars, or much more for a larger project.

While you are trying to obtain a feasible firm commitment, you also must work hard on getting your building permit. The difficulty of obtaining a building permit varies among jurisdictions. In some areas it may take as long as several months. Regardless of where your project is located, you will not get your building permit until these other approvals have been obtained:

1.  your project has been approved as consistent with existing zoning (or a variance has been granted);
2.  you have a water and sewer permit;
3.  your site plan has been approved; and
4.  all other technical requirements have been complied with, including approval of soil erosion plan and bond requirements for off-site improvements.

Sometimes getting a building permit is more difficult than obtaining the final financing commitment. One frequent nightmare is discovering that your final plans are not consistent with existing zoning and that you need a zoning variance, which may take as long as six months to obtain. This unfortunate occurrence happens to even the best of developers. Since zoning requirements often are extremely technical, you must rely on your architect to design a building that complies with both the building and zoning codes.

## CLOSING THE CONSTRUCTION LOAN AND STARTING CONSTRUCTION

Closing is the major event in the development industry. In all government-assisted projects and in most privately financed projects, prior to construction loan closing you are acting alone, spending your money to get the project to the closing table. At closing, the lender advances funds that reimburse you for most of your out-of-pocket expenses and agrees to continue to lend funds to cover the cost of constructing the project. Also, at this point the limited partners enter the picture. After closing you have the benefit of using someone else's money, and the risk is shared.

The key word is *risk*. Lenders will agree to share the risk with you only when they determine the project is feasible and can proceed to construction. In private lending there is some latitude as to when this determination is made. When the lender is also a partner and shares in cash flow and appreciation, as is now routine in commercial lending, the lender may agree to advance a portion of the seed money expenses prior to the start of construction. Also being an investor, the lender is willing to accept greater risk, for which there are greater financial benefits. In government-assisted financing, there is no such latitude.

Government lenders are lenders only and have very strict requirements as to when they are able to advance funds. For HUD-insured projects the decision to advance funds occurs only after HUD insurance is in place and the designated HUD official endorses the loan. At this moment the risk associated with the project has been reduced to an acceptable level. The same concept applies to all financing: closing occurs when the lender determines that the risks associated with the project have been reduced to an acceptable level. At this point the project is considered real.

What must be in place for a project to be real? The principle is that everything must be in place. There can be no uncertainties about any matter that could possibly prevent construction from starting. This is why construction loan closing is such an elusive and tension-filled event. Assuring the lender that all matters relating to the development of the project have been taken care of successfully is no easy task. The burden of proof is on you to demonstrate that the project is able to proceed. The key evidence you must provide is listed below:

1.  a firm commitment for permanent financing, with evidence that all conditions have been or will be met;
2.  a firm commitment for construction financing, with similar evidence provided;
3.  a building permit;
4.  an executed construction contract (between the developer and the general contractor) for an amount not to exceed the approved amount for construction in the loan commitment;
5.  construction contract drawings and specifications executed by the developer, the architect, the lender or insurer, the builder, and the bonding company;
6.  a valid executed sales contract, option agreement, disposition agreement, or deed;
7.  evidence of clear title and adequate title insurance;
8.  an executed agreement between the owner and the architect;
9.  evidence of the legality of the mortgagor entity;
10.  evidence of your ability to fund cash equity requirements (a certified check) and working capital requirements (a letter of credit);
11.  performance and payment bonds for the general contractor;
12.  evidence of the builder's risk and hazard insurance;
13.  a survey of the property and a legal description acceptable to the lender/insurer;

14. various legal opinions and certifications that the method of financing is legal and, for government-financed projects, that civil rights laws are being complied with; and

15. an approved management plan, management agreement, and marketing plan.

These documents are evidence that the project can be built; they can be viewed as a precondition to closing. The documents which, in effect, close the loan are the Regulatory Agreement (for government-financed projects), the mortgage (or deed of trust), the mortgage (or deed of trust) note, and the construction loan agreement. Because of their importance, the Regulatory Agreement and the mortgage usually are recorded. The last action in an FHA closing is HUD's endorsement of the mortgage note, signifying that HUD insurance is in effect. When this occurs, the project is real and the money starts flowing from the lender to the developer.

When bond financing is involved, an additional set of documents is required. Evidence must be presented to demonstrate the legality of the agency or instrumentality that is issuing the tax-exempt bonds. In addition, since there is a great deal of variation in the way bond transactions are handled, there are a number of documents that spell out the roles of the parties, especially regarding the use of the bond proceeds. The most important of these documents is the Trust Indenture, which obligates the various participants to perform according to strict rules and procedures. An official offering statement, which explains to the bond purchasers all the pertinent information about the financing, is also required. To protect the bond purchasers, who do not necessarily understand the nature of the real estate risk, legal opinions that all the facts are presented accurately and completely are required from the bond counsel. At a typical bond closing, there are likely to be at least a half-dozen attorneys—bond counsel, underwriter's counsel, counsel for the instrumentality or issuing agency, bond purchasers' counsel (if the bonds are being purchased by only one or two institutions), HUD attorney (if HUD insurance is involved), and the developer's attorney.

Very few closings are easy, since the event of closing is often used as a mechanism for getting people to agree on difficult negotiating points and for obtaining the final approvals without which an ultimate deadline probably could not be obtained. Few loans close because everything has been completely worked out and all parties are ready to close the loan. Rather, loans close because all parties agree to establish a closing date and to work out all remaining problems before or at the time of closing. When the commitment to work out the problems has been made, usually the closing will be completed, though often not without great anxiety.

Once the loan has been closed, all parties are legally obligated to perform according to the rules and procedures established in the documents. Construction can begin at last.

It may be necessary to begin construction before closing occurs to lock in a construction contract prior to a known increase in labor costs or to start before a known increase in financing costs or the expiration of a land purchase agreement, sewer commitment, zoning approval, or the like. The developer is faced with starting construction at his own risk and using his own funds or losing the project altogether. If an FHA firm commitment is in effect and the developer certifies to undo everything that is done should closing never take place, HUD will permit an early start, as will most state agencies and other lenders. There is great risk in such situations, however, and developers should be especially careful about undertaking an early start.

## RAISING THE EQUITY CAPITAL

Syndication could take place either just before or just after closing. In the case of an equity purchase, when the interests of a local partner are being sold to a syndication firm, syndication most likely would take place prior to initial closing. When the developer will also undertake the syndication, it usually occurs after initial closing. Now at last you are ready to syndicate the deal.

# *S i x*
## Syndicating the Deal:
## How a Section 8 Deal Worked

While the Section 8 program is no longer an active federal program, the syndication process that applied to syndicating Section 8 housing projects will continue to exist. Second-user projects such as older Section 236 or 221(d) (3) projects will follow similar syndication procedures, as will many residential rehabilitation projects involving local government support of one kind or another. For this reason it is useful to focus on a case study of how one Section 8 deal worked.

## THE SECTION 8 PROGRAM

The Section 8 Program was the major housing production program of the federal government between 1974 and 1983. The program was a rental assistance program whereby the federal government in effect "guaranteed" the rent of a housing unit by executing a housing assistance payments contract (HAP) with the owner of a low-income housing project. A qualifying low-income tenant paid 30 percent of his income for rent. The difference between that figure and the contract rent of the unit (regulated by HUD-determined fair market rents) was paid for by HUD. There was a Section 8 program for existing housing and a program for new construction and substantial rehabilitation. The primary difference between the two programs was that, in the latter program, the subsidy stayed with the unit and, in the former, the subsidy went with the tenant. Low-income housing syndication utilized the Section 8 program for new construction and substantial rehabilitation.

As originally conceived in the early 1970s, Section 8 was viewed as a way of getting the government out of the financing business. The notion was that with rents guaranteed for up to 20 years by HUD, conventional lenders would be eager to finance new multi-family Section 8 projects. It never worked out that way, largely because inflation pushed conventional interest rates up during the latter part of the decade to a point where the Section 8 allowable rents were simply not high enough to retire the debt under conventional financing. The result was that most Section 8 projects were financed either through the sale of tax-exempt bonds issued by state housing agencies or special local instrumentalities (under the 11(b) program), or through the purchase from the lender of a fixed rate 7.5 percent permanent mortgage by the Government National Mortgage Association (GNMA). Utilizing these programs in the late 1970s resulted in low permanent mortgage loan rates of 7 to 8 percent. The examples cited here are of projects utilizing this below-market financing.

The other key aspects of the Section 8 program were these:

1.   The program was available to private developers, nonprofit developers, and local public housing authorities. It was utilized primarily by private developers.

2.   The program was competitive. HUD announced that funds were available and issued a notification of funding availability (NOFA) at which time developers could respond by submitting Section 8 preliminary proposals. Preliminary architectural drawings were submitted and sponsors had to have control of a specific site or building. Depending on how much Section 8 money was available, HUD selected the best proposals and invited submission of more detailed proposals.

3.   The program was highly regulated. HUD allowed developers to charge fair market rents (FMRs), but determined itself what fair market rents were for a specific market area. HUD also determined the maximum allowable mortgage and analyzed all proposals to assure that they did not exceed reasonable construction and development cost estimates. Developers had to submit affirmative fair housing marketing plans, follow HUD minimum property standards, pay Davis Bacon prevailing wages to construction workers, and comply with regulations on site selection and man-

agement. Also, all costs had to be certified at the end of the construction period. Cash distributions were also regulated to 10 percent for family projects and 6 percent for elderly projects.

4.  Tax laws treated Section 8 projects more liberally in two major ways: first, by allowing the owner to deduct construction interest and loan fees during the construction period rather than amortizing them over a longer period, and, second, by allowing a more liberal forgiveness of the excess depreciation. These provisions gave low-income housing as important edge in the area of tax shelter investment. Section 167(k) of the Tax Code allowed for a five-year write-off for Section 8 substantial rehabilitation expenses. Other laws and regulations treated Section 8 projects more liberally with regard to qualifying for tax-exempt or below-market financing. The inclusion of Section 8 units for at least 20 percent of a project was a requirement for receiving GNMA financing or tax-exempt bond financing. The 11(b) tax-exempt program required Section 8 assistance for all units in a project.

5.  Rents in Section 8 projects were allowed to be adjusted annually without having to obtain special permission from HUD. HUD determined the fixed percentage amount of allowable increase which applied to projects in a geographical area.

6.  Qualifying low-income households included families, handicapped individuals, and elderly couples or elderly individuals whose incomes did not exceed 80 percent of the median income of the metropolitan area (later revised to 50 percent of the median income of the metropolitan area for most households).

In summary, the Section 8 program was a major production program producing hundreds of thousands of low-income housing units throughout the United States between 1974 and 1983. Because of the income tax advantages offered to owners of Section 8 projects and because of the security of the Section 8 housing assistance payments contract, these projects had a special appeal to wealthy individuals looking for a tax shelter. This fact, coupled with the fact that most Section 8 projects did not generate a great deal of cash flow, made them especially attractive as real estate tax shelter investments.

Even though the program no longer is active, lessons can be learned from the past. Focusing on one real syndication is helpful in understanding the basic dynamics which continue to apply in many syndications which emphasize the tax shelter benefit.

As described in Chapter One, there are two basic ways syndication is undertaken. The first and most common way is for the syndicator to arrange for limited partners to make capital contributions directly into the limited partnership, which in turn is responsible for paying all the participants in the project, one of whom, of course, is the original developer, who becomes the general partner and receives a fee for the effort and risk involved. Such deals are made typically on a best-efforts basis whereby the syndicator is not legally obligated to purchase the project should investors not be found. The other way is for the syndicator to purchase the project (except for 1 or 2 percent, which the local general partner will continue to own), and then resell the interests to investors. In this instance, since the syndicator makes a firm commitment to purchase the project, there is less risk to the local sponsor and more risk to the syndication firm.

In this chapter, the example which is used is representative of the latter type of syndication, whereby a project is purchased and resold in a two-step process. In a one-step process where capital contributions are made directly into the partnership, however, the same basic principles would apply regarding the calculation of tax losses. The next chapter deals with such an example. The main difference is that, instead of purchasing units from a syndicator, the investor contributes directly to the limited partnership. The syndication firm receives a fee for its role in the effort rather than calculating its profit in the manner shown in this example. While there are important legal distinctions between the two approaches—especially in the area of risk and financial exposure—the basic way of analyzing the economic benefits of a syndication offering is very similar in both approaches.

In Section 8 syndications, the amount of money the developer made varied from project to project, depending on whether all of the units in the project received Section 8 commitments or whether only a fraction did, or whether the project was new construction or substantial rehabilitation. Equally significant, while there was some variation in the price the developer received from a syndicator (best-efforts prices tended to be higher and also some firms took a more aggressive posture regarding deductions), the profit was also determined by how much of the developer's cash was put into the project. The investment in a project varied considerably. The most important influences, which will be discussed in detail later in this chapter, were these:

1. ***The amount of loan financing available for the project.*** To the extent that a 90 percent loan was not obtainable, additional cash was required from the developer.
2. ***The discounts the developer had to pay for below-market rate premanent financing.*** The developer may have had to pay a discount for GNMA financing or construction financing.
3. ***Other fees.*** The developer may have incurred fees or expenses to third parties which HUD refused to allow. The working capital letters of credit requirements also could vary depending on the lender.

Depending on how well the developer was able to handle these out-of-pocket cash items, many of which were unpredictable and beyond the developer's control, the developer could come out quite well or, in some instances, barely break even. The most important item, therefore, was how well the developer was able to manage these cash outlays. In addition, since the developer was probably responsible for construction cost overruns, if construction cost problems occurred, the developer could lose money. The same held true for initial operating cost deficits, should the project fail to lease-up quickly.

## PRICING A REAL ESTATE TAX SHELTER

Let us examine an example of where the profits were on a typical Section 8 syndication offering. This example uses the pre-1981 tax laws, with the results of the syndication compared later in the chapter to the syndication potentials of the project under the 1981 Economic Recovery Tax Act.

Since the economic value of a limited partnership in assisted housing was primarily determined by tax losses, what determined value was how many losses a project generated: the greater the losses, the greater the economic value of the partnership interests.

The basic methodology utilized to determine the price of the limited partnership shares in the example which follows was this:

## Step One

The total taxable losses were figured for a 20-year period. As discussed in Chapter One, the losses primarily included real estate taxes, loan fees, interest, and depreciation. To these basic losses were added adjustments to account for any investor fees such as the operating deficit guarantee fee, construction guarantee fee, reporting fees, payment of interest on installment payments and, finally, any *step-up* in basis—although not all syndications used this concept, due in part to its relative sophistication and complexity.

The concept of *step-up* is based on the accounting premise that allows an owner to book a project at the amount paid for it. To the extent that this was higher than what the original developer had invested in the project, which it always will be in the case of syndication, the new owners were allowed to increase the value of the property by that amount for purposes of determining depreciation. In other words, they were able to depreciate the additional value of the project generated by their equity investment.

## Step Two

Based on current market factors, a ratio of tax losses to dollars invested was applied to the losses generated by the project. There were usually two ratios utilized. The first was the ratio of the losses to dollars invested during the pay-in period—typically the first five years. The second was the ratio expressed over the 20-year estimated life of the partnership.

Since the tax losses were fairly standard, the more difficult and subtle factor was the ratio applied to those losses. The ratio was, first of all, a function of the market. It depended on what was going on elsewhere within the syndication market, including what other similar, competitive syndicators were offering in the way of tax shelters.

In addition, the ratio applied to a specific project depended in part on the relative merits and risks of that particular project. Investors would accept a lower loss/investment ratio if the project had potential for generating some cash flow or if it seemed to offer long-term appreciation benefits. Similarly, if there was little hope for cash flow or appreciation, the investor was likely to require a higher investment/loss ratio. Items such as the metropolitan area, the neighborhood, and the design of the building entered into determining the exact ratio which would ultimately be applied. The other important item was, of course, the overall risk, specifically the assurance that the limited partner would not have to worry about a foreclosure. An inexperienced or financially weak general partner would cause investors to require a higher ratio of losses to investment.

**ILLUSTRATIVE LOSS/INVESTMENT RATIO
PRE-1981 TAX ACT**

| Pay-in period | New Construction | Substantial Rehabilitation |
|---|---|---|
| 5 years | $1.40–$1.60 to $1.00 | $2.50–$3.00 to $1.00 |
| 20 years | $2.75–$3.00 to $1.00 | $2.50–$3.50 to $1.00 |

In other words, for a new construction project, an investor would expect on the average $1.50 worth of tax losses to report to the IRS for every dollar actually invested in the project during the five-year pay-in period. Over the 20-year period, the losses would average about $2.75 to $3.00 for every $1.00 invested. During the five-year pay-in period, the loss was almost $2.50 for every $1.00 in the case of substantial rehabilitation projects.

### Step Three

Based on the ratio of losses to investment, the overall tax losses were determined and presented to the investor along with other pertinent economic information about the project, including the potential for positive cash flow and the overall benefit to the investor when the project would be sold in year 20. The latter information normally included a variety of schemes based on alternative rates of appreciation. On the basis of this information and other information included in the offering memorandum, the investor decided whether or not to become a limited partner.

### COMINGS TOWERS AND THE TRACY APARTMENTS

This Section 8 syndication deal contained two projects developed in 1978. One we will call Comings Towers, a 10-story highrise, new construction project consisting of 171 one-bedroom units for the elderly and located in a downtown urban renewel area in Washington, D.C. The project was awarded Section 8 allocations for all units and had a permanent loan of $5,540,300 insured by HUD at a permanent interest rate of 7.5 percent (under the GNMA tandem program). In this particular project, the developer and the syndicator were the same entity.

The second project, which we will call the Tracy Apartments, consisted of 146 units in 10 three-story buildings and one six-story building located in St. Louis. The project involved substantial rehabilitation of existing buildings. In this project, only 20 percent of the units, or 29 apartments, were Section 8 units and could therefore take advantage of the five-year depreciation. Also, unlike Comings Towers, while the syndicator had purchased 90 percent of the equity in the project from a local sponsor, he sold only 70 percent to investors. The project was financed by the state housing finance agency and the mortgage was $3,186,500, bearing a permanent tax-exempt rate of 6.75 percent. Both projects started construction in 1978.

## Benefits to the Limited Partners

For syndication purposes, the two projects were combined in one offering. Each unit of ownership included a 2.71 percent limited partnership interest in Comings Towers and a 2.0 percent limited partnership interest in the Tracy Apartments. The general partner retained a 4.5 percent general partnership interest in the former project and a 4.0 percent interest in the latter.

The tables included in this chapter show the financial data presented to investors in the offering memorandum. These tables have been taken from a real private placement offering memorandum and include figures as they were presented to investors. The names of the projects have been changed in order to protect the anonymity of the sponsors of the project.

Tables 3 and 4 show the losses produced by each project. The taxable losses for the Tracy Apartments were based on 70 percent of the overall losses because only 70 percent of the project was being sold. In Comings Towers, 95 percent of the project was being sold, so the losses were based on 95 percent of total project losses. The total taxable losses for Comings Towers for the 20-year period amounted to some $3,794,900, of which $3,605,400 was attributable to the limited partners (see Table 3). Similarly, the losses for the Tracy Apartments were $2,199,000 total, and $1,539,400 for the limited partners (see Table 4).

Tables 3 and 4 illustrate what constituted the basic taxable losses—construction expenses, construction interest, operating expenses, permanent interest, and mortgage insurance premium and depreciation. To the basic losses were added the step-up basis and the guarantee fees paid by the limited partners to the general partner. The result was an "adjusted total loss" for the two combined projects, as shown in Table 5. This table combines the losses shown in Tables 3 and 4. To these amounts was applied a market ratio averaging 1.85 to 1.0 to determine the investment amount. Table 5 shows a total loss figure attributable to the limited partners for both projects of $3,568,600 during the pay-in period of 5½ years. The assumptions which went into determining depreciation are shown in Table 6.

The ratio applied in this case was higher than the 1.5 to 1.0 ratio then normally applied to new construction and lower than the 2.5 and 1.0 ratio then applied to substantial rehabilitation because the syndication included a mixture of new construction and rehabilitation. The average ratio for this particular offering was 3.1 to 1.0 over the 20-year period, a ratio which was typical for the industry at the time.

Table 7 shows the total benefits available for the investors in the project, assuming a 50 percent income tax rate.

Once the ratio and losses were established, the information was presented for each investor unit. In this particular offering, each unit was priced at $55,000; and there were 35 units, the maximum allowed at the time under SEC regulations in order to qualify as a private placement. Some investors were allowed to purchase more than one unit. The $55,000 breaks down as shown in Table 8.

The next two tables present the net benefits available to potential investors in the 50 percent and 70 percent marginal income tax brackets. Table 9 shows the benefits to someone in the 50 percent bracket. Table 10 shows the benefits to someone in the 70 percent bracket. Table 9 shows, for example, that at the end of the twentieth year, an investor putting up $55,000 over a five-year pay-in period would have received over $170,000 in tax losses which could be reported on the individual's tax return. For someone in the 50 percent bracket, this amounted to a net savings of over $85,000 (.5 × $170,000). For someone in the 70 percent bracket, this amounted to a net savings of $119,000 (.7 × $170,000). These benefits are tax benefits only and do not take into consideration cash distributions or capital gains taxes realized when the project is sold. Tables 9 and 10 also present information regarding potential cash distributions and show the cumulative net benefit of tax savings plus appreciation. For someone in the 70 percent bracket, assuming that the net investment was invested in tax-exempt bonds at 6 percent, in year 20, the investor would have received a net profit of over $153,000. For someone in the 50 percent bracket, the net profit would be about $71,000.

Table 11 presents additional information on cash flow available for distribution to all limited partners (also shown in Tables 9 and 10). The amount is insignificant compared to the tax benefits generated and has virtually no impact on the financial return to the investor.

One important item, of course, that has not been covered is the potential for long-term appreciation benefits or long-term tax liabilities. Syndication offering memoranda also present this information, and this is shown for Comings Towers and the Tracy Apartments in Tables 12 and 13.

In this example, the syndicator assumed that the project would be sold for the amount outstanding on the mortgage loan plus $1. The rationale for this assumption is that in the event of a foreclosure, a lender will bid the property in for the amount of the outstanding loan. Thus the loan amount plus one dollar represents a worst-case situation. In the year 1999, there would be a capital gain (in this case figured on the basis of 35 percent because it was syndicated prior to the Economic Recovery Act of 1981) of $1,634,000. The reason for the capital gains tax, of course, is the depreciation taken on the building since the tax is figured on selling price *less* the adjusted basis (acquisition or development cost less depreciation). For each of the separate 35 investors, this translates to a tax of $46,694 due in 1999. In the meantime, since substantial tax savings would be generated and the taxes due in 1999 would be paid back in 1999 dollars—the value of which is likely to be much less than their value at the time of the initial investment—the tax liability is not an overriding concern.

In this example, the benefits to someone in the 70 percent bracket are in fact quite astonishing. As Table 10 points out, since the project generated losses of $9,800 in the first year and since

## TABLE 3
## PROJECTED TAXABLE LOSS: COMINGS TOWERS (Excluding Gain on Sale of Project)

| Year | Total Income | Construction Expenses | Construction Interest | Operating Expenses* | Permanent Interest and Mortgage Insurance Premium | Depreciation | Total Expenses | Total Taxable Loss (Income) | Taxable Loss (Income) at 95.0%** |
|---|---|---|---|---|---|---|---|---|---|
| 1978 | $ 188,700 | $74,200 | $154,700 | $ 57,100 | $ 0 | $ 121,700 | $ 407,700 | $ 219,000 | $ 208,100 |
| 1979 | 754,900 | 0 | 0 | 268,100 | 442,600 | 478,100 | 1,188,800 | 433,900 | 412,200 |
| 1980 | 754,900 | 0 | 0 | 259,000 | 440,600 | 443,800 | 1,143,400 | 388,500 | 369,100 |
| 1981 | 754,900 | 0 | 0 | 259,000 | 438,600 | 409,700 | 1,107,300 | 352,400 | 334,800 |
| 1982 | 754,900 | 0 | 0 | 259,000 | 436,500 | 375,400 | 1,070,900 | 316,000 | 300,200 |
| 1983 | 754,900 | 0 | 0 | 258,700 | 434,100 | 341,000 | 1,033,800 | 278,900 | 265,000 |
| 1984 | 778,200 | 0 | 0 | 258,000 | 431,600 | 311,800 | 1,001,400 | 223,200 | 212,000 |
| 1985 | 778,200 | 0 | 0 | 258,000 | 428,900 | 319,700 | 1,006,600 | 228,400 | 217,000 |
| 1986 | 778,200 | 0 | 0 | 258,000 | 425,900 | 303,300 | 987,200 | 209,000 | 198,600 |
| 1987 | 778,200 | 0 | 0 | 258,000 | 422,800 | 287,100 | 967,900 | 189,700 | 180,200 |
| 1988 | 778,200 | 0 | 0 | 258,000 | 419,400 | 270,700 | 948,100 | 169,900 | 161,400 |
| 1989 | 778,200 | 0 | 0 | 258,000 | 415,700 | 254,500 | 928,200 | 150,000 | 142,500 |
| 1990 | 778,200 | 0 | 0 | 258,000 | 411,700 | 261,100 | 930,800 | 152,600 | 145,000 |
| 1991 | 778,200 | 0 | 0 | 258,000 | 407,500 | 243,200 | 908,700 | 130,500 | 124,000 |
| 1992 | 778,200 | 0 | 0 | 258,000 | 402,900 | 225,400 | 886,300 | 108,100 | 102,700 |
| 1993 | 778,200 | 0 | 0 | 258,000 | 398,000 | 207,700 | 863,700 | 85,500 | 81,200 |
| 1994 | 778,200 | 0 | 0 | 258,000 | 392,600 | 189,800 | 840,400 | 62,200 | 59,100 |
| 1995 | 778,200 | 0 | 0 | 258,000 | 386,900 | 194,200 | 839,100 | 60,900 | 57,900 |
| 1996 | 778,200 | 0 | 0 | 258,000 | 380,700 | 176,200 | 814,900 | 36,700 | 34,900 |
| 1997 | 778,200 | 0 | 0 | 258,000 | 374,000 | 158,400 | 790,400 | 12,200 | 11,600 |
| 1998 | 778,200 | 0 | 0 | 258,000 | 366,800 | 140,700 | 765,500 | (12,700) | (12,100) |
| TOTAL | $15,636,200 | $74,200 | $154,700 | $5,230,900 | $8,257,800 | $5,713,500 | $19,431,100 | $3,794,900 | $3,605,400 |

*Includes amortization of fees.

**This represents the amount of loss allocable to investors.

**Source:** Private placement offering memorandum. The author has changed the name of the project to preserve anonymity.

100

## TABLE 4
### PROJECTED TAXABLE LOSS: TRACY APARTMENTS (Excluding Gain on Sale of Project)

| Year | Total Income | Construction Expenses | Construction Interest | Operating Expenses* | Permanent Interest and Mortgage Insurance Premium | Depreciation | Total Expenses | Total Taxable Loss (Income) | Taxable Loss (Income) at 70.0%** |
|---|---|---|---|---|---|---|---|---|---|
| 1978 | $ 39,600 | $ 38,300 | $ 31,800 | $ 10,900 | $ 0 | $ 41,100 | $ 122,100 | $ 82,500 | $ 57,800 |
| 1979 | 390,000 | 57,200 | 69,600 | 119,700 | 96,100 | 402,500 | 745,100 | 355,100 | 248,600 |
| 1980 | 394,000 | 3,200 | 5,600 | 122,400 | 229,600 | 381,300 | 742,100 | 348,100 | 243,700 |
| 1981 | 394,000 | 3,200 | 5,600 | 122,400 | 228,000 | 355,100 | 714,300 | 320,300 | 224,200 |
| 1982 | 394,000 | 100 | 300 | 122,400 | 226,300 | 329,200 | 678,300 | 284,300 | 199,000 |
| 1983 | 394,000 | 100 | 300 | 122,100 | 224,300 | 292,000 | 638,800 | 244,800 | 171,400 |
| 1984 | 406,100 | 0 | 0 | 121,400 | 222,300 | 168,000 | 511,700 | 105,600 | 73,900 |
| 1985 | 406,100 | 0 | 0 | 121,400 | 220,000 | 168,500 | 509,900 | 103,800 | 72,700 |
| 1986 | 406,100 | 0 | 0 | 121,400 | 217,700 | 157,300 | 496,400 | 90,300 | 63,200 |
| 1987 | 406,100 | 0 | 0 | 121,400 | 215,300 | 146,400 | 483,100 | 77,000 | 53,900 |
| 1988 | 406,100 | 0 | 0 | 123,600 | 212,700 | 135,100 | 471,400 | 65,300 | 45,700 |
| 1989 | 406,100 | 0 | 0 | 127,900 | 210,100 | 124,300 | 462,300 | 56,200 | 39,300 |
| 1990 | 406,100 | 0 | 0 | 127,900 | 207,600 | 126,600 | 462,100 | 56,000 | 39,200 |
| 1991 | 406,100 | 0 | 0 | 127,900 | 204,900 | 116,200 | 449,000 | 42,900 | 30,000 |
| 1992 | 406,100 | 0 | 0 | 127,900 | 202,100 | 106,200 | 436,200 | 30,100 | 21,100 |
| 1993 | 406,100 | 0 | 0 | 127,900 | 198,900 | 95,700 | 422,500 | 16,400 | 11,500 |
| 1994 | 406,100 | 0 | 0 | 127,900 | 195,600 | 85,700 | 409,200 | 3,100 | 2,200 |
| 1995 | 406,100 | 0 | 0 | 127,900 | 192,000 | 86,800 | 406,700 | 600 | 400 |
| 1996 | 406,100 | 0 | 0 | 127,900 | 188,300 | 76,500 | 392,700 | (13,400) | (9,400) |
| 1997 | 406,100 | 0 | 0 | 127,900 | 184,300 | 66,300 | 378,500 | (27,600) | (19,300) |
| 1998 | 406,100 | 0 | 0 | 127,900 | 179,800 | 56,000 | 363,700 | (42,400) | (29,700) |
| TOTAL | $8,097,100 | $102,100 | $113,200 | $2,508,100 | $4,055,900 | $3,516,800 | $10,296,100 | $2,199,000 | $1,539,400 |

*Includes amortization of fees.

**This represents the amount of loss allocable to investors.

101

# TABLE 5
## COMINGS TOWERS AND TRACY APARTMENTS
## COMBINED OFFERING

| Year | Adjusted total tax loss including fees and step-up in basis | Loss to Investment Ratio | Investment amount |
|------|------|------|------|
| 1 | $ 343,800 | 1.51 to 1 | $ 227,500 |
| 2 | 839,500 | 2.1  to 1 | 409,500 |
| 3 | 757,000 | 2.1  to 1 | 367,500 |
| 4 | 627,700 | 1.9  to 1 | 322,000 |
| 5 | 543,000 | 1.7  to 1 | 315,000 |
| 6 | 457,600 | 1.6  to 1 | 283,500 |
| TOTAL | $3,568,600 | 1.85 to 1 | $1,925,000 |
| Comings Towers Portion | $2,390,962 | 1.85 to 1 | $1,289,400 |
| Tracy Apartments Portion | $1,177,638 | 1.85 to 1 | $ 635,600 |

**Source:** Private placement offering memorandum. The project names have been changed to preserve anonimity.

## TABLE 6
## COMINGS TOWERS AND TRACY APARTMENTS

| Component | Life | Method | Investors' share of Comings Towers at 95% | Investors' share of Tracy Apartments at 70% | Total |
|---|---|---|---|---|---|
| Building shell | 40 | SYD* | $2,026,100 | $ 0 | $2,026,100* |
| Building shell | 25 | 125% | 0 | 75,300 | 75,300 |
| Rehabilitation expenditures | 25 | 167(k) | 0 | 391,000 | 391,000 |
| Mechanical systems | 25 | SYD | 2,247,000 | 1,100,300 | 3,347,300 |
| Site improvements | 25 | SYD | 255,900 | 165,800 | 421,700 |
| Cabinets and specialties | 10 | SYD | 0 | 75,400 | 75,400 |
| Decorating and appliances | 10 | SYD | 38,800 | 0 | 38,800 |
| Decorating and appliances | 5 | SYD | 0 | 165,800 | 165,800 |
| Personal property | 5 | SYD | 287,400 | 0 | 287,400 |
| Basis (step up) adjustments | 30 | SYD | 984,600 | 0 | 984,600 |
| Basis (step up) adjustments | 25 | SYD | 0 | 457,500 | 457,500 |
| TOTAL | | | $5,839,800 | $2,431,100 | $8,270,900 |

*Sum-of-the-year digits. This method is similar to the declining balance method of depreciation and was eliminated by the Economic Recovery Tax Act of 1981.

**Source:** Private placement offering memorandum.

## TABLE 7
### SUMMARY OF PROJECTED INVESTMENT AND RELATED TAX EFFECTS*

| Year | Investment Amount | Investors' Projected Tax Loss (Income) | Investor Fees | Installment Interest at 8% | Investors' Total Projected Tax Loss (Income) | Tax Savings at 50% Rate | Potential Cash Distribution | Potential Total Benefit | Cumulative Total Benefit |
|---|---|---|---|---|---|---|---|---|---|
| 1978 | $ 227,500 | $ 265,900 | $ 43,100 | $ 34,800 | $ 343,800 | $ 171,900 | $ 0 | $ 171,900 | $ 171,900 |
| 1979 | 409,500 | 660,800 | 91,200 | 87,500 | 839,500 | 419,750 | 0 | 419,750 | 591,650 |
| 1980 | 367,500 | 612,800 | 75,200 | 69,000 | 757,000 | 378,500 | 0 | 378,550 | 970,150 |
| 1981 | 322,000 | 559,000 | 21,200 | 47,500 | 627,700 | 313,850 | 0 | 313,850 | 1,284,000 |
| 1982 | 315,000 | 499,200 | 19,300 | 24,500 | 543,000 | 271,500 | 0 | 271,500 | 1,555,500 |
| 1983 | 283,500 | 436,400 | 19,300 | 1,900 | 457,600 | 228,800 | 0 | 228,800 | 1,784,300 |
| 1984 | 0 | 285,900 | 19,300 | 0 | 305,200 | 152,600 | 30,600 | 183,200 | 1,967,500 |
| 1985 | 0 | 289,700 | 19,300 | 0 | 309,000 | 154,500 | 30,600 | 185,100 | 2,152,600 |
| 1986 | 0 | 261,800 | 19,300 | 0 | 281,100 | 140,550 | 30,600 | 171,150 | 2,323,750 |
| 1987 | 0 | 234,100 | 19,300 | 0 | 253,400 | 126,700 | 30,600 | 157,300 | 2,481,050 |

| Year | | | | | | | | | |
|---|---|---|---|---|---|---|---|---|---|
| 1988 | 0 | 207,100 | 19,300 | 0 | 226,400 | 113,200 | 30,600 | 143,800 | 2,624,850 |
| 1989 | 0 | 181,800 | 19,300 | 0 | 201,100 | 100,550 | 30,600 | 131,150 | 2,756,000 |
| 1990 | 0 | 184,200 | 19,300 | 0 | 203,500 | 101,750 | 30,600 | 132,350 | 2,888,350 |
| 1991 | 0 | 154,000 | 19,300 | 0 | 173,300 | 86,650 | 30,600 | 117,250 | 3,005,600 |
| 1992 | 0 | 123,800 | 19,300 | 0 | 143,100 | 71,550 | 30,600 | 102,150 | 3,107,750 |
| 1993 | 0 | 92,700 | 19,300 | 0 | 112,000 | 56,000 | 30,600 | 86,600 | 3,194,350 |
| 1994 | 0 | 61,300 | 19,300 | 0 | 80,600 | 40,300 | 30,600 | 70,900 | 3,265,250 |
| 1995 | 0 | 58,300 | 19,300 | 0 | 77,600 | 38,800 | 30,600 | 69,400 | 3,334,650 |
| 1996 | 0 | 25,500 | 19,300 | 0 | 44,800 | 22,400 | 30,600 | 53,000 | 3,387,650 |
| 1997 | 0 | (7,700) | 19,300 | 0 | 11,600 | 5,800 | 30,600 | 36,400 | 3,424,050 |
| 1998 | 0 | (41,800) | 19,300 | 0 | (22,500) | (11,250) | 30,600 | 19,350 | 3,443,400 |
| TOTAL | $1,925,000 | $5,144,800 | $558,800 | $265,200 | $5,968,800 | $2,984,400 | $459,000 | $3,443,400 | |

Total Losses     $5,968,800

Total Investment  1,925,000

Ratio           3.1 to 1

*Assuming 50% tax rate, minimum tax on tax preference items not included.

**Source:** Private placement offering memorandum.

105

the investor's investment the first year was $6,500, the tax savings more than offset the initial investment (.70 × $9,800 = $6,860). In other words, the first year the investor got more than the initial investment back in tax savings. The second year the situation improved. The investment was $11,700; yet the total losses received were $24,000. The net tax savings was .70 × $24,000 = $16,800, or a profit of $5,100 ($16,800–$11,700). And so it goes through each year of the five-year pay-in period, after which time there was no investment and the net profit increased. As this deal was structured, it was really a no-lose situation for someone in the highest tax bracket, and it was not bad for someone in the 50 percent bracket either—at the end of the five-year pay-in period the investor was still slightly behind, but only to the extent of about $4,000.

There is no question that such an arrangement was (and still is) extremely attractive for high-income investors looking for tax shelter, even if they were likely to pay capital gains taxes of almost $47,000 toward the end of the period, as is shown in the example in Table 13.

Although the internal rate of return method is rarely used to analyze the potential benefits of low-income housing tax shelter syndications, the IRR analysis can easily be used in this manner; and, for the sake of comparison, it is useful to see what the results are. For simplicity, let us assume that the entire $55,000 investment was put up in year 1. The basic equation works as follows:

### COMINGS TOWERS
### TRACY APARTMENTS
Initial investment amount: $55,000

| Year | Benefits 50% rate | 70% rate |
|------|---------|----------|
| 1 | $ 4,900 | $ 6,860 |
| 2 | 12,000 | 16,800 |
| 3 | 10,800 | 15,120 |
| 4 | 8,950 | 12,530 |
| 5 | 7,750 | 10,850 |
| 6 | 6,550 | 9,170 |
| 7 | 5,250 | 6,990 |
| 8 | 5,300 | 7,060 |

(continued on page 116)

### TABLE 8
### COMINGS TOWERS/TRACY APARTMENTS
### PAYMENTS BY THE INVESTORS

| Due Date | Total Payment Per Unit (a) | Principal Payment | Interest Payment | Fees* |
|---|---|---|---|---|
| Upon closing of the offering of units | $ 6,500 | $ 4,274 | $ 994 | $1,232 |
| February 1 | 11,700 | 6,591 | 2,500 | 2,609 |
| February 1 | 10,500 | 6,563 | 1,972 | 1,965 |
| February 1 | 9,200 | 7,786 | 1,360 | 54 |
| February 1 | 9,000 | 8,300 | 700 | 0 |
| February 1 | 8,100 | 8,046 | 54 | 0 |
| TOTAL | $55,000 | $41,560 | $7,580 | $5,860 |

*Includes construction cost overrun guarantee fee, operating deficit guarantee fee, and administrative and reporting fee.

**Source:** Private placement offering memorandum.

## TABLE 9
### INVESTMENT TAX LOSSES AND POTENTIAL BENEFITS FOR A $55,000 INVESTOR IN THE 70% TAX BRACKET

| Year | Investment Date | Investment Amount* | Projected Tax Losses (Income)** | Ratio of Losses to Investment | Projected Tax Savings at 70% Rate | Potential Cash Distribution | Total Annual Benefit | Annual Net Investment | Cumulative Net Investment | Interest at 6% on Cumulative Net Investment*** | Cumulative Net Investment Including Interest at 6%*** |
|---|---|---|---|---|---|---|---|---|---|---|---|
| 1978 | 9/1/78 | $ (6,500) | $ 9,800 | 1.5 | $ 6,860 | $ 0 | $ 6,860 | $ 360 | $ 360 | $ 0 | $ 360 |
| 1979 | 2/1/79 | (11,700) | 24,000 | 2.1 | 16,800 | 0 | 16,800 | 5,100 | 5,460 | 22 | 5,482 |
| 1980 | 2/1/80 | (10,500) | 21,600 | 2.1 | 15,120 | 0 | 15,120 | 4,620 | 10,080 | 329 | 10,430 |
| 1981 | 2/1/81 | (9,200) | 17,900 | 1.9 | 12,530 | 0 | 12,530 | 3,330 | 13,410 | 626 | 14,386 |
| 1982 | 2/1/82 | (9,000) | 15,500 | 1.7 | 10,850 | 0 | 10,850 | 1,850 | 15,260 | 863 | 17,100 |
| 1983 | 2/1/83 | (8,100) | 13,100 | 1.6 | 9,170 | 0 | 9,170 | 1,070 | 16,330 | 1,026 | 19,195 |
| 1984 | | | 8,700 | | 6,090 | 900 | 6,990 | 6,990 | 23,320 | 1,152 | 27,337 |
| 1985 | | | 8,800 | | 6,160 | 900 | 7,060 | 7,060 | 30,380 | 1,640 | 36,037 |
| 1986 | | | 8,000 | | 5,600 | 900 | 6,500 | 6,500 | 36,880 | 2,162 | 44,700 |
| 1987 | | | 7,200 | | 5,040 | 900 | 5,940 | 5,940 | 42,820 | 2,682 | 53,322 |

| Year | | | | | | | | |
|------|------|------|-----|-------|-------|--------|-------|---------|
| 1988 | 6,500 | 4,550 | 900 | 5,450 | 5,450 | 48,270 | 3,199 | 61,971 |
| 1989 | 5,700 | 3,990 | 900 | 4,890 | 4,890 | 53,160 | 3,718 | 70,579 |
| 1990 | 5,800 | 4,060 | 900 | 4,960 | 4,960 | 58,120 | 4,235 | 79,774 |
| 1991 | 5,000 | 3,500 | 900 | 4,400 | 4,400 | 62,520 | 4,786 | 88,960 |
| 1992 | 4,100 | 2,870 | 900 | 3,770 | 3,770 | 66,290 | 5,338 | 98,068 |
| 1993 | 3,200 | 2,240 | 900 | 3,140 | 3,140 | 69,430 | 5,884 | 107,092 |
| 1994 | 2,300 | 1,610 | 900 | 2,510 | 2,510 | 71,940 | 6,426 | 116,028 |
| 1995 | 2,200 | 1,540 | 900 | 2,440 | 2,440 | 74,380 | 6,962 | 125,429 |
| 1996 | 1,300 | 910 | 900 | 1,810 | 1,810 | 76,190 | 7,526 | 134,765 |
| 1997 | 300 | 210 | 900 | 1,110 | 1,110 | 77,300 | 8,086 | 143,961 |
| 1998 | (600) | (420) | 900 | 480 | 480 | 77,780 | 8,638 | 153,079 |
| TOTAL | $(55,000) $170,400   3.1 | $119,280 | $13,500 | $132,780 | $77,780 | | $75,299 | |
| CAPITAL GAIN (IN YEAR 1999)—$128,900 | | | | | | | | |

*Investment amount is the total cost to the investor. This includes installment interest and investor fees.

**The projected tax losses include an allocable share of the installment interest expense and investor fees. These are personal expenses to the investors.

***This assumes the "annual net investment" earns a 6 percent return from a tax-free investment.

**Source:** Private placement offering memorandum.

## TABLE 10
### INVESTMENT TAX LOSSES AND POTENTIAL BENEFITS FOR A $55,000 INVESTOR IN THE 50% TAX BRACKET

| Year | Investment Date | Investment Amount* | Projected Tax Losses (Income)** | Ratio of Losses to Investment | Projected Tax Savings at 50% Rate | Potential Cash Distribution | Total Annual Benefit | Annual Net Investment | Cumulative Net Investment | Interest at 6% on Cumulative Net Investment*** | Cumulative Net Investment Including Interest at 6%*** |
|---|---|---|---|---|---|---|---|---|---|---|---|
| 1978 | 9/1/78 | $ (6,500) | $ 9,800 | 1.5 | $ 4,900 | $ 0 | $ 4,900 | $ (1,600) | $ (1,600) | $ 0 | $ (1,600) |
| 1979 | 2/1/79 | (11,700) | 24,000 | 2.1 | 12,000 | 0 | 12,000 | 300 | (1,300) | (96) | (1,396) |
| 1980 | 2/1/80 | (10,500) | 21,600 | 2.1 | 10,800 | 0 | 10,800 | 300 | (1,000) | (84) | (1,180) |
| 1981 | 2/1/81 | (9,200) | 17,900 | 1.9 | 8,950 | 0 | 8,950 | (250) | (1,250) | (71) | (1,501) |
| 1982 | 2/1/82 | (9,000) | 15,500 | 1.7 | 7,750 | 0 | 7,750 | (1,250) | (2,500) | (90) | (2,841) |
| 1983 | 2/1/83 | (8,100) | 13,100 | 1.6 | 6,550 | 0 | 6,550 | (1,550) | (4,050) | (170) | (4,561) |
| 1984 | | | 8,700 | | 4,350 | 900 | 5,250 | 5,250 | 1,200 | (274) | 415 |
| 1985 | | | 8,800 | | 4,400 | 900 | 5,300 | 5,300 | 6,500 | 25 | 5,740 |
| 1986 | | | 8,000 | | 4,000 | 900 | 4,900 | 4,900 | 11,400 | 344 | 10,985 |
| 1987 | | | 7,200 | | 3,600 | 900 | 4,500 | 4,500 | 15,900 | 659 | 16,144 |

| Year | | | | | | | | |
|---|---:|---:|---:|---:|---:|---:|---:|---:|
| 1988 | 6,500 | 3,250 | 900 | 4,150 | 4,150 | 20,050 | 969 | 21,262 |
| 1989 | 5,700 | 2,850 | 900 | 3,750 | 3,750 | 23,800 | 1,276 | 26,288 |
| 1990 | 5,800 | 2,900 | 900 | 3,800 | 3,800 | 27,600 | 1,577 | 31,665 |
| 1991 | 5,000 | 2,500 | 900 | 3,400 | 3,400 | 31,000 | 1,900 | 36,965 |
| 1992 | 4,100 | 2,050 | 900 | 2,950 | 2,950 | 33,950 | 2,218 | 42,133 |
| 1993 | 3,200 | 1,600 | 900 | 2,500 | 2,500 | 36,450 | 2,528 | 47,161 |
| 1994 | 2,300 | 1,150 | 900 | 2,050 | 2,050 | 38,500 | 2,830 | 52,041 |
| 1995 | 2,200 | 1,100 | 900 | 2,000 | 2,000 | 40,500 | 3,122 | 57,163 |
| 1996 | 1,300 | 650 | 900 | 1,550 | 1,550 | 42,050 | 3,430 | 62,143 |
| 1997 | 300 | 150 | 900 | 1,050 | 1,050 | 43,100 | 3,729 | 66,922 |
| 1998 | (600) | (300) | 900 | 600 | 600 | 43,700 | 4,015 | 71,537 |
| TOTAL | $(55,000) $170,400 | $85,200 | $13,500 | $98,700 | $43,700 | | $27,837 | |
| | 3.1 | | | | | | | |
| CAPITAL GAIN (IN YEAR 1999)—$128,900 | | | | | | | | |

*Investment amount is the total cost of the investor. This includes installment interest and investor fees.

**The projected tax losses include an allocable share of the installment interest expense and investor fees. These are personal expenses to the investors.

***This assumes the "annual net investment" earns a 6 percent return from a tax-free investment.

**Source:** Private placement offering memorandum.

# TABLE 11
## POTENTIAL CASH FLOW FROM PROJECT OPERATIONS
### (After 1984)

| | Comings Towers | Tracy Apartments | Total |
|---|---|---|---|
| GROSS RENTAL INCOME | $819,200 | $432,100 | $1,251,300 |
| VACANCY FACTOR | (41,000) | (26,000) | (67,000) |
| EFFECTIVE GROSS RENT | $778,200 | $406,100 | $1,184,300 |
| OPERATING EXPENSES | (251,800) | (120,200) | (372,000) |
| REPLACEMENT RESERVES | (24,300) | (12,700) | (37,000) |
| NET INCOME | $502,100 | $273,100 | $ 409,000 |
| DEBT SERVICE (INCLUDING MORTGAGE INSURANCE PREMIUM | (465,200) | (251,900) | (775,300) |
| TOTAL POTENTIAL CASH FLOW AT 100% | $ 36,900 | $ 21,300 | $ 58,200 |
| PERCENTAGE INTEREST SOLD | 95.0% | 70.0% | 85.9% |
| POTENTIAL CASH FLOW TO INVESTORS | $ 35,100 | $ 14,900 | $ 50,000 |
| ADMIN. AND REPORTING FEE (FROM CASH DISTRIBUTIONS) | (12,900) | (6,400) | (19,300) |
| POTENTIAL CASH DISTRIBUTION | $ 22,200 | $ 8,500 | $ 30,700 |

**Source:** Private placement offering memorandum.

112

## TABLE 12
## INVESTORS' SHARE OF EXCESS DEPRECIATION AND TAX LIABILITY IN THE EVENT OF SALE*

| Year | ANNUAL TAX PREFERENCE | | | TAX ON SALE** | | |
|---|---|---|---|---|---|---|
| | Comings Towers | Tracy Apartments | Total Tax Preference | Comings Towers | Tracy Apartments | Total Tax On Sale |
| 1978 | $ 43,200 | $ 12,800 | $ 56,000 | $ 0 | $ 0 | $ 0 |
| 1979 | 170,200 | 126,500 | 296,700 | 0 | 0 | 0 |
| 1980 | 157,600 | 121,900 | 279,500 | 0 | 0 | 0 |
| 1981 | 144,800 | 116,400 | 261,200 | 426,700 | 320,500 | 747,200 |
| 1982 | 132,100 | 110,500 | 242,600 | 517,400 | 394,600 | 912,000 |
| 1983 | 119,400 | 97,000 | 216,400 | 593,900 | 454,700 | 1,048,600 |
| 1984 | 106,700 | 36,600 | 143,300 | 717,800 | 493,400 | 1,211,200 |
| 1985 | 94,000 | 31,100 | 125,100 | 838,800 | 529,400 | 1,368,200 |
| 1986 | 81,300 | 25,500 | 106,800 | 949,000 | 560,100 | 1,509,100 |
| 1987 | 68,500 | 19,800 | 88,300 | 1,006,000 | 574,800 | 1,580,800 |
| 1988 | 55,900 | 14,200 | 70,100 | 1,042,900 | 581,600 | 1,624,500 |
| 1989 | 44,000 | 9,100 | 53,100 | 1,065,500 | 585,400 | 1,650,900 |
| 1990 | 32,500 | 4,400 | 36,900 | 1,083,100 | 588,400 | 1,671,500 |
| 1991 | 22,800 | 0 | 22,800 | 1,089,000 | 587,800 | 1,676,800 |
| 1992 | 18,100 | 0 | 18,100 | 1,084,500 | 583,800 | 1,668,300 |
| 1993 | 13,500 | 0 | 13,500 | 1,071,400 | 576,300 | 1,647,700 |
| 1994 | 10,500 | 0 | 10,500 | 1,051,000 | 565,600 | 1,616,600 |
| 1995 | 8,100 | 0 | 8,100 | 1,061,000 | 558,200 | 1,619,200 |
| 1996 | 5,600 | 0 | 5,600 | 1,085,400 | 551,900 | 1,637,300 |
| 1997 | 3,100 | 0 | 3,100 | 1,101,700 | 540,800 | 1,642,500 |
| 1998 | 700 | 0 | 700 | 1,109,700 | 524,600 | 1,634,300 |
| TOTAL | $1,332,600 | $725,800 | $2,058,400 | | | |

*To determine the per-unit amount of annual tax preference or tax on sale, divide the amount shown by 35.

**Note: Tax computed as if a sale occurs at the end of each year commencing two years after final close for a price of $1 in excess of the principal value of mortgage. Possible tax on tax preferences arising from capital gain and possible effect on maximum tax on other "earned" income has been disregarded.

**Source:** Private placement offering memorandum.

113

## TABLE 13
## INVESTORS' PROJECTED TAX ON SALE*
### (For Sale in Year 1999)

| | Comings Towers | Tracy Apartments | Total |
|---|---|---|---|
| SALES PROCEEDS: | | | |
| TOTAL PROCEEDS | $ 4,306,801 | $1,713,201 | $ 6,020,002 |
| INVESTORS' SHARE OF MORTGAGE | | | |
| BALANCE | (4,306,800) | (1,713,200) | (6,020,000) |
| NET PROCEEDS | $          1 | $          1 | $          2 |
| CASH DISTRIBUTIONS: | | | |
| TOTAL CASH | $   568,000 | $   244,800 | $   812,800 |
| ADMINISTRATIVE AND REPORTING FEE | (236,500) | (117,300) | (353,800) |
| NET CASH | $   331,500 | $   127,500 | $   459,000 |
| TAX LOSSES: | | | |
| TOTAL LOSSES | $ 4,128,600 | $1,840,200 | $ 5,968,800 |
| ADMINISTRATIVE AND REPORTING FEE | | | |
| (FROM OFFERING PROCEEDS) | (116,000) | (89,000) | (205,000) |
| INSTALLMENT INTEREST | (170,700) | (94,500) | (265,200) |
| NET LOSSES | $ 3,841,900 | $1,656,700 | $ 5,498,600 |
| INVESTMENT | | | |
| TOTAL INVESTMENT | $ 1,289,400 | $   635,600 | $ 1,925,000 |

114

| | | | |
|---|---|---|---|
| ADMINISTRATIVE AND REPORTING FEE (FROM OFFERING PROCEEDS) | (116,000) | (89,000) | (205,000) |
| INSTALLMENT INTEREST | (170,700) | (94,500) | (265,200) |
| NET INVESTMENT | $ 1,002,700 | $ 452,100 | $ 1,454,800 |
| CAPITAL GAIN: (A + B + C − D) | $ 3,170,701 | $1,332,101 | $ 4,502,802 |
| RECAPTURE: | | | |
| EXCESS DEPRECIATION SUBJECT TO RECAPTURE | $ 1,031,900 | $ 312,300 | $ 1,344,200 |
| OTHER DEPRECIATION SUBJECT TO RECAPTURE | 0 | 0 | 0 |
| RECAPTURE PHASEOUT | $(1,031,900) | $ (145,800) | $(1,177,700) |
| NET RECAPTURE | $ 0 | $ 166,500 | $ 166,500 |
| TAX ON SALE: | | | |
| ORDINARY TAX (F AT 70%) | $ 0 | $ 116,600 | $ 116,600 |
| CAPITAL GAIN TAX (E-F AT 35%) | 1,109,700 | 408,000 | 1,517,700 |
| TOTAL TAX ON SALE | $ 1,109,700 | $ 524,600 | $ 1,634,300 |

*To determine the per-unit amount of projected tax on sale, divide the amount shown by 35. Possible tax on tax preferences arising from capital, gain and possible effect on maximum tax on other "earned" income has been disregarded.

**Source:** Private placement offering memorandum.

115

| Year | 50% rate | 70% rate |
|------|----------|----------|
| 9 | 4,900 | 6,500 |
| 10 | 4,500 | 5,940 |
| 11 | 4,150 | 5,450 |
| 12 | 3,750 | 4,890 |
| 13 | 3,800 | 4,960 |
| 14 | 3,400 | 4,400 |
| 15 | 2,950 | 3,770 |
| 16 | 2,500 | 3,140 |
| 17 | 2,050 | 2,510 |
| 18 | 2,000 | 2,440 |
| 19 | 1,550 | 1,810 |
| 20 | 1,050 | 1,110 |
| 21 | – 46,694 | – 46,694 |
| **Total** | **$51,406** | **$85,606** |

These figures, taken from Tables 9, 10, and 13, show positive benefits in tax savings each year through year 20. In year 21, the project must be sold and, if the amount of the selling price were only equivalent to the mortgage *plus $1*, there would be taxes due of almost $47,000 as stated earlier. This scenario, however, represents a worst-case situation. The project could very well appreciate in value—especially if inflation continues and if there is an improvement in the neighborhood in which the project is located. If these projects did appreciate significantly in value, there could very well be sufficient dollars available to pay the capital gains taxes and return additional profit to the investor.

The table shows total benefits during the period of $51,406 for the 50 percent taxpayer and $85,606 for the 70 percent taxpayer, assuming taxes due at sale in year 20. If no taxes were due at sale in year 20 (because the selling price was high enough to produce income to cover the taxes), the total benefits produced would be $98,100 for the 50 percent taxpayer and $132,300 for the 70 percent taxpayer.

In Chapter Three, the concept of internal rate of return (IRR) was introduced. The concept is used when both the initial investment amount and the projected annual financial benefits are known. What is not known is the discount rate (or rate of return) that the annual financial benefits represent in relationship to the initial investment amount. In this example, we know the required initial investment amount, and we know the projected annual financial benefits. Utilizing a computer analysis, we can easily determine the internal rate of return—that is, the discount rate which discounts the stream of financial benefits so that it is roughly equivalent to the amount of the initial investment. In this case it is as follows:

|  | 50% rate | 70% rate |
| --- | --- | --- |
| **Internal Rate of Return** | 4% | 15.4% |

If there is no tax liability in year 21, the internal rate of return improves, especially for the 50-percent taxpayer:

|  | 50% rate | 70% rate |
| --- | --- | --- |
| **Internal Rate of Return** | 9.3% | 16.5% |

What does the internal rate of return analysis show? First it shows that the investment is significantly better for someone in the 70 percent tax bracket than for someone in the 50 percent tax bracket. In fact, if the investor is hit with a substantial tax liability in year 21, the investment really does not make sense for a 50 percent taxpayer. Since there are now no taxpayers in the 70 percent bracket, the value of the tax shelter has been diminished.

The actual internal rate of return is improved by the staging of the investment over a five-year period, however. By doing this the investor leverages the investment each year and is able to significantly improve the internal rate of return. In fact, the staging of the investment over a five-year period is crucial to the marketability of the tax shelter syndication concept. The staging of payments enables the syndicator to present to the investor what is in effect a no-lose deal. The net investment using the five-year pay-in method works out as follows:

### COMINGS TOWERS
### TRACY APARTMENTS

| Year | Investment | Benefit 50% Rate | Benefit 70% Rate | Net 50% | Net 70% |
| --- | --- | --- | --- | --- | --- |
| 1 | $ 6,500 | $ 4,900 | $ 6,860 | $ – 1,600 | $    360 |
| 2 | 11,700 | 12,000 | 16,800 | 300 | 5,100 |
| 3 | 10,500 | 10,800 | 15,120 | 300 | 4,620 |

| Year | Investment | Benefit 50% Rate | Benefit 70% Rate | Net 50% | Net 70% |
|---|---|---|---|---|---|
| 4 | 9,200 | 8,950 | 12,530 | – 250 | 3,330 |
| 5 | 9,000 | 7,750 | 10,850 | – 1,250 | 1,850 |
| 6 | 8,100 | 6,550 | 9,170 | – 1,550 | 1,070 |
| 7 | | 5,250 | 6,990 | 5,250 | 6,990 |
| 8 | | 5,300 | 7,060 | 5,300 | 7,060 |
| 9 | | 4,900 | 6,500 | 4,900 | 6,500 |
| 10 | | 4,500 | 5,940 | 4,500 | 5,940 |
| 11 | | 4,150 | 5,450 | 4,150 | 5,450 |
| 12 | | 3,750 | 4,890 | 3,750 | 4,890 |
| 13 | | 3,800 | 4,960 | 3,800 | 4,960 |
| 14 | | 3,400 | 4,400 | 3,400 | 4,400 |
| 15 | | 2,950 | 3,770 | 2,950 | 3,770 |
| 16 | | 2,500 | 3,140 | 2,500 | 3,140 |
| 17 | | 2,050 | 2,510 | 2,050 | 2,510 |
| 18 | | 2,000 | 2,440 | 2,000 | 2,440 |
| 19 | | 1,550 | 1,810 | 1,550 | 1,810 |
| 20 | | 1,050 | 1,110 | 1,050 | 1,110 |
| 21 | | – 46,694 | – 46,694 | – 46,694 | – 46,694 |
| Total | | $51,406 | $85,606 | $ – 3,594 | $30,606 |

The benefits are dramatically increased; and in the case of the 70 percent taxpayer, staging the pay-in period translates to having no net investment in the project at all. Under this scenario, it is not even possible to calculate an IRR, since there is in fact no net initial investment at all for the 70 percent taxpayer.

The second thing that the IRR tells us is that the assumptions on which the model is based do affect the overall outcome. In the analysis—using the lump-sum payment up front—for the 50 percent taxpayer, the IRR increases from 4 percent to 9.5 percent, depending on whether the investor owes taxes at the end of the project. If net profits were available, the return would be even higher. Since it is very difficult to predict anything some 20 years into the future, the usefulness of the IRR is questionable. This is the main reason that losses to investment ratios are used in its place and is the industry standard for pricing tax shelter real estate securities. At the same time, the IRR does serve a very important purpose. It enables an investor to compare the potential financial return of a tax shelter investment with practically any other type of investment, and it enables the investor to understand how his return might vary depending on the assumptions used in the analysis. As such, it is an extremely useful tool to use along with the losses to investment pricing ratio for analyzing investment opportunities in a tax shelter real estate syndication.

## Benefits to the Developer

We have just seen how the investors benefitted from being limited partners in the Comings Towers and Tracy Apartments limited partnership. What about the developer of the projects?

Of the total syndication offering of $1,925,000, as shown in Table 7, $1,289,400 (67 percent) was attributable to Comings Towers, where 95 percent of the interests were being sold, and $635,000 (35 percent) was attributable to the Tracy Apartments, where only 70 percent of the interests were being sold. Now let us take a look at how the developer/syndicator fared in each case.

## Comings Towers

Because Comings Towers was a direct development project, the syndicator did not purchase interest from a limited partner, but rather invested out-of-pocket dollars in the project himself as the developer. These out-of-pocket dollars invested by the developer/syndicator are commonly referred to as "over-and-above" cash requirements, meaning over and above the mortgage proceeds. These "over-and-above" requirements usually consisted of the following:

1. *The cash equity requirement imposed by HUD.* This figure was HUD's approved *total replacement cost*, that is, all the project costs, as determined by HUD, including the fair market value of the land, less the amount of the HUD-insured loan.

Since HUD insurance provided for a 90 percent loan-to-value ratio, one would normally expect a developer to provide 10 percent of the costs in cash. This was not the case, however, for two reasons. The first was HUD's BSPRA (as discussed in Chapter Four), which allowed the developer/builder to include as a legitimate cost an imputed allowance of 10 percent of all development costs (excluding land costs and a few other minor items). The BSPRA enabled the actual cash equity to be reduced from 10 percent of total replacement costs to between 1 and 4 percent of total replacement costs.

The second reason one cannot assume the developer's equity to be 10 percent of total replacement costs is that there were many very real out-of-pocket costs that HUD did not allow when computing total replacement costs. The most important of these other "over-and-above" items are spelled out in the other items that follow, and were discussed previously in Chapter Four.

2. *The cost of any off-site improvements.* This included sewer extensions, sidewalks, roads, etc.

3. *The cost of discounts paid by the developer for the permanent loan.* Typically, in order to utilize GNMA financing at 7.5 percent, developers had to pay 2.5 percent of the mortgage amount for this privilege. HUD did not acknowledge the 2.5 percent point discount in determining the total project costs.

4. *The cost of any discount paid to the construction lender.* Since there was no subsidy provided by HUD for the construction loan, to the extent that insufficient interest was budgeted for the construction loan in the final HUD-insured loan, the developer would have to make up the difference, out of pocket.

5. *The fee paid to the general contractor.* To qualify for BSPRA, the developer and builder had to have an *identity of interest.* Normally, the builder was a 1 percent limited partner during the construction period only. The contractor's fee was paid out of the developer's own resources as work progressed. Builders' fees typically averaged 4 to 6 percent of the construction contract.

6. *Working capital requirement.* HUD established this at 2 percent of the mortgage amount, and it was deposited with the mortgagee. An irrevocable letter of credit could be substituted for the cash deposit.

7. *Operating deficits during the lease-up period.* This applied to market rate projects more so than to Section 8 projects and did not occur in this project.

8. *The cost of lobby furniture and other movable items.*

9. *Construction cost overruns.*

10. *Any cost overrun on soft-cost items.* This included items such as interest and taxes, to the extent that there were no savings in other soft-cost items to offset them.

11. *Any fees paid to third parties not recognized by HUD.* This included such fees as those paid to housing consultants.

12. *Any costs incurred on HUD-approved items but which exceeded the HUD-allowed expenditures.* HUD often applied certain percentages to such items as architectural fees, recording fees, tap fees, legal fees, etc. If the developer exceeded these allowed line items, the

additional money spent was not recognized as a cost and therefore would come from the developer's own sources.

13. **Escrows.** These were escrows at final closing for real estate taxes, the mortgage insurance premium, and property insurance.

14. **Any excess costs for land.** This applied when land costs exceeded the HUD-appraised fair market value of the land.

It is quite possible for these items to add up rather quickly and for the developer to find that while HUD had issued a theoretical 90 percent loan, the actual cash investment was greater than 10 percent of all the real costs in the project.

Fortunately, in Comings Towers, the developer managed to handle the over-and-above costs rather well. These costs are shown in Table 14. These figures represent the out-of-pocket cash investment. It should be noted that HUD allowed the sponsor to put up a letter of credit for the working capital deposit. In addition, the sponsor incurred overhead expenses in connection with the project, including interest on seed money which was outstanding for approximately 18 months. To the "hard" expenses, therefore, was added a "soft" money overhead figure of 2 percent of $110,806. For purposes of determining the sponsor's total cost, the hard cost figure of $629,649 and the overhead figure of $110,806 were added, for a total investment or cost of $740,455.

Once the cost to the sponsor was determined, the syndicator/developer could determine profit relatively easily. It was based on the following formula, as previously discussed:

**SELLING PRICE**
   *Less* cost of syndication
   *Less* purchase price paid to the developer (or job costs in the case of direct development)
   *Less* interest on sponsor's outstanding funds
   *Equals* profit.

For Comings Towers, the equation above worked out as indicated in Table 15 and amounted to about $1,755 per unit. This figure was about 24 percent of the overall selling price of the equity and, as such, was within the standard range targeted by most syndicators at that time.

It is worth noting that in Section 8 syndications, many of these figures were expressed in shorthand terms as a percentage of the mortgage. While useful in making quick determinations of selling price and purchase price, these percentages are only guidelines because the actual numbers are based on tax losses and actual cash investment rather than what happens to be the mortgage amount. To base profit projections solely as a percentage of the mortgage would be misleading and inaccurate.

### Tracy Apartments

The Tracy Apartments was a more typical straight syndication business deal whereby a local developer invested funds to develop a project. The syndicator and the developer negotiated a business deal prior to closing, enabling the syndicator to purchase the limited partnership interest in the project. In this particular situation, the syndicator purchased 99 percent of the equity from the local developer but sold only 70 percent to investors, keeping 4 percent and selling 25 percent to one of its own subsidiaries. The selling price was based on both the 70 percent received from investors and the 25 percent sold to its own subsidiary. These numbers are shown in Table 16.

The business deal in this situation differed from the direct development example just described. In the Tracy Apartments, the syndicator did not invest any seed money and had little or no day-to-day involvement in the development of the project. All the effort, risk, and over-and-above cash obligations were borne by the local developer. The syndicator came into the picture just prior to initial closing and at that time executed a purchase agreement to buy 99 percent of the project from the local developer. In this particular situation, the price the syndicator agreed to pay was $536,000, payable over a three-year period in three equal installments—one-third at initial closing, one-third at final closing, and one-third at final closing plus one year. This amount translated to approximately 16.8 percent of the mortgage. Having determined the selling price and the purchase price, we can now compute the profit to the syndicator, as shown in Table 17.

The $182,340 amounted to approximately $1,250 per unit for the 146-unit project. The $182,340 also translated to 21.2 percent of the gross selling price, an acceptable profit margin.

How did the local developer fare in this particular situation? The profit made was the amount received from the syndicator over the three-year payment period, less the over-and-above cash investment. The expenses of the local developer are detailed in Table 18.

The local developer's profit was the $536,000 received from the syndicator, less jobs costs of $361,000, or $175,000. This amounted to about $1,200 per unit, or about 5.5 percent of the project mortgage, as shown in Table 19.

Two other things should be pointed out about the local developer. First, since there were no cost increases or overruns, the developer recaptured most of the working capital letter of credit, actually making an additional $60,000. Second, since the developer was responsible for construction cost overruns, a great deal would have been lost if the project got into trouble during the construction period, an occurrence which fortunately did not occur. The $175,000–$250,000 made from syndication was by no means an overly generous amount, given the time spent on the development, the seed money invested, and the risk incurred.

The example just presented is one example of how the syndication process worked in the late 1970s, using a two-step process whereby the syndicator purchased and resold the equity. In the case of making capital contributions directly into the partnership, however, the same basic factors would apply. The sources of funds would consist of the total contributions of the $1,925,000 plus the mortgage proceeds of $5,540,300 for Comings Towers and $3,186,500 for the Tracy Apartments. Since all project costs would have to come out of the total sources of funds, *including the payment of syndication costs and fees,* the balance would be the fee available to the developer, that is, the developer's profit. In this case, the development risk and exposure would have been greater, and for this reason he probably would have received a higher development fee.

## THE 1981 TAX LAW AND TAX SHELTER SYNDICATIONS

There are several ways that tax shelter syndications have been affected by the Economic Recovery Tax Act of 1981. The first way is the impact that the new law has on individual investors. The old law established a maximum tax of 50 percent on wages and salaries

## TABLE 14
## OUT-OF-POCKET COSTS
### (Comings Towers)

| Item | Amount | Percent of Mortgage |
|---|---|---|
| Mortgage Amount | $5,540,300 | |
| Total Replacement Cost as Determined by HUD | $6,155,889 | |
| GNMA discount | $ 138,507 | 2.5% |
| Cash "equity" as determined by HUD: HUD's total replacement cost *less* mortgage *less* BSPRA *equals* cost equity* | 64,571 | 1.2% |
| Working capital deposited with mortgagee | 110,806 | 2.0% |
| Builder's fee | 232,760 | 4.2% |
| Off-site improvements | 17,605 | 0.3% |
| Other miscellaneous items not approved by HUD | 10,000 | 0.2% |
| Final escrows | 55,400 | 1.0% |
| SUBTOTAL | $ 629,649 | 11.4% |
| Add Overhead at 2% | 110,806 | 2.0% |
| TOTAL INVESTMENT | $ 740,455 | 13.4% |

*This figure is unusually low because of urban renewal land value at 500/unit.

## TABLE 15
## PROFIT TO DEVELOPER/SYNDICATOR
### (Comings Towers)

|  | Amount | Percent of Mortgage |
|---|---|---|
| Selling price* | $1,289,400 | 23.2% |
| *Less* cost of syndication | 128,900 | 2.3% |
| *Less* total job cost ($629,649 hard cost plus $110,806 overhead) | 740,455 | 13.4% |
| *Less* interest cost on outstanding cash investment of sponsor (figured at 12%) | 116,500 | 2.1% |
| NET PROFIT | $ 303,545 | 5.4% |
| PER UNIT (for 171 unit project) | $ 1,775 | |

*This represents Comings Towers' share of the total purchase.

## TABLE 16
### TRACY APARTMENTS: SELLING PRICE

|  | Amount | Percent of Mortgage |
|---|---|---|
| Mortgage | $3,186,500 | |
| HUD Replacement Cost | 3,540,555 | |
| Total selling price | $862,600 | 27.0% |
| Percent of project | 95% | |
| Amount from investors | $635,600 | 20.0% |
| Percent of project | 70% | |
| Amount from subsidiary | $224,000 | 70.0% |
| Percent of project | 25% | |

## TABLE 17
### PROFIT TO THE SYNDICATOR
#### (Tracy Apartments)

|  | Amount | Percent of Mortgage |
|---|---|---|
| Selling price | $862,600 | 27.0% |
| *Less* cost of syndication | 86,260 | 2.7% |
| *Less* purchase price | 536,000 | 16.8% |
| *Less* interest on outstanding cash investment (the difference between cash received from investors and cash advanced to local sponsor) (figured at 12%) | 58,000 | 1.8% |
| NET PROFIT | $182,340 | 5.7% |
| PER UNIT (for 146 unit project) | $ 1,248 | 5.7% |

## TABLE 18
## OUT-OF-POCKET COSTS TO THE LOCAL DEVELOPER
### (Tracy Apartments)

| Item | Amount | Percent of Mortgage |
|---|---|---|
| GNMA discount* | $ 0 | 0 |
| Cash equity** | $111,527 | 3.5% |
| Working capital deposited with mortgagee | 63,730 | 2.0% |
| Builder's fee | 118,000 | 3.7% |
| Off-site improvement | 5,500 | 0.2% |
| Other miscellaneous items not approved by the state agency | 25,000 | 0.5% |
| Interest on seed money advanced and overhead expenses during development | 47,213 | 1.5% |
| TOTAL | $361,000 | 11.3% |

*There was no discount since this project was financed by a state housing agency.

**This was higher because of the higher purchase price of the buildings.

## TABLE 19
## PROFIT TO THE LOCAL DEVELOPER

| Tracy Apartments | |
|---|---|
| Fee received from the syndicator | $536,000 |
| *Less* out-of-pocket expenses | 361,000 |
| *Equals* developer profit | $175,000 |
| Per Unit | $ 1,198 |

and 70 percent on unearned income. The 1981 law abolished the higher tax on investment income, so that the maximum income tax is now 50 percent for all taxpayers. The 1981 tax law also eliminated "tax preference" items (which had the effect of moving certain income from the 50 percent rate to the 70 percent rate) and in effect reduced the maximum capital gains rate from 28 percent to 20 percent. Because of the overall reduction in tax rates, therefore, the value of tax shelters is now less than it was earlier for the wealthier investor. For example, for someone in the 70 percent bracket, a $1,000 tax shelter translated to a net economic benefit of $700 (.70 × $1,000 = $700). Now the same $1,000 is worth only $500. This phenomenon affects the ratio of losses to investment generated.

The second factor affecting tax shelter syndications is that since the 1981 tax law allows for greater accelerated depreciation, tax losses are generated more quickly than was previously the case. Instead of a previous average useful life of 35–40 years with the various components being depreciated separately, now a composite 15-year recovery period exists for the entire building, with the recovery period for personal property being five years. Also, a 200 percent declining balance depreciation instead of a sum-of-the-year digits is allowed for low-income housing. The old and new methods presented earlier in Chapter Two are compared again below.

| | RECOVERY PERIOD | | METHOD OF DEPRECIATION | |
|---|---|---|---|---|
| | Old Law | New Law | Old Law | New Law |
| **Building shell** | 40 yrs. | 15 yrs. | SYD* | 200% DB* |
| **Mechanical systems** | 25 yrs. | 15 yrs. | SYD | 200% DB |
| **Rehabilitation costs** | 25 yrs. | 15 yrs. | 5 yrs. | 5 yrs. |
| **Site improvement** | 25 yrs. | 15 yrs. | SYD | 200% DB |
| **Cabinets and specialties** | 10 yrs. | 15 yrs. | SYD | 200% DB |
| **Decorating and appliances** | 10 yrs. | 15 yrs. | SYD | 200% DB |
| **Personal property** | 5 yrs. | 5 yrs. | SYD | 200% DB |

*DB or declining balance was discussed earlier in Chapter Two (page 16 ). SYD or sum-of-the-year digits is a similar method of depreciation which is no longer used because it was eliminated in the Economic Recovery Tax Act of 1981.

It should be noted that the total overall tax losses have not changed. Rather, what has changed is *when* these tax losses are realized. The 1981 tax law accelerates or moves these tax losses forward in time. Because of this fact (and the time value of money noted earlier), the losses have more value to the investor. Comparison of the losses (including fees and installment interest) over the first six years is shown below for the combined offering of Comings Towers and the Tracy Apartments.

| Year | Losses (Old Law) | Losses (1981 Law) |
|------|------------------|-------------------|
| 1 | $ 343,800 | $ 457,800 |
| 2 | 859,500 | 1,256,100 |
| 3 | 757,000 | 1,035,800 |
| 4 | 627,700 | 840,300 |
| 5 | 543,000 | 712,200 |
| 6 | 457,600 | 590,600 |
| Total | $3,568,600 | $4,892,800 |
| Total Through Year 20 | $5,968,800 | $6,882,900 |

In other words, while there have been no changes to the specific project, under the Economic Recovery Act of 1981, Comings Towers and the Tracy Apartments would generate approximately $1,325,000 in additional tax losses over the first six years (or the investor pay-in period). Over the 20-year projected period of ownership, the project would generate an additional $915,000 in losses. The primary reason for this is that instead of being spread out over a 30 to 40-year period, the losses are now squeezed into a 15-year period.

There are two important other effects of the shorter recovery period. The first is that the identical project shows a taxable income more quickly under the 1981 tax law than under the old law. Under the 1981 tax law, Comings Towers and the Tracy Apartments would show a taxable income in year 15 when the capital recovery period had been completed. In the case of the project under the old tax law, the project did not show a taxable income until year 20.

Another major effect is that since the recovery period is shorter, the difference in losses between using the accelerated rate of depreciation and straight-line depreciation phases out more quickly. Since this amount (*excess depreciation*) is taxed at ordinary income rates, most owners will not want to sell the property until there is little excess depreciation. Under the old law, excess depreciation was eliminated in the sixteenth year. Under the 1981 tax law, it occurs in the fifteenth year.

Under the 1981 tax law, significant new early losses are generated. During the first six years, the identical project generates over 37 percent additional tax losses. Although the project started to show a taxable income five years earlier under the 1981 tax law than under the old law, the overall losses over the 20-year period are still 15 percent higher under the 1981 tax law than they would be under the old law.

In this example, the investor is a winner because the ratio of losses to investments has been increased. The investor now receives more losses for every dollar invested. Whereas before $1.80 in tax losses was obtainable for every $1.00 invested during the first six years, assuming the same investment amount the investor now would receive $2.50 of losses for every dollar invested during the same period. Over the 20-year period, the benefits increase from just over $3.00 of losses for every $1.00 invested to approximately $3.60 for every $1.00. However, the investor's gain is modified by the fact that the same individual is probably in a lower tax bracket, and thus the losses themselves have less value to the investor.

## Benefits to the Developer Under the 1981 Tax Law

In this particular example, the developer/syndicator emerge no better and no worse off than before. The total investment contributions by the limited partners amount to $1,925,000 in each case. This amount is based on the estimation by the syndicator that $2.50 of losses are required to support each dollar of investment during the pay-in period. However, this estimate is very conservative. Should the market for tax shelter syndications turn out to be significantly better than this, the developer and syndicator would also emerge with additional profit.

Let us consider Comings Towers and the Tracy Apartments in terms of the one-step capital contributions model rather than the two-step equity purchase model. Going back to the earlier exam-

·ple presented in Chapter One, the sources of funds that are available to cover all project costs consist of two parts: the mortgage loan and the equity contributions provided by the investors. Since the mortgage loans remain the same in either case, the extent to which equity contributions are increased means more money for the developer and syndicator, assuming all other costs remain the same. Under the capital contributions approach outlined in Chapter One, every project must account for all funds according to the following format:

**SOURCES OF FUNDS**
**Equity contributions from limited partners**
  *Plus* **mortgage loan**
  *Equals* **total source of funds.**

**APPLICATIONS OF FUNDS**
**Project costs**
**Land**
**Construction cost and construction fees**
**Interest**
**Financing fees and discounts**
**Financing discounts**
**Legal fees**
**Initial operating deficit and lease-up expense**
  *Plus* **syndication costs and fees**
  *Plus* **developer fees**
  *Equals* **total application of funds**

Another way of looking at the equation is as follows:

**TOTAL SOURCES OF FUNDS**
  *Less* **all project costs, excluding developer's fees**
  *Equals* **amount of money available to the developer for his fee**

Under the 1981 tax law, therefore, should it turn out in this example that the ratio of 2.5 to 1.0 during the pay-in period was more generous than it need be in order to attract investors, the result would be that more equity capital would be raised. Assuming all other costs remain the same, the result would be to increase the amount available to the developer. The following chart shows what the overall result would be to the developer under the 1981 tax law under varying assumptions about the market for tax shelters expressed in losses to investment ratios.

| Market Assumption | Total 6-Year Project Losses | Total Equity Raised | Developer Profit |
|---|---|---|---|
| $2.54 losses to $1.00 investment | $4,892,800 | $1,925,000 | — |
| $2.35 losses to $1.00 investment | 4,892,800 | 2,082,042 | $157,042 |
| $2.25 losses to $1.00 investment | 4,892,800 | 2,174,577 | 249,577 |
| $2.00 losses to $1.00 investment | 4,892,000 | 2,446,400 | 521,400 |
| $1.85 losses to $1.00 investment | 4,892,800 | 2,644,755 | 719,755 |

In reality, of course, it is unlikely that all other costs would remain the same. The cost of syndication would increase, as would the syndicator's fee (which would be a percentage of total equity funds raised), both of which would reduce the amount available to the developer. At the same time, the example is useful for showing the basic relationships involved. Since the market for tax shelters is dynamic and changing, the actual amount of equity raised from a tax shelter syndication will vary from time to time (depending on the market for real estate securities) and from project to project. Generally speaking, developers will do no worse under the 1981 tax law and will probably do considerably better, assuming that factors affecting other project costs do not change for the worse.

The problem is, of course, that in the development of real estate projects, very little remains the same. The nature of permanent financing is in a constant state of flux, as is the availability of future government assistance. For this reason you should be warned against making conclusions for potential new projects on the basis of the example presented here. The only things that will remain constant are the basic principles that are summarized below:

- that investors will become limited partners and make equity contributions to projects that they perceive as producing economic benefits to them;
- that these benefits consist of cash flow return, appreciation, and tax benefits;
- that some investments will be made that are based exclusively on the tax benefit;
- that these benefits must be competitive with other similar opportunities and with other non-tax-shelter investments;
- that, in determining the economic feasibility of a syndication, the sources of funds and the application of funds must always be equal and that the developer's fee is what is left over after all other applications have been subtracted from the sources of funds.

While in the past Section 8 syndications have enjoyed the priviledged status of being the most attractive tax shelter investment, the 1981 tax has significantly changed the rules of the game. The next chapter examines other opportunities that were created by the Economic Recovery Act of 1981.

# *S e v e n*
## Syndicating the Deal: Commercial and Historical Examples

Times, of course, have changed from the days of Section 8 syndications. Long-term federal rental assistance in the form of a Section 8 Housing Assistance Payment Contract is no longer available, nor is the type of low-interest, permanent financing that assured the feasibility of so many Section 8 projects. In its place we have "new world" financing, consisting of shorter loan terms for permanent financing, often with variable rates pegged to basic interest indicators such as the prime rate. Also, lenders now often participate in the deal, receiving portions of cash flow above debt service, as well as receiving a share of the profits when the project is ultimately sold. In addition since there are no long-term government rent guarantees, the market support for the project is increasingly important. Tenants must be willing and able to pay the required rents or else the project (or a portion of it) might stand vacant, thus not generating the income presented in the financial projections. On the positive side, the 1981 Economic Recovery Tax Act has provided additional incentives, especially with regard to producing tax benefits. The result of these changes is that a brand-new ball game exists for syndicating real estate properties in the 1980s. This chapter deals with two opportunities for real estate syndication in the 1980s. The first is an older commercial property requiring substantial rehabilitation. The second is the same commercial property as an historically certified property.

## THE COMMERCIAL DEAL

The building is located within eight blocks of the central business district in Washington, D.C., which was thriving in 1981, the time the project was conceived. The project is especially useful because it illustrates both the effects of the 1981 tax law, the changes in the nature of permanent financing, the way syndication deals are likely to be structured in the 1980s, and the kind of public/private partnerships that are likely to be required when rehabilitating high-risk properties in marginal areas.

The building was an old warehouse. It had stood vacant for a number of years and as such was not only a neighborhood eyesore but from time to time was a haven for drug addicts, gangs, and derelicts. The general neighborhood surrounding the warehouse, however, had recently undergone considerable revitalization. A number of row houses in the area had been converted to expensive condominiums and sold to young professionals, and two very attractive new Section 8 projects had been recently completed in the adjacent block. The warehouse itself, however, was located in a block with similar commercial buildings and was viewed by many people—including local officials—as being the key to achieving commerical revitalization of what years ago was a thriving commercial area, but which at the current time was shabby and under-utilized. For this reason, local officials agreed to submit an Urban Development Action Grant (UDAG) application to HUD for the purpose of *leveraging* conventional financing: that is, providing additional funds in order to make the project feasible.

In this case, a small developer saw that an opportunity existed and negotiated an option agreement with the building's owner to acquire the property for approximately $12.60 per square foot of total gross building area, or $434,750 for the 34,500-square-foot building.

The starting point of any syndication is the project itself. The primary issues that will determine whether or not the project is feasible are the total economic benefits that the specific project will produce upon completion and whether the benefits are sufficiently high to attract workable financing and sufficient equity capital. If the answer to both of these questions is yes, the project will likely move forward; if the answer is no, the project will not proceed.

It is as simple as that. Implicit in the two questions is the requirement that the economic benefits satisfy two actors besides the original investor: the permanent lender and the potential limited partners. These two actors are very different and are likely to be attracted by different economic benefits. Most syndications, therefore, attempt to structure a business deal that addresses the different needs of each actor. We shall see how this happened in the case of this project.

## THE CONCEPT

As discussed in Chapter Four, any development project begins with an idea or concept. The idea or concept is then translated into a specific physical development program that fits a specific site or building. The physical program is then tested as to the economic benefits it is likely to produce, using economic models that identify all project costs and revenues. If the initial test shows positive economic benefits, the developer moves to the next phases of the development process as presented in Chapter Five.

The idea for this vacant warehouse was to convert the building into office space. Since the building was not in the central business district, it must somehow attract office tenants who otherwise would be attracted to offices in buildings more centrally located. The developer believed he could accomplish this objective by providing attractively designed space and by charging rents which were substantially below the rents charged for similar space in the central business district.

This proposed concept raises the initial issue of marketability, which is the most fundamental question any development project must address: Is there a market for the project? In Section 8 housing, the question of market support was relatively insignificant, since in effect the rents for the units were guaranteed by HUD. In the case of any other project (either commercial or residential) that depends on the users of the space paying the charges for the space out of their own resources, the market factor is critical. Ultimately, the burden of proof will be on the developer to convince both the lender and the potential limited partners that a market in fact does exist and that assumptions regarding the income that the project will produce are valid.

Because the question of market support is so critical (and unfortunately can so easily be overlooked when focusing solely on tax benefits), the first step a developer must take is to compile the necessary information in order to make valid assumptions regarding the income the project will produce and in order to support these assumptions when presenting the project to the other actors. In many instances (when the developer is experienced and when the market support is well-documented and generally recognized) a formal market survey may not be necessary. In other instances (when there is some question about the developer's track record or the strength of the market) a formal market survey is essential and will probably be required by the lender and the syndication firm. Usually the requirement will stipulate that the study be undertaken by an independent consulting firm specializing in such work.

In this project, after surveying office space in the immediate area and in the central business district and assessing the overall strength of the office market, the developer projected that in approximately 18 months from the initial study—the time at which the project would be at the midpoint of initial lease-up—prospective office tenants would be willing to move into the building and pay over $20 per square foot for the space they occupied. The developer contended that this figure would be more than 30 percent below the prices of similar space in the downtown area projected for that period and would be sufficiently competitive to attract tenants. The developer also projected that the rents charged initially would be increased on the average about 8 percent per annum on a *net* basis, that is, 8 percent above annual increases in operating costs.

In terms of testing the economic feasibility of the project, the developer used the rent of $509,210 (just over $20 per square foot) and the projected escalation of 8 percent per year. Taken together, these two assumptions were the basis for determining two of the three economic benefits—the cash flow benefit and the appreciation benefit.

The warehouse contained a total gross floor area of 34,500 square feet. After rehabilitation and conversion, 29,945 square feet would be available to lease to tenants, as estimated by the developer with help from his architect. The balance of the space would be used for common hallways, elevators, stairways, and equipment areas. The total potential income available to the project was, as stated above $509,210 per year (24,945 square feet ÷ $509,210 = 20.41 per square foot). Assuming a normal turnover, vacancy, and collection loss allowance of 5 percent, the developer projected that the actual income that would be realized would be $483,750 (95 percent × $509,210 = $483,750) in the first year of full occupancy. This figure was the starting point for determining the total economic value of this building, as it is the starting point for any income-producing real estate development project, both commercial and residential.

The next question was how much net income would be available to satisfy all the actors in the deal, that is, the owners (the developer plus the limited partners) and the lender or lenders. Since the owner of the building must provide basic services to the tenants and maintain the building, out of the gross income must first be subtracted all costs paid by the owner for operating and maintaining the building. In this area more research is often needed and normally will be required by the lender and the syndication firm. The developer must compile a reasonable estimate of operating costs (projected to the initial occupancy period) and present adequate documentation supporting those costs. Such costs typically include real estate taxes, insurance, utilities, payroll, maintenance, security, and the like, as discussed in Chapter Four. In the case of this project, the developer estimated the operating costs would be $5.00 per square foot of total building space, as shown below:

### PROJECTED ANNUAL OPERATING COSTS

|                        | Per Square Foot | Total      |
|------------------------|-----------------|------------|
| Real estate taxes      | $1.50           | $ 51,750   |
| Insurance              | .30             | $ 10,350   |
| Electricity and fuel   | 1.42            | 48,990     |
| Water                  |                 |            |
| Char service (cleaning)| .90             | 31,050     |
| Capital reserve        | .06             | 2,070      |
| Management fee         | .44             | 15,180     |
| Miscellaneous          | .38             | 13,110     |
|                        | $5.00           | $172,500   |

Once he accomplished this task, he was then able to determine the net income available to the project, as has been discussed previously:

**POTENTIAL GROSS INCOME**
  *Less* **vacancy and collection loss**
  *Equals* **effective gross income**
  *Less* **operating and maintenance costs**
  *Equals* **net income to the project**


This net income produced the principal economic benefit to the various actors or participants. Because of tax law, it is clearly not the only benefit; and it is in some respects less important now than it was prior to the 1981 tax law because of the post-1981 tax benefits. At the same time, however, the net income figure determines a minimum threshold of economic feasibility for any project. At the very least, the income must be sufficiently high in order to satisfy the permanent lender and to put the limited partners in a break-even situation (as is the case in many Section 8 projects) in terms of cash flow. Ideally, it should be sufficiently high to produce some cash benefits for everyone.

One helpful way of understanding the concept is to view this net income from the project as going into a large pot. The actors will be dipping into the pot and taking out the available income. How much the permanent lender is willing to lend and how much investors are willing to contribute depends on these three things— how much money is in the pot, how fast the money is likely to increase over time, and, as we shall discuss, how many tax benefits are also in the pot.

The first actor that must be satisfied is the permanent lender. The lender will be the first to dip into the pot to take out the income, and the lender's requirements will largely determine the way the overall deal is structured. Because permanent financing is the most critical factor in any development project and because many of the old rules and assumptions about permanent financing no longer apply, once the developer is able to determine the potential benefits available, the first person usually approached is the lender. Because the lender probably cannot benefit from tax losses, the lender is typically interested solely in the pot of money available to dip into. The lender will carefully evaluate both the developer's capability and the developer's assumptions about potential income and operating costs and will determine how much money to lend the developer and under what terms and conditions. The amount of money loaned is based on how much money the lender thinks is going to be in the pot each year. This concept was presented in Chapter Four. The loan in essence does not have anything to do with project costs, but rather with the income that will be available for paying back the loan after the project is operating. If a lot of money is available, the lender will make a large loan. If there is very little money available, the loan will be much smaller.

After reviewing the developer's projections and making an analysis, the lender determined that this project would support a $1,600,000 loan. The lender proposed an interest rate of 16 percent, to be adjusted on a periodic basis, based on the current 90-day Treasury bill rate. The lender also stipulated that his bank would receive 30 percent of all distributions (or cash flow) and 30 percent of the residual value of the building when it was sold. The lender informed the developer that this requirement was due to the high-risk nature of the project. After shopping for better deals and finding none, the developer determined that this was the best deal he could get and decided to take it, though somewhat reluctantly.

Chapter Four also introduced the concept that lenders calculate the amount of money they are willing to lend by determining an economic value of the project and by making a loan based on a percentage of the economic value of the project. Economic value is calculated by dividing the net income available to the project by a rate (called the *capitalization rate,* as discussed in Chapter Three), which represents the aggregate before-tax yield requirement of both the lenders and the owners of the project. The capitalization rate used in this instance was 14.589 percent calculated as follows:

**Lender portion at 16.7% (annual return to lender including principal and interest) × 75% of project value**
  **Owner's portion at 8.255% return × 25% of project value**
  **Lender = 16.70% × .75 = 12.525%**
  **Owner = 8.255% × .25 =  2.064%**

  **Capitalization Rate     14.589%**

The lender thus calculated the economic value by taking the $311,250 net income available for both lender and owner and dividing this amount by the capitalization rate of 14.589 percent, yielding a total economic value of $2,133,456. The bank's loan was for 75 percent of value, or 75 percent × $2,133,456, for $1,600,000.

In other words, in figuring the permanent loan, a bank typically works backward. The lender looks first to the pot of money available and asks how much that pot of money will support, given the various requirements of those contributing the funds—that is, the lender and the owner. When lenders participate in the cash flow of the project, often they are willing to negotiate a lower interest rate. This was not the case in this project, however, mainly because of the high risk of the undertaking.

The important thing to the developer at this point, however, is that he has been able to identify one major source of funds—a mortgage loan from a lender. Since the loan is based on the economic value of the project (that is, the capitalized value of the net cash flow), not the actual cost to develop the project, the difference between the actual total cost to develop the project (including whatever development fee he hopes to earn for all his hard work) and the mortgage loan is what must be raised from other sources, either from additional loans or from equity capital. The equity capital may be from the developer's own financial resources. In the case of syndication, equity capital will come from the limited partners.

Let us now turn to the question of costs. Although project costs have nothing to do with economic value or the loan the bank is willing to make, they have a lot to do with project feasibility. As explained earlier, if the costs associated with developing the project exceed the combined sources of funds (from the lenders, the developer, and the limited partners) that can be raised on the basis of the economic benefits that the project produces, then the project is not feasible. In other words, we are back to the initial formula presented in Chapter One. Total sources of funds must equal total applications of funds. If total sources of funds exceed total applications, additional money is available to the developer. If total sources are less than total applications, the difference must come from more equity. If more equity cannot be raised (or is not justified on the economic merits of the project), then the project is not feasible.

At the same time that the developer was figuring net income and economic value, he was figuring the total costs to develop the project. At his own expense, the developer hired an architect to prepare a schematic plan and enlisted a general contractor to provide cost estimates. The projected total project costs were as follows:

## TOTAL PROJECT COSTS

|  | Amount | |
|---|---|---|
| Acquisition | $ 434,750 | ($12.60/sf)* |
| Rehabilitation | 1,440,000 | ($41.73/sf) |
| Site work | 50,000 | ($ 1.47/sf) |
| A&E (Architecture and Engineering) | 54,000 | ($ 1.56/sf) |
| Financing cost during construction | 228,915 | ($ 6.63/sf) |
| Leasing commissions | 49,890 | ($ 1.45/sf) |
| Tenant allowances | 49,890 | ($ 1.45/sf) |
| Syndication costs/ development fee | 153,555 | ($ 4.44/sf) |
| **Total Development Costs** | **$2,461,000** | **($71.33/sf)** |

*(sf) square foot

Since the overall success of any development project is dependent upon the validity of these cost estimates, it is extremely important that they be done carefully and accurately. Since the developer as general partner will typically be the one to whom others will look to cover construction cost overruns and initial operating deficits, it is imperative that the developer provide considerable cushion or contingency in all the major cost areas. Overruns will come out of the developer's pocket.

The total estimated costs for this project totaled $2,461,000, including contingencies in each line item, the cost of syndication, and a small developer's fee. The best loan the developer could secure was $1,600,000, leaving additional cash requirements of $861,000. In order for the project to be feasible, the developer had to raise this additional amount. What were the choices available to him? First, the developer could try to raise the entire amount through capital contributions from limited partners. Second, the developer could try to get additional financing. Or, third, the developer could try to combine the two approaches, securing some additional financing and raising additional equity capital.

The final approach is what the developer did in this instance. After consulting with an expert in tax syndication, the developer decided to structure a deal to raise equity capital from partners largely on the basis of the tax benefits. A deal was worked out whereby the developer and the bank together would take half the cash flow and appreciation (30 percent to the bank, 20 percent to the developer) and none of the tax benefits. The developer would try to enlist 22 partners, who together would contribute all of the equity capital, receive all of the tax benefits, and together share in the remaining 50 percent of the cash flow and appreciation. The deal worked out as shown below. Two friends (limited A and B) were enlisted first, for $30,000 and $20,000, respectively. The balance would come from 20 other partners investing $15,000 each.

### DISTRIBUTION OF BENEFITS

| Partner | Equity Investment | Cash Flow | Tax Benefits | Capital Gains |
|---|---|---|---|---|
| Bank (first trust) | $      0 | 30.0% | 0.0% | 30.0% |
| General partner | 0 | 20.0% | 0.0% | 20.0% |
| Limited A | 30,000 | 5.4% | 10.8% | 5.4% |
| Limited B | 20,000 | 3.6% | 7.2% | 3.6% |
| 20 others (at $15,000 each) | 300,000 | 2.05% (each) | 4.1% (each) | 2.05% (each) |

In order to determine how much could be raised from the limited partners, the developer first had to determine what these benefits were worth to the limited partners. With help from a syndication firm, he determined that for this specific deal, given the high risks and the location, the amount was $350,000. As the table shows, however, the returns to the limited partners on an after-tax basis are impressive; and it is quite possible that for these same returns, investors would be willing to put up more than $350,000. As stated earlier, the amount of equity that can be raised varies depending on the market for tax shelter securities, the quality and experience of the developer, and the general risk associated with the specific project. Because of the neighborhood, which was on the upswing but still shabby and a remote location for office space, and the fact that the developer was relatively small, the judgment was made that this deal would require these generous benefits in order to attract limited partners. Also a contributing factor was that at the same time, the developer was able to get the owner to take back a 12 percent second trust of $111,000 for five years and to get a HUD Urban Development Action Grant loan of $400,000, deferred for five years. This additional financing would enable the developer to pay back the UDAG loan after repaying the second trust to the owner. By working out this relatively sophisticated leveraged financing, the developer was able to establish sufficient sources of funds to match the anticipated applications, as shown in Table 20.

In short, the deal worked. What made the deal work was a combination of financing, including participation in cash flow and appreciation by the permanent lender; a short-term second trust purchase money mortgage provided by the seller, which was then leveraged by a deferred third trust loan from the public sector; and limited partner equity contributions based primarily on the tax benefits produced by the project. Let us turn to these tax benefits now.

Once the developer was able to determine the available financing, the basic economic relationship of the project, and the requirements for equity capital, he then proceeded to raise equity capital. It is at this point that a syndication firm is usually necessary, although, with the help of an experienced tax attorney and accountant, it is not always necessary to employ a syndication firm. In the case of small syndications, such firms may not be interested in taking on the task. Moreover, in such smaller syndications, since there may not be enough cash that can be generated to cover the costs associated with using such firms, the developer may not have much choice in the matter.

If a syndication firm is used, the firm generally will assume the responsibilities of meeting the SEC disclosure requirements and of marketing the real estate securities (by selling the securities itself if the firm is a registered broker-dealer, or by employing such a dealer, as explained in Chapter Three). If a firm is not used, the developer will have to rely on his own attorney and accountant and his own ability to market the securities. Because of the seriousness involved in not meeting the SEC requirements and complying with federal securities laws and state blue-sky laws, a developer should be extremely cautious in trying to undertake the task of syndication without professional assistance.

As described in Chapter Two, the vehicle for marketing the se-

## TABLE 20
## COMMERCIAL REHABILITATION: SOURCES
## AND APPLICATIONS OF FUNDS

| Sources of Funds | Amount |
|---|---|
| | $2,461,000 Project<br>34,500 sf gross<br>29,945 sf net |
| First trust at 16% (floating), 20 years, from bank | $1,600,000 |
| Second trust at 12%, five years, from owner | 111,000 |
| Third trust, no interest, UDAG, five-year deferred payment | 400,000 |
| Equity | 350,000 |
| TOTAL FUNDS AVAILABLE | $2,461,000 |

| Uses of Funds | Amount | |
|---|---|---|
| Acquisition | $ 434,750 | $12.60/sf |
| Rehabilitation | 1,440,000 | 41.73/sf |
| Site work | 50,000 | 1.47/sf |
| A & E | 54,000 | 1.56/sf |
| Financing cost during construction | 228,915 | 6.63/sf |
| Leasing commissions | 49,890 | 1.45/sf |
| Tenant allowances | 49,890 | 1.45/sf |
| Contingency/development fee | 153,555 | 4.44/sf |
| TOTAL DEVELOPMENT COSTS | $2,461,000 | $71.33/sf |

**Source:** Private placement offering memorandum.

curities is the offering memorandum. The offering memorandum in the case of commercial properties will be similar to the offering memorandum used for marketing Section 8 projects. All the information about the developer, the project, the market, the fees, and so on, must be presented. What will be different will be the way in which the economic benefits to the limited partners are presented. In the case of Section 8 projects, the economic benefits are presented in terms of the ratio of tax benefits to dollars invested, as shown in the preceding chapter. Since rehabilitation commercial investments will combine tax credits, tax deductions, cash flow, and appreciation, typically all of these benefits will be presented to the investor. The tables that follow are actual figures included in the private placement offering memorandum and show how these benefits were presented for this project. Interestingly, the internal rate of return was not calculated in the offering memorandum, although it could have been, as is discussed later in this chapter.

Table 21 shows the projected cash flow for the project and the projected increases in cash flow in subsequent years. The developer projected an 8 percent net increase in operating income (that is, an increase 8 percent above any increases in operating costs). The cash flow was projected to go down in year 6, when the UDAG payments of $124,117 went into effect and the second trust loan payments of $32,566 were completed but increased substantially after that time.

## Investor Benefits

And now at last to the tax benefits available to the limited partners. There are two principal tax benefits. The first is the Investment Tax Credit, which is based on 20 percent of all rehabilitation costs. Since this building was over 40 years old, was being rehabilitated as a commercial structure, and the rehabilitation costs exceeded the basis (or price paid for the building), the project qualified for the Investment Tax Credit. The second tax benefit is the tax deduction from the individual tax return determined by interest deductions and the annual capital recovery factor. For tax purposes,

> **NET INCOME (rents received less operating costs)**
> *Less* **interest**
> *Less* **capital recovery (or depreciation)**
> *Equals* **profit or loss for tax purposes**

## TABLE 21
## COMMERCIAL REHABILITATION:
## CASH FLOW

|  | **Amount** |
|---|---|
| Potential gross income at $20.41/sf (24,945 net sq. ft.) | $509,210 |
| Effective gross income at 95% | 483,750 |
| *Less* operating costs at $5.00/sf | (172,500) |
| *Equals* net income | 311,250 |
| *Less* debt service on first trust | (267,122) |
| *Less* debt service on second trust | (32,566) |
| *Less* UDAG loan (deferred until year 6) | 0 |
| *Equals* total cash flow before income taxes for: | |
| Year 1 | 11,562 |
| Year 2* | 36,462 |
| Year 3 | 63,354 |
| Year 4 | 92,397 |
| Year 5 | 123,764 |
| Year 6 | 66,090 |
| Year 7 | 102,676 |
| Year 8 | 142,190 |
| Year 9 | 184,864 |
| Year 10 | 230,952 |

*Assume 8 percent net increase in revenue annually.
**Source:** Private placement offering memorandum.

The annual deductions for the first five years are shown in Table 22. During the first five years, the developer estimated that the project would generate $613,524 in tax losses, with positive taxable income not appearing until year 6. Table 23 shows the combined economic benefits of the tax credit and the annual tax deductions. In summary, after five years, the net after-tax value of the tax benefits would be worth $544,362 to someone in the 50 percent bracket. After subtracting the $350,000 initial investment, a total after-tax profit of $194,362 would be realized, without taking into account any positive cash flow or appreciation.

Table 24 shows the total potential economic benefits available to the limited partner under this scheme. Over the projected 10-year period, the total projected return represents a 294 percent return on the initial investment of $15,000 for each of the additional 20 limited partners prior to selling the property. If the property were resold in the tenth year, the limited partners would also receive 2.05 percent of any proceeds; and there would be no recapture of excess depreciation, since accelerated depreciation was not used. The potential returns to the limited partners were in fact astounding, assuming, of course, the developer's projections were accurate.

Just as we calculated the internal rate of return for the Section 8 deal in Chapter Six, it is possible to calculate the internal rate of return in this example as well.

First of all, a sale price must be calculated for the project in year 10. According to the developer, the net income before debt service at that time would be $606,500 (the first year net income compounded at 8 percent per year). Assuming a capitalization rate at that time of 12.5 percent, the economic value of the project would be $4,852,000 ($606,500 ÷ 12.5). The after-tax picture would be as follows:

| | |
|---|---|
| **GROSS SALE PRICE** | **$4,852,000** |
| *Less* **cost of sale at 5%** | 242,600 |
| *Equals* **net proceeds** | **$4,609,400** |
| *Less* **capital gains taxes at 20% of gain** | 785,392 |
| *Equals* **cash available** | 3,824,008 |
| *Less* **first trust** | 1,600,000 |
| *Less* **UDAG loan** | 400,000 |

| | |
|---|---|
| *Equals* net proceeds | 1,824,008 |
| Partners' share at 2.05% | $ 37,392 |

**To figure capital gain:**

| | | |
|---|---|---|
| Adjusted sales proceeds | | $4,609,400 |
| *Less* adjusted basis | | |
| Initial basis | $2,461,000 | |
| *Less* investment tax credit | 187,000 | |
| *Less* capital recovery (depreciation) | 1,591,560 | |
| Adjusted basis | | 682,440 |
| *Equals* capital gain | | $3,926,900 |

Given the after-tax profits at the time of sale, it is possible to calculate the internal rate of return from the stream of benefits shown below:

| Year | Benefit (Investment) |
|---|---|
| 0 | ($15,000) initial investment |
| 1 | 13,441 |
| 2 | 3,699 |
| 3 | 3,955 |
| 4 | 4,294 |
| 5 | 3,700 |
| 6 | 677 |
| 7 | 1,052 |
| 8 | 1,457 |
| 9 | 1,894 |
| 10 | 2,367 + $37,392 = $39,759 |

This internal rate of return (as based on the information provided in the offering memorandum) shows an astonishing internal rate of return of over 45 percent.

Too good to be true? Quite possibly. What if the developer's projections were not accurate? What if he could not get the proposed rent for the space, or if it took him much longer to lease the building than anticipated? What if it cost much more to rehabilitate the building than anticipated? What if the permanent loan rate (which is floating) went up? What if he underestimated his operating costs? Any of these factors could seriously jeopardize the economic

## TABLE 22
## COMMERCIAL REHABILITATION: TAX SITUATION

|  | First Year Annual Amount |
|---|---|
| Net income | $311,250 |
| *Less interest* on first trust | 256,000 |
| *Less interest* on second trust | 14,640 |
| *Less* depreciation of: |  |
| shell $250,000 basis (15 years) | 18,267 |
| structural rehabilitation of $749,000 (15 years)* | 49,920 |
| "Personal property" of $504,000 (five years)** | 100,800 |
| Construction period interest and fees of $405,690 (10 years) | 40,569 |
| TOTAL "LOSSES" FROM DEPRECIATION | $209,556 |
| TOTAL TAX WRITE-OFF | $480,196 |
| *Equals* annual profit (loss) for tax purposes |  |
| Year 1 | ($168,946) |
| Year 2 | (144,046) |
| Year 3 | (129,634) |
| Year 4 | (117,154) |
| Year 5 | (56,744) |
| TOTAL | ($613,524) |

*Tax credit of $187,000 subtracted from basis.

**The 10 percent tax credit is not subtracted from personal property write-off.

**Source:** Private placement offering memorandum.

## TABLE 23
## COMMERCIAL REHABILITATION: SUMMARY
## OF TAX BENEFITS
### (Five-Year Period)

| | Amount | Net Value to Individual in 50% Bracket |
|---|---|---|
| Investment tax credit of 20% for structural rehabilitation costs (20% × $936,000) | $187,200 | $187,200 |
| Investment tax credit of 10% for "personal property" rehabilitation (10% × $504,000) | 50,400 | 50,400 |
| Cumulative five-year losses | 613,524 | 306,762 |
| Cumulative net value of tax losses plus tax credit | — | 544,362 |
| Investment | 350,000 | 350,000 |
| Excess over initial investment | — | 194,362 |
| Ratio of total five-year deductions to initial investment of $350,000 | $1.75 to (of deductions) | $1.00 (of investment) |

**Source:** Private placement offering memorandum.

## TABLE 24
### COMMERCIAL REHABILITATION: SUMMARY OF BENEFITS TO $15,000 LIMITED PARTNERS

| Year | Investment | Cash Flow at 2.05% | Net Value of Tax Savings or (Taxes Due) at 4.1% | Net Value of Tax Credit at 4.1% | Annual Total Benefits | Annual Return on Investment | Cumulative Return on Investment* |
|---|---|---|---|---|---|---|---|
| 0 | $15,000 | $ 0 | $ 0 | $ 0 | $ 0 | 0% | 0% |
| 1 | 0 | 237 | 3,463 | 9,741 | 13,441 | 90 | 90 |
| 2 | 0 | 747 | 2,952 | 0 | 3,699 | 25 | 115 |
| 3 | 0 | 1,298 | 2,657 | 0 | 3,995 | 26 | 141 |
| 4 | 0 | 1,893 | 2,401 | 0 | 4,294 | 29 | 170 |
| 5 | 0 | 2,537 | 1,163 | 0 | 3,700 | 25 | 195 |
| 6 | 0 | 1,354 | (677) | 0 | 677 | 5 | 200 |
| 7 | 0 | 2,104 | (1,052) | 0 | 1,052 | 7 | 207 |
| 8 | 0 | 2,914 | (1,457) | 0 | 1,457 | 9 | 216 |
| 9 | 0 | 3,788 | (1,894) | 0 | 1,894 | 12 | 228 |
| 10 | 0 | 4,734 | (2,367) | 0 | 2,367 | 16 | 244 |
| TOTAL | $15,000 | $21,606 | $ 5,189 | $9,741 | $36,536 | 244% | — |

PLUS 2.05% of capital gains when project is sold or refinanced.

*Assumes 50 percent income bracket.

**Source:** Private placement offering memorandum.

benefits. While the tax benefits would remain the same, there would be the need to supply additional equity capital. Since the initial equity investment would be increased, the return on the investment would be reduced.

One of the important questions that any prudent investor would want to know before becoming a limited partner in such a deal would be who would be responsible for contributing the additional equity capital if the project got into trouble. Normally, construction cost overruns and initial operating deficits are the responsibility of the general partner, but this may not always be the case. Such obligations will be spelled out in the partnership agreement, which should be reviewed by the investor's attorney. Equally important is the issue of the general partner's financial strength. Does the general partner have sufficient funds available to cover overruns and deficits? If not, the limited partners may have no other choice but to provide more equity at some later point.

In other words, although the tax benefits are very generous, the risks associated with many rehabilitation projects are very high. For a project that is unable to lease up at break-even rates, the prospect is for long-term additional annual cash requirements, which is probably an unpleasant enough prospect to offset the potential benefits. In other words, the investment—and indeed the entire project—is not a good idea if the annual income received cannot support the costs of operating and financing the project and cannot provide the required cash to the investors.

It is interesting to note that unlike the Section 8 deal presented in the preceding chapter and the residential deal presented in the next chapter, this remarkable syndication opportunity never closed. After a great deal of hoopla, including large signs stating "This innovative project is being financed by . . . ," the deal fell through as it became apparent that there was no market for the proposed use. The numbers were too good. If in fact the assumptions stated in an offering memorandum are not reasonable and accurate, the entire financial package collapses like a house of cards.

In a situation where there was a strong general partner and where the risks were considered reasonable and generally acceptable, at that time an internal rate of return of between 18 and 22 percent would have been sufficient to entice investors into relatively high-risk projects. Since the internal rate of return is so sensitive to assumptions regarding such items as appreciation, it is often advisable to show investors high and low expectations, given a best-case and worst-case scenario. If they can accept this range of potential benefits, they are likely to invest in a specific deal. In this case, for example, the general partner could have raised substantially more in syndication capital (approximately twice as much) if the assumptions were accurate and the general partner wanted to show investors an internal rate of return of 22 percent. Since the assumptions were woefully inaccurate, the projections were essentially worthless, and the deal fell through. This actually turned out all for the better. While the developer lost several thousand dollars in architectural fees and site option money, within the next year the commercial office market collapsed in Washington, thus virtually assuring the demise of developer, investors, and lenders if this ill-conceived project had gone forward.

## THE WAREHOUSE AS AN
## HISTORICAL PROPERTY

The factors that apply to renovating commercial projects also apply to rehabilitating historical structures. The only difference is that if the project is a certified historical structure or is located in a certified historical district and is certified by the National Park Service as being significant to the district, the tax benefits are increased. The process for determining the tax benefits of an historical structure are the same as for a commercial structure, except for these two differences, described earlier in Chapter Three: 1) The tax credit is 25 percent of all rehabilitation costs instead of 20 percent (or 15 percent in the case of a 30 to 39-year-old building) for older commercial properties; and 2) in figuring the annual capital recovery factor, the amount of the tax credit is not subtracted from the basis. (In 1982 this was subsequently changed so that one-half of the credit was subtracted from the basis.)

Tables 25 through 27 show the benefits to the same $15,000 limited partner using the same assumptions with the only change being that historical benefits are used instead of the commercial benefits.

In Table 25, the deductions are increased from $613,524 during the first five years to $691,404. The reason for this is that the

## TABLE 25
## HISTORICAL REHABILITATION: TAX SITUATION

|  | First-Year Annual Amount |
| --- | --- |
| Net income | $311,250 |
| *Less interest* on first trust | 256,000 |
| *Less interest* on second trust | 14,640 |
| *Less* depreciation of: | |
| shell $250,000 basis (15 years) | 18,267 |
| structural rehabilitation of $936,000 (15 years) | 62,400 |
| "personal property" of $504,000 (five years) | 100,800 |
| construction period interest and fees (10 years) | 40,569 |
| Total "losses" from depreciation | $222,036 |
| TOTAL TAX WRITE-OFF | $492,676 |
| *Equals* annual profit (loss) for tax purposes | |
| Year 1 | ($181,426) |
| Year 2 | (169,006) |
| Year 3 | (142,114) |
| Year 4 | (129,634) |
| Year 5 | (69,224) |
| TOTAL | ($691,404) |

**Source:** Private placement offering memorandum.

## TABLE 26
## HISTORICAL REHABILITATION:
## SUMMARY OF TAX BENEFITS
### (Five-Year Period)

| | Amount | Net Value to Individual in 50% Bracket |
|---|---|---|
| Investment tax credit of 25% for structural rehabilitation costs (25% × $936,000) | $234,000 | $234,000 |
| Investment tax credit of 10% for "personal property" rehabilitation (10% × $504,000) | 50,400 | 50,400 |
| Cumulative five-year "losses" | 691,404 | 345,702 |
| Cumulative net value of five-year losses plus tax credit | — | 630,102 |
| Investment | 350,000 | 350,000 |
| Excess over initial investment | — | 280,102 |
| Ratio of total five-year deductions to initial investment of $350,000 | $1.97 to (of deduction) | $1.00 (of investment) |

**Source:** Private placement offering memorandum.

## TABLE 27
### HISTORICAL REHABILITATION: SUMMARY OF BENEFITS TO $15,000 LIMITED PARTNERS

| Year | Investment | Cash Flow at 2.05% | Net Value of Tax Savings or (Taxes Due) at 4.1% | Net Value of Tax Credit at 4.1% | Annual Total Benefits | Annual Return on Investment | Cumulative Return on Investment |
|------|-----------|-------------------|------------------------------------------------|--------------------------------|----------------------|----------------------------|-------------------------------|
| 0 | $15,000 | $ 0 | $ 0 | $ 0 | $ 0 | 0% | 0% |
| 1 | 0 | 237 | 3,719 | 11,660 | 15,616 | 104 | 104 |
| 2 | 0 | 747 | 3,464 | 0 | 4,211 | 28 | 132 |
| 3 | 0 | 1,298 | 2,913 | 0 | 4,211 | 28 | 160 |
| 4 | 0 | 1,893 | 2,657 | 0 | 4,550 | 30 | 190 |
| 5 | 0 | 2,537 | 1,419 | 0 | 3,956 | 26 | 216 |
| 6 | 0 | 1,354 | (677) | 0 | 677 | 5 | 221 |
| 7 | 0 | 2,104 | (1,052) | 0 | 1,052 | 7 | 228 |
| 8 | 0 | 2,914 | (1,457) | 0 | 1,457 | 9 | 237 |
| 9 | 0 | 3,788 | (1,894) | 0 | 1,894 | 12 | 249 |
| 10 | 0 | 4,734 | (2,367) | 0 | 2,367 | 16 | 265 |
| TOTAL | $15,000 | $21,606 | $ 6,725 | $11,660 | $39,991 | 265% | — |

**Source:** Private placement offering memorandum.

157

rehabilitation tax credit was not subtracted from the basis in figuring the annual capital recovery amount. The tax credit was increased from $187,000 to $234,000, as shown in Table 26, since it is based on 25 percent of rehabilitation costs. Finally, Table 27 shows the annual return to the $15,000 limited partners, amounting to a cumulative return over 10 years of 265 percent. In the first year alone, the return amounted to 104 percent of the original investment.

## COMPARISON OF COMMERCIAL REHABILITATION AND HISTORICAL REHABILITATION

| Same Property | | |
| --- | --- | --- |
| | Commercial | Historical |
| Initial investment | $15,000 | $15,000 |
| 10-year cash flow | 21,606 | 21,606 |
| 10-year net value of tax losses | 5,189 | 6,725 |
| Net value of tax credits | 9,741 | 11,600 |
| Total 10-year benefit | $36,536 | $39,991 |
| Cumulative return | 244% | 265% |

In other words, the tax benefits are better for an historical property than for a rehabilitated older commercial structure. While the example just described shows the benefits accruing to the investor, in reality the benefits would probably accrue to the general partner. Rather than keeping the investment at $15,000, the general partner could raise the equity requirement so that the after-tax net benefits to the investor would be equivalent in either case. The result would be that the general partner would receive more equity capital and would increase the development fee. In short, the developer would make more money.

There is one warning about historical properties. The property must be listed on the National Register of Historic Places or must be located in an historical district and be determined to be of significance to the district. If the property is on the register or is determined to be significant to the district, then in order to participate in the tax benefits, certain standards must be followed and the rehabilitation work must be certified by the National Park Service. The key actor in the process of historical preservation is the State Historical Preservation Officer (SHPO), who should be contacted prior to considering any rehabilitation of historic structures. Another interesting aspect of the law is that if an older commercial structure is located within an historical district, the commercial structure is presumed to be of historical significance and will not qualify for the commercial rehabilitation tax credit until a determination has been made by the National Park Service regarding the historical status of the building. In other words, for an older commercial building located in an historical district, an owner may not have a choice regarding which tax incentives to use.

## SUMMARY: THE KEY TO RAISING EQUITY CAPITAL IS PRICING THE ECONOMIC BENEFITS

What comes through in the examples presented in this chapter and the Section 8 project in Chapter Five is the fact that there is very wide latitude regarding both the interpretation of the various economic benefits that a project will produce and the value of the benefits to limited partners. In the case of Section 8 projects, the benefits were exclusively tax benefits; and since the market risk factors were minimal (because of HUD Housing Assistance Payments), there was a great deal of similarity between the pricing of equity for such projects. Tax losses were calculated for a period of time, and standard market ratios were applied to these loss factors. It is relatively easy to express the amount of equity that could be raised as percentages of the mortgage—30–35 percent for substantial rehabilitation, 25–27 percent for new construction, and so on—and this was typically done as a shorthand way of determining equity capital.

Commercial and historical properties, however, are quite different because there is likely to be substantial market risk involved, and because many projects are likely to produce cash flow and appreciation benefits in addition to tax benefits. Also the permanent lender is likely to claim a substantial portion of the cash flow and appreciation benefits. The result is that every deal is different. While it is relatively easy to determine the tax benefits produced by a commercial or historical property, the value of these benefits to investors (that is, what the benefit can be sold for) will vary significantly from project to project, depending on the risk involved in the undertaking and what other potential economic benefits are available for investors. In undertaking any project that a developer hopes to syndicate, it is extremely important to enlist at the outset professionals who are knowledgeable about current syndication markets to assess the value of the limited partnership interests for a specific project.

The role of the developer is not to price the value of the equity, but rather to put together a viable project that produces the greatest economic benefits.

# *E i g h t*

## Syndicating the Deal: An Historical Residential Property Example

In the absence of federal deep subsidy housing programs, there is the implication that development and syndication of rental housing may no longer be viable. This is not necessarily the case, however. Local or state governments, for instance, may step in with subsidies or leveraged financing to replace, at least in part, the previous role of the federal government. Also, there will be an increasing number of syndications involving government-assisted second-user properties such as Section 236 and Section 221(d)(3) properties, as discussed in Chapter Three. There will also be syndication of residential historical properties. Such an example is the subject of this chapter.

This particular example was a 315-unit older apartment house, also located in the Washington metropolitan area. These numbers were formulated at the stage of testing preliminary economic feasibility and actual syndication had not yet taken place. The building was on the National Register of Historic Places and as such qualified for the 25 percent Investment Tax Credit.

In the preceding chapter, we talked about how the basic assumptions regarding rental income must be valid and how without the generation of cash flow, the tax benefits will lose their appeal because of the requirements for additional equity capital from limited partners. In other words, the basic market must be present in order to produce sufficient rents to cover project financing and debt service. In many instances, this will be a major problem in rental housing, since often the market will not be present to support the rents required to make the deal work.

One way of getting around the potential shortfall in necessary rental income is to plan for a conversion to condominiums in the mid-term future—typically between five and ten years away. Such an assumption can be extremely dangerous, however, and a planned condominium conversion concept should be undertaken only in areas where condominium conversion is clearly a viable alternative. In this project, the concept made considerable sense because there was already a great deal of condominium conversion activity in the immediate area; and the project, which itself had a great deal of charm, was clearly a candidate for condominium conversion. In fact, were it not for the historical classification of the building, the project would have been converted at that time. By operating the property as a rental property for at least five years, however, the owners could use the investment tax credits, which are available only to owners of income-producing properties.

The basic deal was this: the building would be acquired from the previous lender, who had foreclosed on the property, by a joint venture consisting of a strong developer as general partner, who had reached an agreement with the tenants' association. Because the project was in foreclosure and because of strict laws in the District of Columbia requiring the permission of the tenants in order for a project to be converted to a condominium, the acquisition price was well below what probably would have been the fair market price at that time. This fact helped assure the feasibility of the deal. The other key variable was short-term conventional financing for five years at 15 percent. What made the permanent lender willing to agree to the loan was the additional provision that when the project was sold as condominium units, the lender would receive 25 percent of the net profit available at the time.

The costs required to rehabilitate the project, including generous relocation allowances to the tenants, were as follows:

| Costs | Total | Per Unit |
|---|---|---|
| Acquisition: | $ 3,350,000 | $10,635 |
| Land | 1,675,000 | 5,317 |
| Building | 1,675,000 | 5,317 |
| | | |
| Rehabilitation Costs: | | |
| Residential | 4,335,500 | 13,763 |
| Commercial | 241,900 | 768 |
| Total | 4,577,400 | 14,531 |

| | | |
|---|--:|--:|
| **Soft Costs:** | | |
| Interest | 1,999,200 | 6,347 |
| Loan fees | 294,000 | 933 |
| Architectural and | | |
|    Engineering | 90,000 | 286 |
| Legal | 75,000 | 238 |
| Taxes | 100,000 | 317 |
| Insurance | 40,000 | 127 |
| **Total** | 2,598,200 | 8,248 |
| Marketing | 125,000 | 397 |
| Overhead | 280,000 | 889 |
| **Tenants** | | |
| 30 members | 225,000 | 714 |
| 27 nonmembers | 67,500 | 214 |
| Tenant obligations | 60,000 | 190 |
| **Total** | 352,500 | 1,119 |
| **TOTAL COSTS** | **$11,283,100** | **$35,819** |

In putting together the deal and assessing basic economic feasibility of the syndication, these next steps were taken:

1. On the basis of a market study, rents were projected for the project after rehabilitation. The market rents—including the commercial income from several small shops—are shown below and compared with the subsidized rents which would be maintained for 40 existing tenants. To this figure was added the commercial income:

| Tenant Units | Number | Square Feet Per Unit | Total | Rent/ Square Foot | Unit Rent | Total Rent |
|---|---|---|---|---|---|---|
| Efficiency | 5 | 310 | 1,550 | $.80 | $248 | $ 1,240 |
| 1 BR | 30 | 660 | 19,800 | .51 | 337 | 10,110 |
| 2 BR | 5 | 960 | 4,800 | .49 | 467 | 2,335 |
| Subtotal | 40 | 626 | 26,150 | .52 | 342 | 13,685 |

**Annual Total Rent**            $164,220

| Market Units | Number | Square Feet Per Unit | Total | Rent/ Square Foot | Unit Rent | Total Rent |
|---|---|---|---|---|---|---|
| Efficiency | 81 | 310 | 25,110 | $1.03 | $320 | $ 25,920 |
| 1 BR | 141 | 660 | 93,060 | .82 | 541 | 76,309 |
| 2 BR | 45 | 960 | 43,200 | .75 | 720 | 32,400 |
| 2 BR/Den | 8 | 1,190 | 9,520 | .67 | 800 | 6,400 |
| Subtotal | 275 | 626 | 170,890 | .83 | 513 | 141,029 |
| | | | | | | |
| Total | 315 | 626 | 197,040 | | | |

Annual Total Rent                                                    $1,692,350

Total Residential Income $1,856,570

Other Income                       32,620

Commercial Income              116,112

Total Annual Income         $2,005,302

2.  The next step was to estimate the costs of operating and maintaining the building as a rental property. After undertaking the necessary research in order to determine operating costs, the following budget was prepared:

| Item | Amount |
|---|---|
| Estimated Total Development Cost | $11,200,000 |
| | |
| Operating Costs: Renting | |
| Advertising | 25,000 |
| | $ 25,000 |
| | |
| Administration | |
| Office salaries | 25,000 |
| Office expenses | 12,000 |
| Management fee | 80,212 |
| Manager's salary | 16,500 |
| Legal | 2,000 |
| Audit | 4,500 |

| | | |
|---|---:|---:|
| Telephone | 3,500 | |
| Benefits | 4,150 | |
| Payroll taxes | 3,320 | |
| Workmen's compensation | 2,905 | |
| Total | | $154,087 |

**Operating**

| | | |
|---|---:|---:|
| Janitorial supplies | 4,700 | |
| Electricity | 135,000 | |
| Water and sewer | 37,500 | |
| Exterminating | 1,400 | |
| Trash | 6,750 | |
| Total | | $185,350 |

**Maintenance**

| | | |
|---|---:|---:|
| Security payroll | 45,000 | |
| Grounds supplies | 500 | |
| Maintenance payroll | 50,000 | |
| Repairs materials | 8,000 | |
| Repairs contract | 2,000 | |
| Elevator contract | 7,200 | |
| HVAC contract | 3,400 | |
| Decorating | 16,000 | |
| Equipment repair | 700 | |
| Appliance repair | 600 | |
| Window washing | 5,500 | |
| Benefits | 9,500 | |
| Payroll taxes | 7,600 | |
| Workmen's compensation | 6,650 | |
| Total | | $162,650 |

**Taxes and Insurance**

| | | |
|---|---:|---:|
| Real estate taxes | 100,265 | |
| Insurance | 18,500 | |
| Reserves | 48,000 | |
| Total | | $166,765 |
| **TOTAL OPERATING** | | **$693,852** |
| Per unit | | $ 2,203 |
| Per square foot | | $ 3.36 |

3. Then the developer identified the basic assumptions underlying the economic model. The key assumptions were these:

- that the total costs, excluding developer fees or syndication costs, would be $11,283,100, as shown above;
- that total costs assumed a rehabilitation loan of $9,800,000 at 15 percent interest for 24 months, with the interest capitalized and included in the total rehabilitation costs;
- that the net residential area that was available for sale or rent was 170,890 square feet for all market-rate units and 26,150 for units to be sold to the tenants at below-market prices;
- that if the project units were sold as condominiums, the market price per unit at that time was $90 per square foot;
- that units would be sold to the 40 tenants at $55 per square foot, with no price escalation for five years;
- that condominium prices would inflate at about 7 percent per year, as would both operating costs and rental income; and
- that a permanent lender would make a permanent loan of $9,800,000 available based on 15 percent interest only for five years, with 25 percent participation in the profits at the time of condominium conversion.

4. The developer next formulated the basic business deal, whereby the various benefits were distributed among all the participants—general partner, limited partners, and lender. The deal was as follows:

**BUSINESS DEAL**

| Cash Flow | Participation |
|---|---|
| General partner | 5% |
| Limited partners | 95 |
| Lender | 0 |

| Tax Losses | |
|---|---|
| General partner | 5% |
| Limited partner | 95 |
| Lender | 0 |

| Residuals | |
|---|---|
| General partner | 50% |
| Limited partners | 25 |
| Lender | 25 |

### Investment Tax Credit

**Limited partners**            **100%**

This arrangement is very similar to the arrangement presented in Chapter Seven, and both are typical of the kind of financing available at the time the project was analyzed.

The *cash flow,* of course, is what is available after operating costs and debt service have been paid. The limited partners got 95 percent of this amount. *Tax losses* are determined by the net income less interest, less capital recovery. The *net residuals* include what is available when the units are sold as condominiums, some five years into the future, according to the same formula introduced in Chapter Seven:

**GROSS SALES PROCEEDS**
    *Less* **cost of sale**
    *Less* **capital gains taxes**
    *Less* **mortgage due**
    *Equals* **net profits (or "residuals" available**
    **for distribution)**

In converting the project to a condominium five years into the future, the owners would have two choices. They could convert the project themselves and sell directly to home purchasers, or they could sell to a third-party condominium converter. In the former case, they would pay taxes on the basis of ordinary income tax rates rather than capital gains tax rates since the income would be considered business income. While it may be possible to structure the deal whereby the capital gains tax would apply (by subdividing the project into 315 separate limited partnerships), such an arrangement is quite complicated and possibly would not be allowed by the IRS. In figuring taxes on the basis of capital gains, therefore, the safest assumption is that the project would be sold to a third-party condominium converter, in which case the selling price would be based on a wholesale, in contrast to a retail, sale's price, the latter being somewhat higher than the former (in order to give the third-party condominium converter room for profit).

The final benefit is the Investment Tax Credit, based on 25 percent of all rehabilitation costs. Because this project is a residential project, in contrast to a commercial project, no Investment Tax Credit is available for personal property rehabilitation expenditures, as was the case with commercial deals in Chapter Seven. The Investment Tax Credit for this project is $1,895,150 (.25 × $7,580,000—the amount of allowable rehabilitation costs).

Because the project was developed after the 1982 tax act, one-half of the Investment Tax Credit was subtracted from the basis in figuring the adjusted basis for the property, as shown below:

| | |
|---|---:|
| **TOTAL COSTS** | **$11,283,100** |
| *Less* **land** | **1,675,000** |
| *Less* **tenant costs** | **352,500** |
| *Less* **one-half** | |
| **Investment Tax Credit** | **947,575** |
| *Equals* **adjusted basis** | **8,308,025** |

5.   Having estimated the rent levels, operating costs, projected sales prices, and Investment Tax Credit, the developer was able to project the financial benefits produced by the project. These are shown in Table 28.

These benefits do not take into consideration the benefits to be generated from the sale of the project in year 5. To figure this, the projected sales revenue was estimated for each year for the next five years (see Table 29).

Assuming that the project was sold in year 5, the net amount available for distribution would be $9,902,797, which would be distributed 50 percent to the general partner, 25 percent to the lender, and 25 percent to the limited partners. (If there were 35 limited partners, each would get .7 percent of the net profits.)

6.   The developer next made two separate projections, the first showing the total financial benefits to the limted partners, and the second showing the total financial benefits to the lender. These are shown below and represent the essence of the basic syndication financial data:

**SUMMARY BENEFITS**

| Limited Partners | 1984 | 1985 | 1986 | 1987 | 1988 |
|---|---|---|---|---|---|
| Investment | | | | | |
| Tax Credit | $1,895,150 | | | | |
| Cash flow | (165,330) | (79,149) | 13,066 | 111,736 | 217,312 |
| Tax benefits | 345,753 | 302,662 | 256,554 | 207,220 | 154,431 |
| Residuals | | | | | 2,475,699 |
| Total | 2,075,573 | 223,513 | 269,620 | 318,956 | 2,847,442 |

| | |
|---|---|
| Discount rate | |
| (IRR) | .23 |
| Present value | 3,130,851 |

| Lender | | | | | |
|---|---|---|---|---|---|
| Interest | 1,470,000 | 1,470,000 | 1,470,000 | 1,470,000 | 1,470,000 |
| Residuals | | | | | 2,475,699 |
| Loan | | | | | 9,800,000 |
| Total | 1,470,00 | 1,470,000 | 1,470,000 | 1,470,000 | 13,745,699 |

| Discount rate | |
|---|---|
| (IRR) | .185 |
| Present value | 9,798,929 |

The internal rate of return for the limited partners amounted to 23 percent; the lender's internal rate of return was 18.5 percent. Both rates were more than adequate to attract participants in the deal, if the assumptions on which the projections were based were valid.

In calculating the initial investment for the limited partners, the developer backed into or solved for this amount by *discounting* the financial benefits using a discount rate of 23 percent. The amount was $3,130,851, or about $3.1 million. Remember that this number was derived during the initial feasibility analysis. When the deal was actually syndicated, in all probability this number would be adjusted depending on various refinements of the cost and market data and the market conditions for real estate securities at the time of actual syndication. The final pricing would also spread out the capital contributions from the limited partners over a three to five-year period.

Now at last the developer had the information he needed in order to estimate the sources and applications of funds. The sources of funds included the $9,800,000 loan from the lender and the $3,100,000 equity contributions from the limited partners. The applications of funds included all project costs identified earlier, plus the cost of syndication. What was left over is what was available for the developer.

In this example, therefore, the developer stood to make a substantial amount, both in the way of a development fee and at the time of condominium sale, at which time the developer would get one-half of the net sale proceeds.

Here again, a warning should be issued—beware of the accuracy of the basic assumptions and the rehabilitation cost estimates. In this case, while the rent and sale figures seemed

## TABLE 28
## FINANCIAL BENEFITS OF HISTORICAL RESIDENTIAL PROPERTY

| Cash Flow | 1984 | 1985 | 1986 | 1987 | 1988 |
|---|---|---|---|---|---|
| Gross income | $2,145,674 | $2,295,871 | $2,456,582 | $2,628,542 | $2,812,540 |
| Effective Gross Income | 2,038,390 | 2,181,077 | 2,333,753 | 2,497,115 | 2,671,913 |
| Operating costs | (742,422) | (794,391) | (849,999) | (909,499) | (973,164) |
| Net income | 1,295,968 | 1,386,686 | 1,483,754 | 1,587,617 | 1,698,750 |
| Debt service | (1,470,000) | (1,470,000) | (1,470,000) | (1,470,000) | (1,470,000) |
| Cash flow | (174,032) | (83,314) | 13,754 | 117,617 | 228,750 |
| Cumulative cash flow | (174,032) | (257,346) | (243,592) | (125,976) | 102,774 |
| *After Taxes* | | | | | |
| Net Income | 1,295,968 | 1,386,686 | 1,483,754 | 1,587,617 | 1,698,750 |
| *Less* interest | 1,470,000 | 1,470,000 | 1,470,000 | 1,470,000 | 1,470,000 |
| *Less* capital recovery (depreciation) | 553,868 | 553,868 | 553,868 | 553,868 | 553,868 |
| Profit (loss) | (727,900) | (637,183) | (540,115) | (436,252) | (325,119) |
| Investment tax credit | 1,895,150 | | | | |
| Total Benefits | 2,085,068 | 235,277 | 283,811 | 335,742 | 391,309 |

**Source:** Owner's initial feasibility analysis.

These benefits do not take into consideration the benefits to be generated from the sale of the project in year 5. To figure this, the projected sales revenue was estimated for each year for the next five years (see Table 29).

## TABLE 29
### BENEFITS GENERATED FOR NEXT FIVE YEARS

| Condo Conversion Potential | 1984 | 1985 | 1986 | 1987 | 1988 |
|---|---|---|---|---|---|
| Sales revenues | $16,456,707 | $17,608,676 | $18,841,284 | $20,160,174 | $21,571,386 |
| Tenant revenues | 1,438,250 | 1,438,250 | 1,438,250 | 1,438,250 | 1,438,250 |
| *Less* sales costs | (894,748) | (952,346) | (1,013,977) | (1,079,921) | (1,150,482) |
| Net revenues | 17,000,209 | 18,094,580 | 19,265,557 | 20,518,503 | 21,859,154 |
| *Less* capital gains taxes | (1,738,437) | (1,735,764) | (1,859,185) | (1,999,001) | (2,156,357) |
| *Less* mortgage | (9,800,000) | (9,800,000) | (9,800,000) | (9,800,000) | (9,800,000) |
| Cash available | 5,461,772 | 6,558,816 | 7,606,372 | 8,719,502 | 9,902,797 |
| ITC subject to recapture | (1,516,120) | (1,137,090) | (758,060) | (379,030) | 0 |
| *Less* ITC recapture (50% tax bracket) | 758,060 | 568,545 | 379,030 | 189,515 | 0 |
| Net after ITC recapture | 4,703,712 | 5,990,271 | 7,227,342 | 8,529,987 | 9,902,797 |

**Source:** Owner's initial feasibility analysis.

**SOURCES OF FUNDS**

| | |
|---|---:|
| Equity contributions | $ 3,100,000 |
| Loan proceeds | 9,800,000 |
| Total sources | $12,900,000 |

**APPLICATIONS OF FUNDS**

| | |
|---|---:|
| Acquisition | $ 3,350,000 |
| Rehabilitation hard costs | 4,577,400 |
| Rehabilitation soft costs | 2,598,200 |
| Marketing costs | 125,000 |
| Developer overhead | 280,000 |
| Tenant cost | 352,500 |
| Total project cost | $11,283,100 |
| Syndication costs and fees at 18% of syndication | $ 682,000 |
| Amount available to the developer for developer fees | $ 934,900 |
| Per unit | $ 2,967 |
| Total applications | $12,900,000 |

reasonable and accurate, the developer at this preliminary stage did not have a firm estimate regarding rehabilitation costs. Before the deal could be syndicated, the rehabilitation cost estimates would have to be final and complete. To the extent that these costs increased, the amount of the initial developer's fee would be reduced (though it would not be a dollar-for-dollar loss since additional costs would generate a larger basis and hence more losses). Nevertheless, at the preliminary financial feasibility stage, this deal looked very good. With reasonable assumptions regarding current cost, operating, and income factors, the project clearly produced substantial benefits which would attract the three principal parties necessary to make the deal work—general partner, limited partners, and lender. This is, in a nutshell, what determines financial feasibility for a syndication project: generating enough financial benefits to make everyone happy.

# *N i n e*
## Conclusion

This book has emphasized the financial aspects of real estate syndication. Money, of course, is what the development and syndication process is all about. As many developers often put it, it's how you keep score. As has been pointed out throughout this book, the syndication fee earned by a general partner is what is received from limited partners who purchase a potential stream of financial benefits. In other words, since the developer sells to others future financial benefits that otherwise would be available exclusively to the developer, the developer is able to receive a fee to cover his overhead and produce a profit. Therefore, the fee that is received is, first and foremost, a function of the value of the potential stream of financial benefits. The greater the benefits, the higher the fee that goes to the developer. Thus the developer's fee does not necessarily relate to the amount of work that has been put into the undertaking. In theory there is no limit to what a developer can receive from limited partners, as long as the financial benefits are there to justify the payments.

However, the fees charged by the general partner must be disclosed fully in the offering memorandum. Because of this, the fees must be justified. As discussed in Chapter One, rather than one's fee being stipulated, there are usually a variety of fees. There are two reasons for this. The first is to meet the reasonableness test, thus demonstrating to potential investors that there is justification for the fees involved. Hence, an organization fee, a construction management fee, a construction guarantee fee, a lease-up fee and so on are necessary. The second reason is the need to structure the fees so that they can be of greatest benefit to the limited partner with regard to the investor's own tax situation. Most fees are therefore structured in such a way that they are an expense item rather than a development cost item, since in the latter case they would be capitalized and amortized as part of the overall development costs. In some cases, however, such as historical or older commercial properties, it is often more advantageous for fees to be capitalized so that they are eligible for the Investment Tax Credit. In those deals it is not uncommon for the developer fees to be more in construction-related items (which are capitalized) and less in lease-up and management-related items (which are expensed).

As the examples in this book have shown, there are no firm rules either with regard to what fees are charged or with regard to how the various benefits are distributed between the general partner and the investors. ***The underlying principal is that investors will pay to participate in a limited partnership depending on the benefits likely to be received and the risks associated with receiving those benefits.*** This is really the only hard-and-fast rule in the industry. If the financial benefits are available to support a large capital contribution, as a developer-general partner, you have a considerable amount of discretion as to what you call the various fees and how you structure them.

In joint venture situations, how you share the development fee between two or more general partners is negotiable. The four key factors affecting the division of the fees are: (1) what you bring to the table in terms of making the deal work (site control, ability to get financing, local approvals, etc.); (2) how much work and expertise you put into developing the project; (3) how much money you put into the deal; and (4) how much risk you take on. All four rules are very important. Generally speaking, the development fees are shared according to the principle "to each according to one's contribution," with "contribution" defined both in terms of tangible and intangible items. With regard to potential areas of conflict in the decision-making process, usually the "golden rule" applies: those with the gold make the rules. Whoever has the most money in the deal will usually have the final say.

You will recall that another aspect of the development fees received by the general partner is that usually these fees are received over a period of time (typically three to six years) as the capital contributions from investors are paid in. This again is more a function of marketing the securities than anything else. First of all, investors are often people with very high annual incomes and not necessarily with a great deal of liquid net worth. By spreading out the capital contributions over a period of years, a syndicator can reach a broader market. Second and more important, the primary marketing appeal, especially of tax shelter syndications, is to gear the payments to the individual's income tax liability. Thus a 2 to 1 loss ratio each year means that the investor in the 50 percent tax bracket is no worse off than he or she would be if the limited partner had no investment and paid full income taxes to the government. It is in fact a no-lose situation for the investor and as such is a very strong factor in marketing the securities.

The final factor affecting how much money a general partner makes is how much of the syndication process the general partner takes on. If the general partner is experienced and has the ability to structure and market the limited partnership interests, additional profit centers are available. Since the fee paid to a syndication firm for structuring and marketing the real estate securities often amounts to as much as 20 to 25 percent of the equity raised, the additional profits are significant, as are the responsibilities and risks associated with this part of the business. Unfortunately, there are few shortcuts or easy dollars to be made in real estate syndication. Generally speaking, a developer or development firm is better off doing what it knows how to do—that is, developing the project—and not taking on the task of structuring and marketing the real estate securities unless it has proven expertise in this area.

The three case studies presented in Chapters Six, Seven and Eight are examples of three different types of syndication deals. While there are not likely to be many government-assisted housing syndications like Coming Towers and the Tracy Apartments, the structuring of these deals is similar to what will be used in the resyndication of older HUD-insured properties. The key difference is that that secondary purchase money (that is, financing provided by the owner) financing will be used to increase the tax basis of the property without altering the day-to-day project economics since the secondary financing allows both principal and interest payments to be deferred until a time in the distant future. Because of the complexities and potential tax risks of such projects, both developers and investors should be extremely careful in getting involved in these deals.

The other case studies are probably more typical of the types of deals that are likely to be developed in the 1980s. In these examples the various economic benefits produced by the project were identified and then distributed among the various participants in the deal. No two deals will be the same. Rather, what will be the same is the way the basic process works: identifying the benefits, distributing the benefits according to a formula which is reasonable, and then selling the benefits to limited partners who invest money up-front in order to receive the stream of future benefits.

Real estate development and real estate syndication are obviously not for everyone. The two essential ingredients needed in order to be a developer are expertise and money. Expertise can often be acquired through the use of consultants. Money, on the other hand, is something you either have or do not have. If you do not have it, then it is often necessary to associate or joint venture with a firm or individual who does have it. For this reason joint ventures are commonplace in the development industry, with one firm or individual providing the expertise and the other the seed money, working capital, and net worth required to develop the project.

How much money is needed in order to undertake a specific project? First, you need enough seed money to get the project to the closing table. Second, you need enough money to provide the necessary guarantees to the limited partners and lenders on such items as operating deficits and construction overruns and to qualify for financing. The seed money requirements are these:

1. *The deposit required to hold a property until the loan closing.* If you already own the property or do not have to put up a deposit, you are in luck, since this is often a fairly substantial sum.
2. *The fee due the architect.* This amount includes both his fee for the preliminary work and the amount you will owe him for the working drawings if the project never closes. At the outset, a written agreement should be executed with the architect for both the preliminary work and the design work. If you cannot afford to pay what you agree to pay, you have no business moving ahead.
3. *The fee for other preliminary work.* This may include the topographical and boundary survey, test borings, or structural engineering survey.

4. *The fee for any other outside consultants.* These may assist you on such items as preparing the initial market and feasibility study, the loan package, and the application for historical certification, and securing financing and raising capital. Some professionals may agree to make their fee contingent upon a loan's closing. If this is the case, so much the better. However, all agreements should be in writing, and you must be prepared and able to live up to the agreements if the project fails.

In order to determine the net worth requirements, it is necessary to determine the requirements of the specific lender or insurer whose requirements vary depending on the amount of the loan and the risks associated with the project.

In recent times a wide variety of firms and individuals have gotten involved in the development and syndication process—including non-profit community groups and community-based development corporations. Such trends have been healthy and should continue. No specific project, however, is any better than the financial rewards and risks associated with the specific project and the strength and expertise of the development team. I hope this book has given the reader a basic understanding of how the process works and has provided the tools required to evaluate specific real estate deals from the perspective of developer, investor, lender, or some other participant in the business of real estate development and syndication.

# *APPENDIXES*

# A/   ACRS Cost Recovery Tables for Real Estate All Real Estate (Except Low-Income Housing)

| Recovery Year is: | 1 | 2 | 3 | 4 | 5 | 6 | 7 | 8 | 9 | 10 | 11 | 12 |
|---|---|---|---|---|---|---|---|---|---|---|---|---|
| 1 | 12% | 11% | 10% | 9% | 8% | 7% | 6% | 5% | 4% | 3% | 2% | 1% |
| 2 | 10 | 10 | 11 | 11 | 11 | 11 | 11 | 11 | 11 | 11 | 11 | 12 |
| 3 | 9 | 9 | 9 | 9 | 10 | 10 | 10 | 10 | 10 | 10 | 10 | 10 |
| 4 | 8 | 8 | 8 | 8 | 8 | 8 | 9 | 9 | 9 | 9 | 9 | 9 |
| 5 | 7 | 7 | 7 | 7 | 7 | 7 | 8 | 8 | 8 | 8 | 8 | 8 |
| 6 | 6 | 6 | 6 | 6 | 7 | 7 | 7 | 7 | 7 | 7 | 7 | 7 |
| 7 | 6 | 6 | 6 | 6 | 6 | 6 | 6 | 6 | 6 | 6 | 6 | 6 |
| 8 | 6 | 6 | 6 | 6 | 6 | 6 | 5 | 6 | 6 | 6 | 6 | 6 |
| 9 | 6 | 6 | 6 | 6 | 5 | 6 | 5 | 5 | 5 | 6 | 6 | 6 |
| 10 | 5 | 6 | 5 | 6 | 5 | 5 | 5 | 5 | 5 | 5 | 6 | 5 |
| 11 | 5 | 5 | 5 | 5 | 5 | 5 | 5 | 5 | 5 | 5 | 5 | 5 |
| 12 | 5 | 5 | 5 | 5 | 5 | 5 | 5 | 5 | 5 | 5 | 5 | 5 |
| 13 | 5 | 5 | 5 | 5 | 5 | 5 | 5 | 5 | 5 | 5 | 5 | 5 |
| 14 | 5 | 5 | 5 | 5 | 5 | 5 | 5 | 5 | 5 | 5 | 5 | 5 |
| 15 | 5 | 5 | 5 | 5 | 5 | 5 | 5 | 5 | 5 | 5 | 5 | 5 |
| 16 | — | — | 1 | 1 | 2 | 2 | 3 | 3 | 4 | 4 | 4 | 5 |

**Note:** (Use the Column for the Month in the First Year the Property is Placed in Service)

**Source:** These are the figures provided by the IRS for computing depreciation.

# B/ ACRS Cost Recovery Tables for Real Estate Low-Income Housing

| If the Recovery Year is: | The applicable percentage is: | | | | | | | | | | | |
|---|---|---|---|---|---|---|---|---|---|---|---|---|
| | 1 | 2 | 3 | 4 | 5 | 6 | 7 | 8 | 9 | 10 | 11 | 12 |
| 1 | 13% | 12% | 11% | 10% | 9% | 8% | 7% | 6% | 4% | 3% | 2% | 1% |
| 2 | 12 | 12 | 12 | 12 | 12 | 12 | 12 | 13 | 13 | 13 | 13 | 13 |
| 3 | 10 | 10 | 10 | 10 | 11 | 11 | 11 | 11 | 11 | 11 | 11 | 11 |
| 4 | 9 | 9 | 9 | 9 | 9 | 9 | 9 | 9 | 10 | 10 | 10 | 10 |
| | 8 | 8 | 8 | 8 | 8 | 8 | 8 | 8 | 8 | 8 | 8 | 9 |
| 6 | 7 | 7 | 7 | 7 | 7 | 7 | 7 | 7 | 7 | 7 | 7 | 7 |
| 7 | 6 | 6 | 6 | 6 | 6 | 6 | 6 | 6 | 6 | 6 | 6 | 6 |
| 8 | 5 | 5 | 5 | 5 | 5 | 5 | 5 | 5 | 5 | 5 | 6 | 6 |
| 9 | 5 | 5 | 5 | 5 | 5 | 5 | 5 | 5 | 5 | 5 | 5 | 5 |
| 10 | 5 | 5 | 5 | 5 | 5 | 5 | 5 | 5 | 5 | 5 | 5 | 5 |
| 11 | 4 | 5 | 5 | 5 | 5 | 5 | 5 | 5 | 5 | 5 | 5 | 5 |
| 12 | 4 | 4 | 4 | 5 | 4 | 5 | 5 | 5 | 5 | 5 | 5 | 5 |
| 13 | 4 | 4 | 4 | 4 | 4 | 4 | 5 | 4 | 5 | 5 | 5 | 5 |
| 14 | 4 | 4 | 4 | 4 | 4 | 4 | 4 | 4 | 4 | 4 | 4 | 4 |
| 15 | 4 | 4 | 4 | 4 | 4 | 4 | 4 | 4 | 4 | 4 | 4 | 4 |
| 16 | — | — | 1 | 1 | 2 | 2 | 2 | 3 | 3 | 3 | 4 | 4 |

**Notes:** Use the Column for the Month in the First Year the Property is Placed in Service. These tables do not apply for short taxable years of less than 12 months.

**Source:** These are the figures provided by the IRS for low-income housing depreciation.

# C/ Typical Offering Memorandum for Private Placement Syndication

*Table of Contents*

Investor Services Fees
Basis Adjustment
Depreciation
Original User Requirement
Depreciation Recapture
Sale or Foreclosure of the Properties
Sale or Other Disposition of Partnership Interests
Sale of Property to Tenants (Rollover)
Liquidation and Dissolution of the Partnerships
Foreign Tax Credits and Foreign Source Income
Excess Investment Interest—Interest on Certain Obligations
Activities Not Engaged In for Profit
Minimum Tax on Tax Preferences
Maximum Tax Rate/Rate Adjustments
Alternative Minimum Tax/Capital Gains
Taxation at Death
Other Tax Aspects
The Partnership Agreements and Interests in the Partnerships
The Purchase Agreement and Distribution of Cash to Investors
Documents Available for Inspection
Terms of Purchase and Method of Sale
Method of Sale
Procedure for Subscribing
Payments by the Investors
Investor Representations
Default by the Investor
Acquisition of Units by Key Employees of NCHP
Glossary of Terms

Exhibits

A—Financial Projections
B—General Partner Financial Statements
C—Prior Performance Tables
D—Operation and Management of the General Partner
     Annual Report
     Directors of the Corporation
     Executive Officers of the Corporation
E—Purchase Agreement
F—Limited Partnership Agreement of Comings Towers Associates
G—Draft Amendment to Limited Partnership Agreement of
     Comings Towers Associates
H—Limited Partnership Agreement of Tracy Apartments Associates

I—Draft Amendment to Limited Partnership Agreement of Tracy
Apartments Associates

**Source:** Contents of private placement offering memorandum used
for the example in chapter 6.

# D/ Present Value of $1 Per Period (Discount Rates)

| Year | 12% | 14% | 15% | 16% | 18% | 20% | 25% | 30% |
|------|-----|-----|-----|-----|-----|-----|-----|-----|
| 1 | .893 | .877 | .870 | .862 | .847 | .833 | .800 | .769 |
| 2 | .797 | .769 | .756 | .743 | .718 | .694 | .640 | .592 |
| 3 | .712 | .675 | .658 | .641 | .609 | .579 | .512 | .455 |
| 4 | .636 | .592 | .572 | .552 | .516 | .482 | .410 | .350 |
| 5 | .567 | .519 | .497 | .476 | .437 | .402 | .320 | .269 |
| 6 | .507 | .456 | .432 | .410 | .370 | .335 | .262 | .207 |
| 7 | .452 | .400 | .376 | .354 | .314 | .279 | .210 | .159 |
| 8 | .404 | .351 | .327 | .305 | .266 | .233 | .168 | .123 |
| 9 | .361 | .308 | .284 | .263 | .226 | .194 | .134 | .094 |
| 10 | .322 | .270 | .247 | .227 | .191 | .162 | .107 | .073 |
| 11 | ..287 | .237 | .215 | .195 | .162 | .135 | .086 | .056 |
| 12 | .257 | .208 | .187 | .168 | .137 | .112 | .069 | .043 |
| 13 | .229 | .182 | .163 | .145 | .116 | .093 | .055 | .033 |
| 14 | .205 | .160 | .141 | .125 | .099 | .078 | .044 | .025 |
| 15 | .183 | .140 | .123 | .108 | .084 | .065 | .035 | .020 |
| 16 | .163 | .123 | .107 | .093 | .071 | .054 | .028 | .015 |
| 17 | .146 | .108 | .093 | .080 | .060 | .045 | .023 | .012 |
| 18 | .130 | .095 | .081 | .089 | .051 | .038 | .018 | .009 |
| 19 | .116 | .083 | .070 | .060 | .043 | .031 | .014 | .007 |
| 20 | .104 | .073 | .061 | .051 | .037 | .026 | .012 | .005 |
| 25 | .059 | .038 | .030 | .024 | .016 | .010 | .004 | .001 |
| 30 | .033 | .020 | .015 | .012 | .007 | .004 | .001 | .000 |

**Source:** Standard discount tables.

# E/ Partnership Agreement and Certificate of Limited Partnership

NAME OF PARTNERSHIP: Rehab Associates

NAME OF PROJECT: Tenth Street, N.W.

LOCATION: Washington, D.C.

## TABLE OF CONTENTS

## AGREEMENT AND CERTIFICATE
## OF LIMITED PARTNERSHIP

NAME OF PARTNERSHIP: REHAB ASSOCIATES

NAME OF PROJECT: TENTH STREET, N.W.

LOCATION: WASHINGTON, D.C.

This Agreement and Certificate of Limited Partnership is made and entered into on the day and year written below by and among the undersigned parties in accordance with the Limited Partnership Act of the District of Columbia.

NOW, THEREFORE, in consideration of the premises and the mutual covenants herein contained, the parties hereby agree and certify as follows:

## ARTICLE I
## SCOPE, PURPOSES, AND POWERS

### Section 1.01. Scope
Any previous Agreement for the formation, organization and governance of the Partnership is hereby superseded and amended by substituting the within Agreement therefor in its entirety.

### Section 1.02. Name and Address
The Partnership shall be conducted under the name of Associates. The principal office and place of business of the Partnership shall be:

c/o   REHAB ASSOCIATES
10th Street, N.W.
Washington, D.C.

### Section 1.03. Purposes and Objectives
The purposes and objectives of the Partnership are to acquire, own, develop, rehabilitate, maintain, operate and manage primarily for families and individuals of low and moderate income a housing project (the "Project") identified as follows:

Name: Harris House
Location: 10th Street, N.W., Washington, D.C.

Number of Dwelling Units: 100 Units
Financing Program: District of Columbia Department of
Housing and Community Development
interim and permanent financing with
100% Section 8 rental assistance—
existing program.

### Section 1.04. Powers

The Partnership is empowered and authorized:

(A) to option, purchase, or otherwise acquire any property, real or personal, in fee or under lease, and any interest therein or pertinent thereto, which may be necessary or appropriate for the accomplishment of the purposes and objectives of the Partnership;

(B) to enter into a Contract of Sale with the District of Columbia Department of Housing and Community Development ("DHCD") and to perform and carry out the terms of the Contract of Sale and the requirements of the 14th Street Urban Renewal Plan as applicable;

(C) to develop and rehabilitate the property acquired by the Partnership with off-site and on-site improvements, and to rehabilitate, own, maintain, operate and manage the housing units and other facilities relating thereto which, together, constitute the Project;

(D) to assist and further the construction, rehabilitation, maintenance and management of housing for qualified tenants;

(E) to raise and provide such funds as may be necessary to achieve the purposes and objectives of the Partnership and to borrow funds, execute and issue mortgage notes and other evidences of indebtedness, and secure the same by mortgages, deeds of trust, pledges or other liens; provided, however, that the Partnership shall have no power or authority to execute a mortgage loan note other than a non-recourse mortgage loan note which contains exculpatory clauses to the effect that neigher the Partnership nor the Partners shall have any personal liability for the mortgage debt or for any deficiency judgment which may be entered upon foreclosure of the said mortgage debt, and that the mortgagee shall look only to the mortgaged property for collection of any sum due under or in connection with the mortgage note;

(F) to apply for and obtain DHCD and/or other Federal or local government agencies' mortgage financing, interest subsidy, rent supplement and housing assistance payments and other assistance provided by Federal and local law;

(G) to sell, lease or otherwise dispose of the Project, or any part thereof, subject to the restrictions hereinafter contained; and

(H) to enter into, perform and carry out contracts, and engage in other activities, which may be necessary and proper for the protection and benefit of the Partnership and the accomplishment of its purpose and objectives.

### Section 1.05. Term

The Partnership shall commence upon the filing of this Agreement and Certificate of Limited Partnership and shall terminate on December 31, 2032, unless it is dissolved at an earlier date as provided in Section 9.01 hereof.

### Section 1.06. Partners

The general and limited partners shall be the entities or persons listed in Exhibit A, annexed hereto and made a part hereof, as the same may be amended from time to time. The General Partners shown on Exhibit A are referred to in this Agreement as the "General Partner" or the "General Partners" as the context may require. The Limited Partners shown on Exhibit A are referred to in this Agreement as the "Limited Partner" or as "Limited Partners" as the context may require. Unless the context otherwise clearly indicates, the terms "Partner" and "Partners" shall include all of the General and Limited Partners. The addresses of the Partners are shown on Exhibit A below the name of each respective partner. All references in this Agreement to Exhibit A are references to Exhibit A as amended and in effect from time to time.

## ARTICLE II
## CONTRIBUTIONS TO CAPITAL

### Section 2.01. Contribution by the General Partners

The General Partners have contributed to the capital of the Partnership all right, title and interest each may have had with respect to the Property including:

(A) The rights to acquire the Property;
(B) Contracts and understandings with an architect, builder and consultant with respect to the development of the Project;
(C) Rights in and to the DHCD commitment to provide the construction and permanent financing for the Project;
(D) Right to the HUD Assignment of Section 8 Annual Contribution and Agreement to Enter Into Housing Assistance Payments Contract.
(E) All other rights, assets or interests related to the Property and the improvements. Said contributions have been made subject to the Partnership's obligation to reimburse, to the extent actually recov-

ered from mortgage proceeds, any advances by the General Partners which are recognized as "project costs". Contributions by each General Partner to the capital of the Partnership pursuant to this Section 2.01 have been assigned the value of Two Thousand Dollars ($2,000) for purposes of the establishment of each General Partner's capital account.

## Section 2.02. Limited Partners' Capital Contribution

(A) The Limited Partners shall contribute to the capital of the Partnership an aggregate amount of Eighty Thousand Dollars ($80,000).
(B) The aggregate of the foregoing cash contribution shall be made by the said Limited Partners, *pro rata,* as follows:
  (1) Forty Thousand Dollars ($40,000) shall be due and payable upon the execution of this Agreement. In the event that a Limited Partner transfers a portion of his/her limited partnership interest subsequent to the execution of this Agreement, the transferee of the limited partnership interest shall reimburse the transferor an amount equal to that portion of the capital contribution attributable to the limited partnership interest transferred.
  (2) Twenty Thousand Dollars ($20,000) shall be due and payable August 1, 1983 or within fifteen (15) days after the General Partners have given written notice that the Certificate of Occupancy has been issued, whichever shall later occur.
  (3) Twenty Thousand Dollars ($20,000) shall be due and payable August 1, 1984, or upon the anniversary date of the achievement of the conditions for the second payment, whichever shall later occur.
(C) The Limited Partners' capital contributions (2) and (3) shall be evidenced by interest bearing notes payable to the Partnership and delivered upon execution of this Agreement or any Amendment thereto. Such notes shall provide that payment shall be stayed for any period during which the General Partners shall be in default under the terms of this Agreement.
(D) The amount of cash to be contributed to the capital of the Partnership by each Partner is shown on Exhibit A hereto.
(E) No Limited Partner (in his/her capacity as a Limited Partner) shall be required to make any additional capital contributions, or shall be personally liable for any losses, debts, obligations or liabilities of the Partnership beyond the amount set forth opposite his/her name in Exhibit A hereto.
(F) The General Partners, shall bear all financial risk and expense in conjunction with the development, construction of the Project and syndication of the Partnership interests.

(G) The General Partners may advance to the Partnership such funds as may be necessary over and above the proceeds of the mortgage loan, and the capital contributions of the Partners to effect settlement, and to complete rehabilitation of the Project.

### Section 2.03. Initial Percentage Interests
The parties shall have the following respective partnership interests:
(A) The General Partners, and their respective interest in the Partnership ("Percentage Interest") are:

> 1.0  Joseph T. Howell
> 1.0  Faye Godwin

(B) The Limited Partners and their respective interest in the Partnership ("Percentage Interest") are:

> 48.5  Joseph T. Howell
> 0.5  Cardiac Construction
> 49.0  Faye Godwin

### Section 2.04. Capital Accounts
(A) A capital account shall be established for each Partner. The account shall be credited with the amount of such capital contributions, and with that Partner's share of Partnership income, gains and profits. Each Partner's capital account shall be debited with that Partner's share of losses and distributions.
(B) Upon the transfer by any Partner of all or any part of its Percentage Interest, the proportionate amount of the capital account of the transferor shall be transferred to the transferee; provided, however, that no such transfer shall relieve the transferor of its obligation to pay into the Partnership its required capital contribution.

### Section 2.05. Return of Contributions
No Partner shall be entitled to demand the return of its capital contribution, except as provided herein.

### ARTICLE III
### RIGHTS, POWERS AND OBLIGATIONS OF THE
### GENERAL PARTNER

### Section 3.01. Management of Business
The Partnership shall be managed and its business shall be controlled solely by Faye Godwin as a General Partner, subject to the terms and conditions of this Agreement.

Without limiting the generality of the foregoing, Faye Godwin may, on behalf of the Partnership, without the consent of any other Partner except as otherwise specifically provided in this Agreement, exercise the power to employ on behalf of the Partnership such persons, firms, partnerships or corporations, including any Partner or a firm, partnership or corporation of which any Partner is an owner of an equity interest or in which an individual related to any Partner is an employee or owner of an equity interest, as Ms. Godwin shall deem advisable for the proper operation of the business of the Partnership, such employment to be undertaken upon such terms and for such compensation as Ms. Godwin in her sole judgement, shall determine and upon competitively reasonable terms.

### Section 3.02. Action by General Partners

(A) The General Partners shall promptly take any and all action which may be necessary or appropriate to perfect and maintain the Partnership as a Limited Partnership under laws of the District of Columbia.

(B) The General Partners shall devote such time and attention to the Partnership business as may be necessary for the proper performance of the duties hereunder. The General Partners may, however, engage in and hold interests in other business ventures of every kind and description for their own account including, without limitation, other low and moderate income housing projects whether or not such business ventures are in direct or indirect competition with the Project and whether or not the Partnership also has an interest therein.

### Section 3.03. Liability to Partnership and Limited Partners

The General Partners shall not be liable, responsible or accountable in damages or otherwise to the Partnership or any Limited Partner for any act performed by them in good faith and reasonably believed by them to be within the scope of the authority conferred on them by this Agreement and in the best interests of the Partnership, except for acts of malfeasance, gross negligence or fraud.

### Section 3.04. Indemnification of General Partners

The General Partners shall be entitled to indemnity from the Partnership for any act performed by them in good faith and reasonably believed to be within the scope of the authority conferred on them by this Agreement and in the best interests of the Partnership, except for acts of malfeasance, gross negligence or fraud; provided, however, that any indemnity under this Section shall be paid out of and to the extent of Partnership assets only.

### Section 3.05. Power of Attorney

(A) Each Limited Partner hereby irrevocably constitutes and appoints Ms. Godwin as a General Partner, his true and lawful attorney, in his name, place and stead, to make, execute, acknowledge and file such instruments as may be necessary to the conduct of the Partnership business including without limitation, deeds of conveyance of real property or interests therein, but not including any amendment to the Limited Partnership Agreement or Certificate of Limited Partnership, except as may be necessary to effectuate the provisions of Article VIII hereof.

(B) It is expressly intended by each of the Partners that the foregoing power of attorney is coupled with an interest.

(C) The said power of attorney shall survive an assignment by any Partner of the whole or part of its Percentage Interest until such time as the assignee has been substituted as a Partner.

(D) The said power of attorney shall also, to the extent permitted by law, survive the merger, bankruptcy, receivership or dissolution of a Partner.

(E) Each Partner shall execute such instruments as Ms. Godwin may request in order to give evidence of, and to effectuate, the granting of this power of attorney, whether by executing a separate counterpart or otherwise.

(F) All Partners shall assist and cooperate with Ms. Godwin if and when they determine to sell a portion of their respective interest in the Partnership to the investors, and they hereby agree to grant Ms. Godwin the power of attorney, as provided in this Section, to effectuate such sale and substitution of investors as Limited Partners of the Partnership.

**ARTICLE IV**
**DEVELOPMENT TEAM**

### Section 4.01. Selection

The members of the Development Team selected are as follows:

(A) Certified Public Accountants: Numbers Inc.

(B) Consultant Services: Howell Associates

(C) Insurance Agent: City and Town Insurance

(D) Management Agent: Property Services Inc.

(E) Architect: Design Associates

(F) Title Services: First Title Insurance Company

(G) Attorney: Bill Harris

(H) General Contractor: Cardiac Construction

## ARTICLE V
## POWERS AND RESPONSIBILITIES OF THE GENERAL PARTNERS

### Section 5.01. Functions of the General Partners
The General Partners shall be responsible for maintaining constructive amicable relationships with members of the Development Team, DHCD, and other government agencies having jurisdiction over the Project, and representatives of the community in which the Project is located.

### Section 5.02. Accounting
The General Partners shall cause the Partnership to conform its accounting procedures and reporting timetables to the requirements of DHCD.

### Section 5.03. Insurance
(A) The General Partners shall cause the Partnership to obtain and keep in force such insurance, in such amounts, on such terms, and with such carriers, as will protect the Partnership and its property with the broadest coverage at the lowest cost.

### Section 5.04. Overhead
No part of the office overhead or administrative expenses of any General Partner shall be deemed an expense of the Partnership.

## ARTICLE VI
## RIGHTS AND OBLIGATIONS OF LIMITED PARTNERS

### Section 6.01. Powers of Limited Partners
No Limited Partner shall have any power or authority to, or responsibility for, the conduct of the business or management of the affairs of the Partnership.

### Section 6.02. Liability of Limited Partners
No Limited Partner shall be obligated to provide any contributions to the capital of the Partnership in addition to those specified in Exhibit

A to this Agreement and no Limited Partner shall be obligated to make any loan to the Partnership. No Limited Partner shall have any personal liability with respect to the liabilities or obligation of the Partnership.

### Section 6.03. Rights of Limited Partners

Each Limited Partner shall have the same right as a General Partner:

(A) to have the Partnership books kept at the principal place of business of the Partnership, and to inspect and copy them at any reasonable time;

(B) to receive on demand true and full information of all things affecting the Partnership, and a formal account of the Partnership affairs whenever circumstances render it just and reasonable; and

(C) to petition a court for dissolution and winding up of the Partnership in accordance with law and the terms of this Agreement.

### Section 6.04. Outside Activities

Each Limited Partner may engage and hold interests in business ventures of every kind and description other than the Project for its own account including, without limitation, other low and moderate income housing projects. Neither the Partnership nor any of the Partners shall have any rights by virtue of this Agreement in such independent business ventures.

## ARTICLE VII
## ALLOCATIONS, ELECTIONS AND DISTRIBUTIONS

### Section 7.01. Allocations

(A) All income, gains, profits, losses, deductions and credits of the Partnership shall be allocated among the Partners in proportion to their respective Percentage Interests.

(B) In the event of a valid transfer of all or part of a Partner's Percentage Interest pursuant to Article VIII hereof, all income, gains, profits, losses, deductions and credits of the Partnership, and all distributions shall be allocated between the transferor and the transferee pro rata in accordance with the number of days in the Partnership fiscal year before and after the transfer; provided, however, that nothing herein shall preclude the transferor and transferee from making, as between themselves, special provisions for extraordinary or nonrecurring allocations of income, gains, profits, losses, deductions, credits or distributions.

(C) If any Partner transfers all or part of its Percentage Interest at a profit, any basis adjustment allocable to such profit, whether made under Section 754 of the Internal Revenue Code of otherwise, shall be allocated solely to the transferee. Where such transfer is made prior to completion of the Project and determination of the total cost (tax basis) of the transferee's allocable share of Partnership assets transferred, such determination shall not take into account costs associated with the management and operation of the Project.

(D) In the event of transfers aggregating 50% or more of the total Percentage Interests in the Partnership within any period of twelve months, resulting in termination of the Partnership under Section 708 of the Internal Revenue Code, the gain or loss and depreciation with respect to the increase in the adjusted basis of the recontributed assets shall be allocated to the transferees.

## Section 7.02. Elections

(A) In the event of a transfer of all or part of a Percentage Interest, the Partnership shall elect pursuant to Section 754 of the Internal Revenue Code to adjust the basis of the Partnership property.

(B) All other elections required or permitted to be made by the Partnership shall be made in such manner as will, in the opinion of the Partnership's auditors, be most advantageous to the Limited Partners holding more than 50% of the aggregate Percentage Interests held by all Partners.

(C) No Partner shall take any action or refuse to take any action which would cause the Partnership to forfeit the benefits of any tax election previously made or agreed to be made.

## Section 7.03. Distribution of Proceeds of Refinancing and Sale

(A) The net proceeds resulting from the refinancing of any mortgage loan on the Project or from the sale or taking by eminent domain of all or substantially all the assets of the Partnership, or from the liquidation of the said assets prior to the dissolution Partnership, shall be distributed and applied in the following priority and to the following extents:

(1) to the payment of liabilities other than loans by Partners, including the costs and expenses of such refinancing, sale or liquidation;

(2) to the setting up of any reserves which the General Partners may deem reasonably necessary for any contingent or unforeseen liabilities or obligations of the Partnership, provided said reserves are paid to a bank or trust company as escrowee, to be held by the escrowee for the purpose of disbursing such reserves in payment of the aforementioned Partnership liabilities or obligations and, at the expiration of such period as Ms. Godwin deems advisable, distributing the balance thereafter remaining in the manner hereinafter provided;

(3) to the repayment of loans by Partners;

(4) to the Partners in proportion to their respective Percentage Interests.

(B) In settling the accounts of the Partnership after dissolution, its assets shall be applied in the order of priority set forth in the then existing Uniform Limited Partnership Law of the District of Columbia.

### Section 7.04. Prohibition of Distributions

No distribution shall be made in violation of the Federal law or the Uniform Limited Partnership Act of the District of Columbia, or any other applicable law.

## ARTICLE VIII
## TRANSFER OF INTERESTS; ADMISSION OF PARTNERS

### Section 8.01. Transferability

(A) The term "transfer" when used in this Agreement with respect to a Percentage Interest includes a sale, assignment, pledge, gift, exchange, transfer by operation of law, or any other disposition.

(B) Upon the death or legal incompetency of an individual partner, the Percentage Interest of that Partner shall descend to and/or vest in his personal representative, in whom shall inure all of the rights and obligations which the Partner possessed. Upon the bankruptcy, insolvency, dissolution or other cessation to exist as a legal entity of a Partner not an individual, the authorized representative of such entity shall succeed to all of the rights and obligations of the Partner, for the purpose of effecting the orderly winding up and disposition of the business of such entity.

(C) Except as provided in subparagraph (B) above, the transferee of a Percentage Interest shall have only the rights, powers and privileges enumerated in Section 8.02 hereof or otherwise provided by law and may not be admitted to the Partnership as a General Partner or Limited Partner except as provided in Sections 8.03 and 8.04 hereof.

(D) Except as provided in sections 8.01(B) herein, the Percentage Interest of any Partner is not transferable, in whole or in part, and any purported transfer of such shall not be valid or effective unless in accordance with the conditions and limitations set forth herein.

(E) The transferor of a Percentage Interest shall be obligated to pay such reasonable expenses, as may be incurred in connection with the transfer of a Percentage Interest and the substitution of the transferee as a partner in the Partnership.

(F) The effective date of any transfer pursuant to Section 8.01(B) shall be the date of the event precipitating said transfer, provided that within a reasonable period of time after such event written notice of such is provided.

### Section 8.02. Rights of Transferee

Except as provided in Section 8.01(B), unless admitted to the Partnership as a General or Limited Partner in accordance with Sections 8.03 or 8.04 hereof, the transferee of a Percentage Interest, or a part thereof, shall not be entitled to any of the rights, powers or privileges of its predecessor in interest, except that it shall be entitled to receive and be credited or debited with its proportionate share of Partnership income, gains, profits, losses, deductions, credits and distributions.

### Section 8.03. Admission of General Partners

A Limited Partner, or the transferee of all or part of the Percentage Interest of a General Partner or a Limited Partner, may be admitted to the Partnership as a General Partner upon furnishing to the General Partners all of the following:

(A) the prior written approval of all Partners, which approval may be granted or denied in each Partner's sole discretion;

(B) such financial statements, guarantees or other assurances as the General Partners may require with regard to the ability of the proposed General Partner to fulfill the financial obligations of a General Partner hereunder;

(C) acceptance, in form satisfactory to the General Partners of all the terms and provisions of this Agreement, and (to the extent required by DHCD or any other government agency) Deed of Trust note, Deed of Trust Loan, and debt service reduction subsidy or housing assistance payments on the same terms and conditions as the other General Partners;

(D) a certified copy of a resolution of its Board of Directors (if it is a corporation) authorizing it to become a General Partner under the terms and conditions of this Agreement.

(E) such other documents or instruments as may be required in order to effect its admission as a General Partner; and

(F) payment of such reasonable expenses as may be incurred in connection with its admission as a General Partner.

### Section 8.04. Admission of Limited Partners

(A) A General Partner, or the Transferee of all or part of the Percentage Interest of a General Partner or a Limited Partner, may be admitted to the Partnership as a Limited Partner upon furnishing to the General Partners all of the following:

(1) the prior written consent of Ms. Godwin and Mr. Howell which consent may be granted or denied in their sole discretion;

(2) acceptance, in form satisfactory to the General Partners of all the terms and conditions of this Agreement the Deed of Trust Note, Deed of Trust, and other documents required in connection with the mortgage loan, and debt service reduction subsidy or housing assistance payments;

(3) a certified copy of a resolution of its Board of Directors (if it is a corporation) authorizing it to become a Limited Partner under the terms and conditions of this Agreement.

(4) a power of attorney substantially identical to that contained in Section 3.05 hereof; and

(5) such other documents or instruments as may be required in order to effect its admission as a Limited Partner.

(B) By executing this Limited Partnership Agreement each Limited Partner consents to the admission of a General Partner, or the transferee of all or part of the Percentage Interest of a General or a Limited Partner, to the Partnership as a Limited Partner provided that the transfer has been effected in compliance with Section 8.01 and that, prior to admission, the information required to be provided to the General Partners pursuant to subsection (A) above has been supplied. In connection therewith, each partner has granted a power of attorney to Ms. Godwin as stated in Section 3.05 hereof, to effectuate such admission.

(C) The effective date of such admission shall be the date of filing of the appropriate Amendment to the Certificate of Limited Partnership.

### Section 8.05. Amendment to the Limited Partnership Agreement and the Certificate of Limited Partnership

Upon the withdrawal of any Partner, Ms. Godwin and Mr. Howell shall take all steps necessary and appropriate to prepare and execute an amendment to this Limited Partnership Agreement and to prepare, execute and record an Amendment to the Certificate of Limited Partnership to reflect such withdrawal and may, for this purpose, execute the power of attorney granted pursuant to Section 3.05 hereof.

### ARTICLE IX
### DISSOLUTION AND LIQUIDATION

### Section 9.01. Dissolution

The Partnership shall be dissolved upon:

(A) the expiration of its term of December 31, 2032.

(B) the retirement, withdrawal, bankruptcy, assignment for the benefit of creditors, dissolution, death, disability or insanity of a General Partner, or any other event which results in such person ceasing to be a General Partner, unless all the remaining General Partners agree to continue the Partnership;

(C) an election to dissolve the Partnership made in writing by all Partners;

(D) the distribution, pursuant to Section 7.05 of this Agreement, of the proceeds of the sale, exchange or other disposition of all or substantially all of the property of the Partnership; provided, however, that if the Partnership receives a purchase money mortgage upon such sale the Partnership shall continue in existence until such mortgage is satisfied, sold or otherwise disposed of; and provided further, however, that if the Project is a Qualified Housing Project, as that term is defined in Section 1039 of the Internal Revenue Code and Regulations, and the sales to the tenants or occupants thereof or to a nonprofit organization formed solely for the benefit of such tenants or occupants, the Partnership shall be terminated at the expiration of the reinvestment period unless the proceeds of the sale have been reinvested in another Qualified Housing Project;

(E) the election by Mr. Howell and Ms. Godwin not to make loans or to contribute to the capital of the Partnership; or

(F) any other event which, under the laws of the District of Columbia, would cause its dissolution.

### Section 9.02. Liquidation

Upon the dissolution of the Partnership, Mr. Howell and Ms. Godwin (which term, for the purpose of this Article, shall include the trustees, receivers or other persons required by law to wind up the affairs of the Partnership) shall cause the cancellation of the Certificate of Limited Partnership, shall liquidate the assets of the Partnership, and shall apply and distribute the proceeds of such liquidation in the order of priority set forth in the then existing Uniform Limited Partnership Law of the District of Columbia.

### Section 9.03. Distribution in Kind

Notwithstanding the provisions of Section 9.02 hereof, if on dissolution of the Partnership Ms. Godwin shall determine that an immediate sale or part or all of the Partnership's assets would be impractical or would cause undue loss to the Partners, Ms. Godwin may, in her absolute discretion, either defer for a reasonable time the liquidation of any assets except those necessary to satisfy liabilities of the Partnership (other than those to Partners) or distribute to the Partners, in lieu of cash, as tenants in common and in proportion to their respective Percentage Interests, undivided interests in such Partnership assets as the General Partners deem not suitable for liquidation. Any distributions in kind shall be subject to such conditions relating to the disposition and management thereof as Ms. Godwin deems reasonable and equitable.

### Section 9.04. Final Statement

As soon as practicable after the dissolution of the Partnership, a final statement of its assets and liabilities shall be prepared by the Partnership auditors and furnished to the Partners.

## ARTICLE X
## BOOKS OF ACCOUNT AND REPORTS

### Section 10.01. Books of Account

The books, records and accounts of the Partnership shall be kept at the principal office of the Partnership or at the office of Howell Associates. All Partners and their duly authorized representatives shall have the right to examine and make copies of the same at all reasonable times.

### Section 10.02. Fiscal Year

The fiscal year of the Partnership shall be the calendar year.

### Section 10.03. Tax Returns

The Partnership auditors, at the expense of the Partnership, shall prepare for approval by Ms. Godwin the timely execution and filing by Ms. Godwin all tax returns of the Partnership.

### Section 10.04. Bank Accounts

(A) The funds of the Partnership shall be deposited in the name of the Partnership in such bank accounts insured by the Federal Deposit Insurance Corporation ("FDIC") as shall be designated by Ms. Godwin.

(B) Ms. Godwin shall have the sole authority, in her discretion, to determine the number and identity of the persons authorized to make withdrawals from the Partnership bank accounts.

## ARTICLE XI
## GENERAL PROVISIONS

### Section 11.01. Identification of Government Agencies, Statutes, Programs and Forms

Any reference in this Agreement, by name or number, to a government, agency, statute, regulation, program, or form shall include any successor or similar department, agency, statute, regulation, program or form.

### Section 11.02. Addresses and Notices

The address of each Partner for all purposes shall be the address set forth on the signature page of this Agreement or such other address of which the General Partners have received written notice. Any notice, demand or request permitted to be given or made hereunder shall be in writing and shall be deemed given or made when delivered in person or when sent to such Partner at such address by first class mail or by telegram or Western Union Mailgram.

### Section 11.03. Titles and Captions

All article and section titles or captions in this Agreement are for convenience only. They shall not be deemed part of this Agreement and in no way define, limit, extend or describe the scope or intent of any provisions hereof.

### Section 11.04. Pronouns and Plurals

Whenever the context may require, any pronoun used herein shall include the corresponding masculine, feminine or neuter forms. The singular form of nouns, pronouns and verbs shall include the plural and vice versa.

### Section 11.05. Further Action

The parties shall execute and deliver all documents, provide all information and take or forbear from all such actions as may be necessary or appropriate to achieve the purposes of this Agreement.

### Section 11.06. Applicable Law

This Agreement shall be construed in accordance with and governed by the laws of the District of Columbia.

### Section 11.07. Binding Effect

This Agreement shall be binding upon and inure to the benefit of the parties and their heirs, executors, administrators, successors, legal representatives and assigns.

### Section 11.08. Integration

This Agreement constitutes the entire agreement, among the parties pertaining to the subject matter hereof, superseding all prior agreements and understandings pertaining thereto; no covenant, representation or condition not expressed in this Agreement shall affect or be deemed to interpret, change or restrict the express provisions hereof.

### Section 11.09. Amendment

Except as provided in Section 3.05 hereof, this Agreement may be modified or amended only with the written approval of all Partners.

### Section 11.10. Creditors

None of the provisions of this Agreement shall be for the benefit of or enforceable by any creditors of the Partnership.

### Section 11.11. Waiver

No failure by any party to insist upon the strict performance of any covenant, duty, agreement, or condition of this Agreement or to exercise any right or remedy consequent upon a breach thereof shall constitute a waiver of any such breach or of such or any other covenant, agreement, term or condition. Any Partner by notice pursuant to Section 11.02 hereof may, but shall be under no obligation to, waive any of its rights or any conditions to its obligations hereunder, or any duty, obligation or covenants of any other Partner. No waiver shall affect or alter the remainder of this Agreement but each and every covenant agreement, term and condition hereof shall continue in full force and effect with respect to any other then existing or subsequent breach.

### Section 11.12. Separability

Any provisions of the Federal law, District or other applicable law which supersede any provisions hereof shall not affect the validity of the balance of this Agreement, and the remaining provisions shall be enforced as if the invalid provisions were deleted.

### Section 11.13. Counterparts

This Agreement may be executed in counterparts, all of which taken together shall constitute one agreement binding on all the parties notwithstanding that all the parties are not signatories to the original or the same counterpart. Each party shall become bound by the Agreement immediately upon affixing his signature hereto, independently of the signature of any other party.

### Section 11.14. Waiver of Partition

Each Partner hereby waives any right to partition of the Partnership property.

### Section 11.15. Authorization and Representation

Each Partner represents to the others and to the Partnership that it has been authorized to execute and deliver this Limited Partnership Agreement and the Certificate of Limited Partnership through the officer signing on his behalf.

## ARTICLE XII
## LAND DISPOSITION AGREEMENT PROVISIONS

Notwithstanding any other provisions of this Agreement, prior to the issuance of a Certificate of Completion for the Project by the District of Columbia Department of Housing and Community Development, no Percentage Interest may be sold, assigned, transferred, pledged, or hypothecated in contravention of the terms and conditions of that certain Contract for Sale of Land for New Construction with the District of Columbia Department of Housing and Community Development, Contract No. DHCD-      dated      1982, pertaining to the Project site.

IN WITNESS WHEREOF, this Agreement and Certificate of Limited Partnership has been duly executed by the Parties as of the day of 1982.

Joseph Howell, Faye Godwin   GENERAL PARTNERS:


Joseph Howell, Faye Godwin   LIMITED PARTNERS:
Cardiac Construction


DISTRICT OF COLUMBIA, ss:

I,      , a Notary Public in and for the jurisdiction aforesaid, do hereby certify that      , whose name is signed to the foregoing and hereunto annexed Agreement and Certificate of Limited Partnership of      Associates as a General and Limited Partner, acknowledged the same before me in my jurisdiction aforesaid.

GIVEN under my hand and official seal this      day of June 1982.

_____
Notary Public

My commission expires: _____

DISTRICT OF COLUMBIA, ss:

I,          , a Notary Public in and for the jurisdiction aforesaid, do hereby certify that          , whose name is signed to the foregoing and hereunto annexed Agreement and Certificate of Limited Partnership of          Associates as a General and Limited Partner, acknowledged the same before me in my jurisdiction aforesaid.

GIVEN under my hand and official seal this          day of June 1982.

_____
Notary Public


My commission expires: _____

# EXHIBIT A

| Name and Addresses | Percentage of Partnership Interest | Value of Initial Capital Contribution |
|---|---|---|
| **GENERAL PARTNERS** | | |
| Joseph Howell | 1.0 | $ 2,000 |
| Faye Godwin | 1.0 | $ 2,000 |
| **LIMITED PARTNERS** | | |
| Joseph Howell | 48.5 ⎫ | |
| Faye Godwin | 0.5 ⎬ | $80,000 |
| Cardiac Construction | 49.0 ⎭ | |

# F/ Key Provisions of the Economic Recovery Tax Act of 1981 and the Tax Equity and Fiscal Responsibility Act of 1982

The main provisions of the 1981 tax act affecting real estate involve the way depreciation is figured and the concept of an investment tax credit. Key provisions are:

*Shorter capital recovery periods and new accelerated depreciation for all real estate.* The 1981 tax law extablished an Accelerated Cost Recovery System (ACRS), which provides for a 15-year "recovery period" for all real property, residential and commercial, new and used. *Composite* ("the whole project"), rather than *component* ("various parts of the building taken separately") depreciation is required, and "salvage value" is not considered. The recovery period for personal property is five years.

Accelerated depreciation is now allowed for real property according to the following schedule:

| | |
|---|---|
| **all commercial** | **= 175% declining balance** |
| **all "market rate" residential** | **= 175% declining balance** |
| **all low-income residential** | **= 200% declining balance** |

*Continued recapture of excess depreciation.* The old law provided generally that, when a project was sold, any excess depreciation (the extent to which accelerated depreciation exceeds straight line) would be treated by the IRS as ordinary income and therefore would be subject to the higher personal income tax rates (as high as 70 percent), in contrast to the lower capital gains rates (then up to 28 percent).

The 1981 law did not change the residential real estate provisions. Excess depreciation was treated as ordinary income. As previously was the case, this recapture "phases out" in the case of low-income housing (but in 15 years instead of 16 years and eight months). However, in the case of commercial properties, all accelerated depreciation, not just the difference between straight-line and accelerated depreciation, is subject to recapture at ordinary income rates.

*New tax incentives for rehabilitation expenditures for historical and commercial buildings.* The old law provided for five-year straight-line depreciation for all rehabilitation expenditures for low-income housing (Section 167(k)), up to $20,000 per unit in rehabilitation costs, and five-year straight-line depreciation for all rehabilitation costs (no dollar limit per unit) for historical buildings (Section 167(0)). In addition, 10 percent "tax credits" were available for the rehabilitation costs associated with older commercial buildings (20 years old or older).

The five-year write-off of costs for historical rehabilitation (Section 167(o)) was replaced by a 25 percent tax credit based on the rehabilitation costs. These conditions, however, must be present:

1.  The building must be on the historical register or in an historical district and, though not necessarily of historical value itself, certified as contributing to the significance of the district. It must be income-producing. Owner-occupied residential dwellings do not qualify.
2.  The rehabilitation costs must exceed $5,000 or the adjusted *basis* of the building (the amount paid for the building less the cost of the land and depreciation). You have to spend more fixing up the building than you paid for it.
3.  The work done must be approved by the National Park Service.
4.  Straight-line 15-year depreciation must be taken. Accelerated depreciation is not allowed. However, one-half of the investment tax credit is subtracted from the basis of the property in determining cost recovery (an amendment in the 1982 tax act).
5.  The tax credit is subject to recapture if the project is sold, but the recapture penalty phases out over a five-year period.
6.  The tax credit can be spread over several years by going back three years or forward 15 years.

The investment tax credit also applies to any commercial building over 30 years old (for which a 15 percent credit is available) or over 40 years old (for which a 20 percent credit is available). The same basic provisions apply to an old commercial building as to an historic building except that, in determining cost recovery, the entire amount of the tax credits must be subtracted from the value of the building to determine the adjusted basis.

In addition to the new ACRS provisions and the investment tax credit, these other provisions of the 1981 act affect investment in real estate:

1.  Owners of low-income housing are allowed to expense construction loan interest (that is, take the deduction for interest as it occurs), financing costs, and fees, rather than amortizing them over a 10-year period, as is required for all other projects (Section 189). However, without Section 8 or an equivalent program, this may be of little value.
2.  The maximum personal income marginal tax rate was reduced from

70 to 50 percent. This and the repeal of the surtax on unearned income reduces the maximum tax rate on long-term capital gains from 28 to 20 percent.

3.  The 1981 tax law extended Rule 167(k) ("the five-year write off") for all low-income rental housing, increasing the limit to $40,000 per unit where there is a certified housing program providing for ultimate home ownership by the tenants in the building.

The big winners that emerged from the Economic Recovery Tax Act of 1981 were the owners of historical buildings (either certified buildings or buildings which are certified as being important to an historical district) and the owners of commercial buildings 30 years old or older which require substantial rehabilitation.

The second big winners were the people who purchase existing commercial properties. Prior to the 1981 law, relatively little tax shelter (straight-line depreciation only) was available for people who purchased these properties. Now, since essentially the same tax shelter is available for almost all properties, existing commercial and residential properties have a new appeal. The relative advantage previously enjoyed by owners of new residential property has disappeared. Where substantial rehabilitation costs are involved, the advantage is clearly with the commercial owner, who can get the investment tax credit.

The one exception is that commercial owners must think twice before they elect to use accelerated depreciation, since all accelerated depreciation is subject to recapture, not just the "excess," as is the case with residential owners.

Low-income housing—whatever that will mean in the absence of Section 8 new construction and substantial rehabilitation—also emerged a winner, but clearly without the relative strong advantage it enjoyed earlier. Higher rates of accelerated depreciation are still allowed (200 percent declining balance instead of 175 percent declining balance for other property), rehabilitation or construction "soft costs" can be expensed, and the 167(k) five-year write-off for rehabilitation costs continues, with a possible $40,000 (instead of $20,000) per-unit maximum.

Finally, existing rental properties can qualify for more rapid depreciation than was previously the case. To take advantage of the new tax law, however, requires starting anew by purchasing an existing property. People who acquired such property before 1981 cannot use the ACRS. "Anti-churning" rules strictly prohibit bringing previously owned property under ACRS by methods such as sale-leaseback arrangements.

Before the new law a new owner of older "second-user" property could do not better than apply 125 percent accelerated depreciation to component "useful lives" ranging from 15 to 30 years. Now the term is

15 years for the entire building, and 175 percent declining balance accelerated depreciation is allowed. Accordingly, it is possible that some existing properties will become attractive as tax shelter investments, as discussed earlier.

With the reduction in effective capital gains tax rates, many owners may be more willing to sell marginal properties. However, it is not clear whether the increased tax benefits will be sufficient to offset the fact that it has become increasingly difficult for older rental properties to generate a sustained positive cash flow. However, getting a tax shelter is one thing; losing real dollars, year after year, is another. The real estate market risks, therefore, are increasingly important.

## TAX EQUITY AND FISCAL RESPONSIBILITY
## ACT OF 1982

While the tax act of 1982, or TEFRA as it is now called, did not have the far-reaching impact on real estate development syndication as did the Economic Recovery Act of 1981, the law did broaden the coverage of calculating a minimum tax for individuals. The minimum tax required under the act is calculated by applying a flat 20 percent rate to a tax base less a specified amount (set in 1982 as $40,000 for married couples and $30,000 for individuals). In applying the minimum tax to the person's tax liability, if the tax due exceeds what is owed using the regular method, then the 20 percent alternative minimum tax applies. In addition, the act provided for increasing the "adjusted gross income calculation" by nine "tax preference items" (including accelerated depreciation in excess over straight-line, all accelerated depreciation on personal property subject to a lease, and several other categories). Thus, wealthy investors will no longer be able to claim that they pay no taxes whatsoever, if in fact this was ever the case.

Other features of TEFRA include adjusting the basis for historical property, requiring that one-half the investment tax credit must come off the basis, as discussed earlier, and establishing strict penalty provisions for noncompliance with tax laws. If there is a substantial underpayment of income taxes, a fine of 10 percent of the underpayment is due plus interest due on the underpayment based on the prime rate. Finally, the law provided for civil penalties for persons or organizations promoting "abusive tax shelters." The law imposed a penalty equal to the greater of $1,000 or 10 percent of the income derived by the person from the activity. In order to assist the IRS in auditing tax shelter returns, the law also required for every partnership to have a *Tax Matters Partner,* who is responsible for dealing with all tax issues and questions on behalf of the limited partnership.

The message behind TEFRA is one of warning: beware of promoting or getting involved in shaky tax shelters. The Congress clearly intends for these types of deals to be stopped; and by all accounts, the IRS is going to pursue such fraudulent deals with increasing intensity.

# G/ Comparison of the Old Tax Law With the Economic Recovery Act of 1981

| Type of Property | Depreciation and Treatment of Rehabilitation Costs | |
| | Old Law | 1981 Law |
| --- | --- | --- |
| New residential rental | 30–40 years, SYD*; construction period fees amortized over 10 years | 15 years, DB**; construction period fees expensed |
| New "low-income" residential rental | 30–40 years, SYD; construction period fees expensed | 15 years, 200% DB; construction period fees expensed |
| Low-income substantial rehabilitation rental | 5-year straight-line for rehabilitation costs (up to $20,000 per unit), SYD for balance, 30–40 years | No change except the limit is increased to $40,000 per unit in some cases; 15-year depreciation for balance |
| Existing residential | 25–30 years, 125% DB | 15 years, 175% DB |
| Existing commercial, no or little rehabilitation | Straight-line | 15 years, 175% DB |
| New commercial | 30–40 years, 150% DB; construction period fees amortized | 15 years, 175% DB; construction period fees amortized |
| Historic buildings | 5-year straight-line for rehabilitation costs, no limit | ITC*** for 25% of rehabilitation costs, 15-year depreciation only |
| Commercial rehabilitation | 10% ITC, straight-line depreciation | 15–20% ITC; 15-year depreciation (basis excludes tax credit) only<br><br>Optional straight-line re- |

| | | covery periods of 15, 35, or 45 years |
| --- | --- | --- |
| | **Recapture** | |
| All residential | All excess depreciation | No change |
| All commercial | All excess depreciation | All accelerated depreciation |

*SYD = sum-of-the-year digits.
**DB = declining balance.
***ITC = Investment Tax Credit.

**Source:** The author.

# H/ FHA Form 2013

Form Approved
OMB No. 2502-0029

**U.S. DEPARTMENT OF HOUSING AND URBAN DEVELOPMENT**
HOUSING-FEDERAL HOUSING COMMISSIONER
## APPLICATION FOR MULTIFAMILY HOUSING PROJECT

### SECTION A · PROJECT IDENTIFICATION

| 1. Name of Project | 2. HUD Project Number *(Mortgage Ins. or Sec. 202)* |
|---|---|
| | 3. HUD Project Number *(Section 8)* |

### SECTION B · PURPOSE OF APPLICATION

TO: The Assistant Secretary for Housing-Federal Housing Commissioner: Application is being made pursuant to Item (a): ☐ 1, ☐ 2, ☐ 3 of Section M, Page 3 hereof. The undersigned desire(s) to participate, with respect to the Property and Program(s) described below. Therefore, it is requested that you give consideration to the information presented herein, for the purpose of loaning and/or approving:

☐ Mortgage Insurance: Section; ___
☐ a Feasibility Letter *(Rehab.)*  ☐ Direct Loan Section 202
☐ a SAMA Letter *(New Const.)*  ☐ Housing Asst. Pymnts. Sec. 8
☐ a Conditional Commitment  ☐ a Preliminary Proposal
☐ a Firm Commitment  ☐ a Final Proposal

Mortgagor: ☐ PM ☐ NP ☐ LD ☐ B–S  Other ___
Financing: ☐ Conventional  ☐ GNMA ☐ Bond ☐ State Agency
Other ___
Mortgage/Loan Amount: $ ___
Interest Rate: Permanent ___ %  Construction ___ %

### SECTION C · LOCATION AND DESCRIPTION OF PROPERTY

| 1. Street Address | 2. Municipality | 3. County | 4. State and ZIP Code | 5. Congressional Dist. |
|---|---|---|---|---|

6. Type of Project: ☐ Proposed ☐ Rehabilitation ☐ Existing  Year Built: 19 ___
7. Number of Units: Revenue: ___ Non-Revenue: ___ TOTAL: ___
8. No. of Buildings
9. List Accessory Buildings  Area ___ Sq. Ft.
10. List Recreation Facilities  Area ___ Sq. Ft.
11. Type of Buildings ☐ Elevator ☐ Walkup ☐ Row (T.H.) ☐ Detached ☐ Semi-Detached
12. No. of Stories
13. No. of Elevators
14. Type of Foundation: ☐ Crawl Space ☐ Partial Bsmt. ☐ Full Basement ☐ Slab on Grade
15. Structural System
16. Floor System
17. Exterior Finish
18. Heating System
19. Air Conditioning System

### SECTION D · INFORMATION CONCERNING LAND OR PROPERTY

1. Date ☐ Acquired ☐ Optioned  / /
2. Price ☐ Purchase ☐ Option  $
3. Additional Cost Paid or Accrued  $
4. Total Cost  $
5. Outstanding Balance  $
6. Relationship Between Seller and Buyer, Business, Personal or Other

7. Site Area ___ Sq. Ft.
8. Zoning *(If recently changed, submit evidence)*
9. If leasehold, show annual ground rent $ ___  lease term, remaining ___ years

10. Off-Site Facilities: Public / Comm. / At Site / Feet from Site
Water ☐ ☐ ☐ ___ft.
Sewer ☐ ☐ ☐ ___ft.
Paving ☐ ☐ ☐ ___ft.
Gas ☐ ☐ ☐ ___ft.
Electrical ☐ ☐ ☐ ___ft.
11. Unusual Site Features: ☐ None ☐ Cuts ☐ Fill ☐ Erosion ☐ Other  ☐ Poor Drainage ☐ Retaining Walls ☐ Rock Foundations ☐ High Water Table
12. Special Assessments: a. ☐ Prepayable ☐ Non-prepayable  b. Principal Balance $ ___  c. Annual Payment $ ___  d. Remaining Terms ___ years

### SECTION E · ESTIMATE OF INCOME

| Unit Type | No. of Living Units | No. of Units Assisted | Living Area *(Sq. Ft.)* | Composition of Units | PBE Not in Rent ($) *(Sec. F-1)* | Unit Rent per Mo. ($) | Total Monthly Unit Rent ($) |
|---|---|---|---|---|---|---|---|
| | | | | | | | |
| | | | | | | | |
| | | | | | | | |
| | | | | | | | |
| | | | | | | | |
| Employee(s) Liv. Units(s) | | | | | | | |
| TOTALS | | | | | | | |

2. TOTAL ESTIMATED MONTHLY RENTALS FOR ALL LIVING UNITS $

3. Number of Parking Spaces ☐ Attended ☐ Self Park  Total Spaces
4. Parking and Other Income *(Not Included in Rent)*
Open Spaces ___ @ $ ___ per month = $ ___
Covered Spaces ___ @ $ ___ per month = $ ___
Laundry ___ Sq. Ft. or Living Units @ ___ per month = $ ___
Other ___ per month = $ ___
TOTAL ANCILLARY INCOME $

5. Commercial Space *(Describe)*
Area-Ground Level ___ sq. ft. @ $ ___ per sq. ft./month = $ ___
Other Levels ___ sq. ft. @ $ ___ per sq. ft./month = $ ___
TOTAL COMMERCIAL $

6. TOTAL ESTIMATED MONTHLY GROSS INCOME AT 100 PERCENT OCCUPANCY  $
7. TOTAL ANNUAL RENT *(Item 6 times 12 months)*  $
8. Gross Floor Area: ___ Sq. Ft.
9. Net Rentable Residential Area: ___ Sq. Ft.
10. Net Rentable Commercial Area: ___ Sq. Ft.

### SECTION F · EQUIPMENT AND SERVICES *(Check Items Included in the Rent, Listed Below)*

Equipment:
☐ Range and Oven ☐ Carpet
☐ Microwave Oven ☐ Drapes
☐ Refrigerator ☐ Swimming Pool
☐ Laundry Facilities ☐ Air Conditioning Equip.
☐ In Common Area ☐ Trash Compactor
☐ In Living Unit ☐ Disposal
☐ L.V. Hookup Only ☐ Other

Services: (Gas / Elect. / Oil)
☐ Heat ☐ ☐ ☐
☐ Hot Water ☐ ☐ ☐
☐ Cooking ☐ ☐
☐ Air Conditioning ☐ ☐
☐ Lights, etc., in Units
☐ Cold Water ☐ Parking
☐ Other

### SECTION F-1 · UTILITIES *(Not in Rent)*

* PERSONAL BENEFIT EXPENSES *(PBE):*
Check Utilities and Services Not Included in the Rent and Paid Directly by the Tenant.
☐ Electricity ☐ Heating ☐ Gas
☐ Decorating ☐ Repairs ☐ Water
Other
Remarks

Previous Edition is Obsolete

223

HUD-92013 (4-81)

| SECTION G - ESTIMATE OF REPLACEMENT COST | | | SECTION I - ESTIMATE OF ANNUAL EXPENSE | | |
|---|---|---|---|---|---|
| **LAND IMPROVEMENTS** | | | **ADMINISTRATIVE** | | |
| 1. Unusual Land Improvements | $ | | 1. Advertising | $ | |
| 2. Other Land Improvements | $ | | 2. Management Fee (____ %) | $ | |
| 3. TOTAL LAND IMPROVEMENTS | | $ | 3. Other | $ | |
| **STRUCTURES** | | | 4. TOTAL ADMINISTRATIVE | | $ |
| 4. Main Buildings | $ | | **OPERATING** | | |
| 5. Accessory Buildings | $ | | 5. Elevator Maintenance Exp. | $ | |
| 6. Garage | $ | | 6. Fuel - Heating | $ | |
| 7. All Other Buildings | $ | | 7. Fuel - Domestic Hotwater | $ | |
| 8. TOTAL STRUCTURES | | $ | 8. Lighting and Misc. Power | $ | |
| 9. SUBTOTAL (Line 3 plus Line 8) | | $ | 9. Water | $ | |
| 10. General Requirements (Line 9 x ____ %) | | $ | 10. Gas | $ | |
| 11. SUBTOTAL (Line 9 plus Line 10) | | $ | 11. Garbage and Trash Removal | $ | |
| **FEES** | | | 12. Payroll | $ | |
| 12. Builder's General Overhead (Line 11 x ____ %) | $ | | 13. Other | $ | |
| 13. Builder's Profit (Line 11 x ____ %) | $ | | 14. TOTAL OPERATING | | $ |
| 14. SUBTOTAL (Sum of Lines 11 through 13) | $ | | **MAINTENANCE** | | |
| 15. Bond Premium | $ | | 15. Decorating | $ | |
| 16. Other Fees | $ | | 16. Repairs | $ | |
| 17. ESTIMATED TOTAL COST OF CONSTRUCTION | $ | | 17. Exterminating | $ | |
| 18. Architect's Fee - Design (Line 14 x ____ %) | $ | | 18. Insurance | $ | |
| 19. Architect's Fee-Supervisory (Line 14 x ____ %) | $ | | 19. Ground Expense | $ | |
| 20. TOTAL FOR ALL IMPROVEMENTS (Sum of Lines 17 through 19) | | $ | 20. Other | $ | |
| 21. Cost per Gross Square Foot $ ____ (Line 20 divided by Item 8, Section E) | | | 21. TOTAL MAINTENANCE | | $ |
| 22. Construction Time ____ Months Plus 2 = ____ Months | | | 22. Replacement Res.: New Const. = (.006 x Line 8, Sec. G Total Struct.) Rehab = (.004 x Mort/Loan Requested in Sec M) | | $ |
| **CHARGES AND FINANCING DURING CONSTRUCTION** | | | 23. SUBTOTAL EXPENSES (Sum of Lines 4, 14, 21 and 22) | | $ |
| 23. Interest on $ ____ @ ____ % for ____ Months | $ | | 24. Real Estate: Est. Assessed Value = $ ____ at $ ____ per $1000 = | $ | |
| 24. Taxes | $ | | 25. Personal Prop. Est. Assessed Value = $ ____ at $ ____ per $1000 = | $ | |
| 25. Insurance | $ | | 26. Employee Payroll Tax | $ | |
| 26. HUD/FHA Mtg. Ins. Pre. (0.5%) | $ | | 27. Other | $ | |
| 27. HUD/FHA Exam. Fee (0.3%) | $ | | 28. Other | $ | |
| 28. HUD/FHA Insp. Fee (0.5%) | $ | | 29. TOTAL TAXES | | $ |
| 29. Financing Fee (___%) | $ | | 30. TOTAL EXPENSES (Line 23 plus Line 29) | | $ |
| 30. FNMA/GNMA Fee ( _%) | $ | | 31. Avg. exp. per unit per annum (PUPA) (Line 30 divided by TOTAL Item 7 Sec. C) | | $ |
| 31. AMPO (2.0%) | $ | | **SECTION J - TOTAL SETTLEMENT REQUIREMENTS** | | |
| 32. Contingency (Sec. 202) (3.0%) | $ | | 1. Development Costs (Line 45, Section G) | | $ |
| 33. Title and Recording | $ | | 2. Cash Req. for Land Debt/Acquisition | | $ |
| 34. TOTAL CHARGES AND FINANCING | | $ | 3. SUBTOTAL (Lines 1 plus 2) | | $ |
| **LEGAL, ORGANIZATION AND AUDIT FEE** | | | 4. Mortgage Amount $ ____ | | |
| 35. Legal | $ | | 5. Development/Cash (Lines 3 minus 4) +/- | | $ |
| 36. Organization | $ | | 6. Initial Operating Deficit | | $ |
| 37. Cost Certification Audit Fee | $ | | 7. Discount Costs | | $ |
| 38. TOTAL LEGAL, ORG. AND AUDIT FEE | | $ | 8. Interest Yield Costs | | $ |
| 39. Builder's and Sponsor's Profit and Risk | | $ | 9. Working Capital (2% of Mortgage Amount) | | $ |
| 40. Consultant Fee (Nonprofit Only) | | $ | 10. Min. Capital Investment (Sec. 202) | | $ |
| 41. Supplemental Management Fund | | $ | 11. Off-Site Construction Costs | | $ |
| 42. Contingency Reserve (Rehabilitation Only) | | $ | 12. Non-Mortgagable Relocation Expenses | | $ |
| 43. Relocation Expenses | | $ | 13. Other | | $ |
| 44. Other | | $ | 14. TOTAL ESTIMATED CASH REQUIRED (Sum of Lines 5 through 13) | | $ |
| 45. TOTAL ESTIMATED DEVELOPMENT COST (Lines 20 + 34 + 38 through 44) | | $ | **FUNDS AVAILABLE FOR CASH REQUIREMENTS** | | |
| 46. Land (Estimated Market Price of Site) ____ sq. ft. @ $ ____ per sq. ft. | | $ | 15. Source of Cash: a. ____ $ ____ b. ____ $ ____ c. ____ $ ____ SUBTOTAL (a + b + c) $ ____ | | |
| 47. TOTAL ESTIMATED REPLACEMENT COST OF PROJECT (Line 43 plus Line 44) | | $ | 16. Source of Fees and Grants: a. ____ $ ____ b. ____ $ ____ c. ____ $ ____ SUBTOTAL (a + b + c) $ ____ | | |
| 48. Average Cost per Living Unit $ ____ (Line 45 divided by Total in Sec. C, Item 7) | | | 17. TOTAL Cash, Fees and Grants (Sum of Items 15 plus 16) | | $ |
| **SECTION H - ANNUAL INCOME COMPUTATIONS** | | | NOTE: Line 17 must equal or exceed Line 14 | | |
| 1. Estimated Project Gross Income (Line 7, Section E, Page 1) | | $ | | | |
| 2. Occupancy (Entire Project) | | ____ % | | | |
| 3. Effective Gross Income (Line 1 x Line 2) | | $ | | | |
| 4. Total Project Expenses (Line 30, Section I) | | $ | | | |
| 5. Net Income to Project (Line 3 minus Line 4) | | $ | | | |
| 6. Expense Ratio (Line 4 divided by Line 3) | | ____ % | | | |

HUD-92013 (4-81)

# Index

# About the Author

Joseph T. Howell is president of Howell Associates, a real estate development consulting firm located in Washington, D.C. Prior to establishing Howell Associates in 1981, Mr. Howell was Director of Development for the National Corporation for Housing Partnerships, where he was responsible for all of the projects for which NCHP was the sole project developer. Mr. Howell brings to this book the experience of a developer with hands-on experience, having been responsible for the development of over 1,500 units of housing. In addition to his development and consulting practice, Mr. Howell has taught at The George Washington University, where in 1981 he was Banneker Professor of Washington Studies, and at the University of the District of Columbia. he is also the author of *Hard Living on Clay Street*, a study of working-class families published by Doubleday Anchor in 1973, which continues to be a popular text in sociology and urban studies courses in many colleges and universities throughout the United States.

Mr. Howell lives in Washington, D.C., with his wife and two children.